*Rolling
on the
River*

Steve Neal

Rolling on the River

THE BEST OF

Steve Neal

With a Foreword by Paul Simon

Southern Illinois
University
Press
CARBONDALE AND
EDWARDSVILLE

Library of Congress Cataloging-in-Publication Data

Neal, Steve, 1949–
Rolling on the river : the best of Steve Neal / Steve Neal ;
foreword by Paul Simon.
p. cm.

1. Politicians—United States Biography.
2. United States—Politics and government—1945–1989.
3. United States—Politics and government—1989–
4. Celebrities—United States Biography.
5. United States—History—1945– Biography. I. Title.
E747.N43 1999
973.9′092′2—dc21
[B]
ISBN 0-8093-2282-X (alk. paper)
99-21324
CIP

For Raymond R. Coffey

and Bernard M. Judge

Contents

Contents

Contents

Contents

Foreword

Only two of the nation's political columnists show a great sense of history: George Will and Steve Neal. George Will is nationally syndicated and widely read. Steve Neal should be more widely read than he is, and this book will enable both his fans and his new readers to gain insight into this remarkable writer and also to gain insight from him.

Both Steve Neal and George Will are interested in sports, but George writes about sports more frequently than Steve. And, even as a former sports reporter, I appreciate Steve's less frequent reference to that part of the nation that entertains us. Occasionally the sports scene does more than entertain us. That occurred when the nation witnessed Jackie Robinson's historic entry into major league baseball and a similar—though less dramatic—smashing of the color barrier when Kenny Washington brought his outstanding ability as a ball carrier into the National Football League. A Steve Neal column urging Kenny Washington's induction into the Hall of Fame prompted me to write to the NFL commissioner and others who I thought might help make that a reality.

But it is the brush with history that marks Steve Neal's writings as distinctive. His love of history has resulted in five books devoted to understanding leading U.S. political figures. It is not only that Steve Neal's columns are frequently seasoned with historical detail, it is also that his sense of history adds perspective to what he writes.

Do I agree with him all the time? No. For example, he is an aficionado of boxing. I believe that any "sport" in which the opponents' aim is to damage each other's brains should be outlawed.

But do I read Steve Neal faithfully? Yes.

One of the nation's fine historians, Barbara Tuchman, died in 1989 at the age of 77. Although she had made significant contributions to our understanding of history, I know of no other of the nation's political columnists who paid her tribute, as Steve Neal did. Her death prompted no front-page headlines, but I am grateful that someone paid Barbara Tuchman the tribute she deserved and perhaps in the process encouraged other budding historians who might some day enrich the nation.

Steve Neal is also willing to do the unconventional. Alderman Thomas Keane served time in federal prison but, during his service on the Chicago City Council, had contributed immensely to the better operation of that city. When Tom Keane turned ninety, Steve Neal had the courage and good sense to pay tribute to him.

Occasionally I had breakfast alone with Cardinal Bernardin, the Roman Catholic prelate in the Chicago area. We talked about the problems each of us faced. By any gauge, he was an outstanding leader, and Steve Neal's column following the death of Cardinal Bernardin captured the man and his essence as well as any tribute I read.

That type of column writing comes with time, but it takes more than time to develop that skill. There is an instinct that good journalists develop—sometimes. Too many fall into the quicksand of cynicism. Too many look only at yesterday's headlines and stories to reach today's conclusions.

Steve Neal is a different, and better, journalist as you will sense as you read the pages of this fine collection.

Paul Simon

Preface

It beats working.

For more than a quarter century, I have been following politicians around and putting them in print. Along the way, I have covered campaigns for offices ranging from alderman to the presidency of the United States. "It's the greatest spectator sport in the country," Mayor Frank Skeffington tells his nephew in Edwin O'Connor's *The Last Hurrah*. "People begin as strangers and in a little while they know the names and numbers of all the players; a little while more, and they're telling the coaches how to run things. They wouldn't play the game for ten thousand dollars, but it's great fun to sit in the stands and look on."

There are few places where the game is played with more intensity than in Chicago where I've had a ringside seat at the political carnival for two decades. Though I grew up in the Pacific Northwest, my grandfather lived in Chicago for nearly a half century and gave me an early education in the city's rich political tradition.

I have been fascinated with politics since the 1960 presidential contest between John F. Kennedy and Richard M. Nixon. When Theodore H. White wrote his classic history of that campaign, I thought it was more compelling than any novel I had ever read. After reading *The Making of the President 1960*, it was my goal to become a political writer.

There were a lot of intermediate stops. I was the sports editor of my high school newspaper and continued to write about sports while working for the athletic department when I attended the University of Oregon. My interest in sports, as well as in music and literature, has never waned, and I continue to write about these subjects even though politics has become my specialty.

I got my first crack at political reporting when I got my first job as a general assignment reporter on the old Oregon Journal. Former senator Wayne L. Morse, whose opposition to the Vietnam war had cost him re-election to a fifth term in 1968, gave me a scoop by confiding that he would attempt a political comeback in 1972.

xiii

When I attended the Columbia University School of Journalism, I had the good fortune to take a course in political writing from Richard Reeves, who was then writing a column for *New York* magazine. Reeves has a wonderful sense of humor, is a natural storyteller, and has a keen understanding of the political arena. More than a generation later, Reeves is still one of the sprightliest writers around. I also learned history from a past master, John A. Garraty, who has been a friend and mentor for three decades.

After Columbia, I joined the *Philadelphia Inquirer* where I worked from June of 1972 until January of 1979. Gene Roberts, who became executive editor several months after my arrival, gave me the opportunity to write about state, local, and national political figures. The controversial and outspoken Frank L. Rizzo was Philadelphia's mayor and dominant newsmaker during this period. I more often covered Rizzo's arch rival, Philadelphia Democratic chairman Peter J. Camiel, who once told me why he would never voluntarily give up public office: "There is nothing as useless as a former mayor, a former officeholder, a former candidate, a former anything. There is just nothing they can do for you."

When I moved to Chicago in 1979, I joined the *Chicago Tribune* and covered Jane M. Byrne's election as the city's first woman mayor. Four years later, I followed Harold Washington's rise to power as Chicago's first African American mayor. In between the Byrne and Washington elections, I worked in the *Tribune*'s Washington bureau and covered Ronald Reagan's successful 1980 presidential campaign and the first two years of his administration. I was at the Washington Hilton on that fateful March afternoon in 1981 when Reagan was shot by John Hinckley.

Since January of 1987, I have written for the *Chicago Sun-Times*. Washington became the first mayor since the late Richard J. Daley to win re-election in 1987. But Washington died later that year, which set the stage for the emergence of a second Mayor Daley. If the Daleys have been the major influence in Democratic politics, former governor James R. Thompson has had a similar impact in the Illinois Republican party. Thompson's former aide, Jim Edgar, and his former lieutenant governor, George H. Ryan, were elected as Thompson's successors.

In writing a political column since 1983, I have tried to make politics accessible and interesting to a general audience. I've tried to keep in mind what Ed Klauber of CBS News said in 1939:

Preface

What news analysts are entitled to do and would do is to eluci-
date and illuminate the news out of common knowledge, or
special knowledge possessed by them or made available to them
by this organization through its sources. They should point out
the facts on both sides, show contradictions with the known
record, and so on. They should bear in mind that in a democracy
it is important that people not only should know but should
understand, and it is the analyst's function to help the listener to
understand, to weigh and to judge, but not to do the judging for
him.

I'd like to thank Nigel Wade, editor of the *Chicago Sun-Times*, for invit-
ing me to write the "Talking Politics" column and for giving me the
permission to reprint my work. Thanks also to Steve Huntley, the editorial page editor, and his predecessors Michelle Stevens and Mark
Hornung; executive editor Larry Green; executive news editor Jocyelyn
Winnecke; and metropolitan editor Don Hayner. My articles on Paul
Robeson, Ronald Reagan, John Updike, and Patsy Cline are reprinted
with permission from the *Philadelphia Inquirer*. My articles on Alan J.
Dixon and Saul Bellow are reprinted with permission from the *Chicago Tribune*. I'd also like to express my appreciation to Southern Illinois University Press director Rick Stetter, managing editor Carol
Burns, editorial director Jim Simmons, acquisitions editor Karl Kageff,
and copyeditor Kathleen Kageff. Thanks also to Mike Lawrence of the
Southern Illinois University at Carbondale Public Policy Institute for
suggesting this project. Lawrence, a veteran statehouse reporter and
former Springfield bureau chief for the *Sun-Times*, wrote for many years
what I considered the best political column in the state. And, most of
all, I want to thank my wife, Susan, and our daughters, Erin and Shannon.

Rolling
on the
River

Lift Every Voice

Marian Anderson

Chicago Sun-Times, 2/26/97

In her hands, she had the whole wide world.

Marian Anderson (1897–1993) was probably the greatest contralto of the 20th century. She was the first African American to sing with the Metropolitan Opera Company and a world-renowned concert artist. On hearing her in the 1930s, the conductor Arturo Toscanini declared: "Yours is a voice one hears once in a hundred years."

Anderson also was a quiet activist for human rights.

"She represented preparation waiting for opportunity," the Rev. Jesse L. Jackson said of Anderson. "When the opportunity came at the Easter Sunday concert, her talent was so obvious and so brilliant that she soared like an eagle."

On Thursday night, Anderson will be celebrated in a 100th birthday tribute at Carnegie Hall at a concert conducted by Robert Shaw. It has been 30 years since a hushed audience thrilled to the magnificence of her voice in her farewell concert at Carnegie Hall. Some of her friends, including Roberta Peters and Isaac Stern, will share their memories.

"At age 10, I heard for the first time, the singing of Marian Anderson on a recording," recalled the soprano Jessye Norman, who is performing in Thursday's tribute. "I listened, thinking, 'This can't be just a voice, so rich and beautiful.' It was a revelation. And I wept."

The soprano Leontyne Price told the *New York Times* that Anderson "inspired me to believe that I could achieve goals that, otherwise, would have been unthought of."

It was on Easter Sunday, 1939, that Anderson gave her famous Lincoln Memorial concert in Washington. Though she had already achieved international fame, she was denied the use of Constitution Hall, the headquarters of the Daughters of the American Revolution, because of her race.

In the wake of this incident, Eleanor Roosevelt resigned from the DAR in support of Anderson. Interior Secretary Harold Ickes arranged for Anderson to sing in the open air at the Lincoln Memorial. Anderson's concert in front of 75,000 people was not only a personal triumph but an important milestone in the struggle for civil rights.

"I am deeply touched," she said that day, "that I can be in any way a symbol of democracy."

I interviewed Anderson 22 years ago this month at her apartment overlooking Central Park on New York's Fifth Avenue. She talked softly and almost hesitantly in a rich voice.

Anderson told me how she had applied to one of Philadelphia's top music schools as a young girl.

"This beautiful young blonde girl behind the window ignored me when it got to be my turn in line. I thought, at first, it was because she didn't notice me. But when I was the only one left, she tossed her head in delight and told me, 'We don't take coloreds.'

"One was naive enough to believe that people didn't enjoy hurting the feelings of another. You might expect this sort of thing at a place where pugilists are fighting. But it was absolutely jolting to me."

Anderson confided that she had been approached by several Hollywood studios seeking her cooperation on movies about her life. But her name wasn't for sale. "One has reservations about any kind of film," she said. "Even with the best of care, film biographies seem to go off a little bit. And I'm sure that my concept of my life is different than people who would make a film."

During her concerts, Anderson sang with her eyes closed. "My feeling was I could shut out everything and concentrate more inwardly on what I was trying to accomplish," she said.

Anderson said that her earliest ambition had been to sing for the Met. But she learned that blacks weren't invited to perform there, and that her career would have to be on the concert stage. "My chance (at the Met) finally came (in 1955)," she said. "But one would have been happy if it had come earlier.

She almost never listened to her recordings. "I always feel that somehow, had I been given one more chance, I could have done better," she said. But nobody did it better.

Paul Robeson
Philadelphia Inquirer, 3/10/74

It may have been the biggest, starriest, brassiest party ever thrown at Carnegie Hall. Zero Mostel was there. So were Angela Davis, Harry Belafonte, James Earl Jones, and Coretta King. They had gathered— along with several thousand others—to celebrate Paul Robeson's 75th birthday.

But there was something a bit peculiar about the whole thing. The guest of honor was absent. Paul Robeson, actor, singer, and civil rights activist, was spending a quiet evening in West Philadelphia where, for the last eight years, he has lived in the seclusion of a Walnut Street rowhouse near 52d Street.

Robeson stayed home when the National Urban League presented him its first Whitney M. Young Memorial Award two years ago. And he wasn't there when Rutgers University dedicated a $5 million student center in his honor the same year. He hasn't been seen in public since 1965.

Robeson has always been something of a maverick. And his proud, stubborn independence has cost him dearly.

Robeson's successes established him as a national hero. People filled theaters to hear him sing "Ol' Man River" or watch him play "The Emperor Jones." Yet Robeson, it seemed to white America, suffered from a terrible language handicap. Although he was fluent in more than 20 languages, ranging from Russian to Swahili, he never understood the meaning of the word "shuffle."

It was bad enough that Robeson openly despised Hollywood and refused to make American films, but it was unheard of for any black actor to speak against racial discrimination as Robeson was doing in the 1930s. When Robeson expressed his admiration for the Soviet Union during World War II, right-wing congressmen branded him a Communist. The State Department finally took away his passport in 1950, when, as a matter of principle, he refused to say whether or not he was a Communist. Robeson said he would sooner go to jail than submit to "an invasion of my right of secret ballot." A witness before the House UnAmerican Activities Committee, at the prompting of Rep. Richard Nixon, suggested that anyone who owned a Robeson record was a security risk. Robeson's name was dropped from "Who's Who in America" and a sports encyclopedia removed his name from two

All-America football teams. Robeson, the onetime hero, was a non-person.

There were, to be sure, a few voices of protest. W. E. B. Du Bois, Black America's distinguished historian-philosopher, asserted: "The persecution of Paul Robeson by the government and people of the United States has been one of the most contemptible happenings in modern history."

But it was effective. Such was the paranoia of the early post-war era that New Deal liberals, who might have provided a rallying point for calmness and sanity, were trying to outlaw the Communist party. Paul Robeson, whose accomplishments had been a source of pride to a generation of Americans, was urged to disown his past and grovel before the witch-hunters. By recanting, he could have continued his career, traveled freely, and cleared the innuendoes and undocumented charges. Robeson could not, and will not, apologize for his political convictions.

The crucifixion of Paul Robeson took place at a time when America's influence in the world was declining. Russia had broken the U.S. monopoly on nuclear weapons. The Korean war frustrated many Americans. Red-baiting demagogue Joseph McCarthy was imposing a reign of terror on thousands of innocent Americans. By manipulating many of these fears, anti-communist demagogues such as Rep. Martin Dies all but destroyed Robeson.

Robeson's defiance of the House UnAmerican Activities Committee, and his refusal to shed his manhood before the witch-hunters, should have been applauded in the black community. It wasn't. Orthodox black political leaders including Walter White, the president of the NAACP, took pains to dissociate themselves from Robeson. His name became a great whisper.

This conspiracy of silence was perhaps the most painful blow, robbing him of his good name, depriving America of one of its greatest artists. It is highly unlikely that Robeson, now an invalid, will ever make another public appearance. His son, Paul Robeson, Jr., says, "He is in command of all of his faculties and not in serious trouble, but doctors say the strain of public appearances is the worst thing that could happen to him."

The injustices against Paul Robeson have not been righted. But there is evidence at long last, that he is undergoing a rehabilitation of sorts. "When people find out even a few of the things he did, it is impossible to maintain the curtain of silence anymore," says Robeson, Jr.

4

His history has all the ingredients of a legend.

He entered Rutgers University in 1915, the third black to attend the institution, which was chartered in 1766. When Robeson arrived in New Brunswick he was the only black on campus.

He was born in Princeton, N. J., the son of a former slave. His father, William Drew Robeson, had escaped from a North Carolina plantation in 1860 and eventually became a Presbyterian minister. His mother, Maria Louisa Bustill, was a member of a Philadelphia family whose ancestry went back to 1732.

Robeson wanted to play college football. He had been a star fullback in high school and seemed to have the size (6 foot 2, 200 pounds) to make the team, and the Rutgers coach was eager to give him a chance. But more than half of the 30-member squad threatened to quit if a black man was allowed to try out for the team. Following a loss to Princeton, Sanford decided to invite Robeson to play. He told the team that he didn't care if anyone quit.

The players made Robeson's first day in practice a nightmare. Years later, he recalled: "On the first play from scrimmage they set about making sure that I wouldn't get on their team. One boy slugged me in the face and smashed my nose, just smashed it. That's been a trouble to me every day since. And then, when I was down, flat on my back, another boy got me with his knee, just came over and fell on me. He managed to dislocate my right shoulder."

With his broken nose, dislocated shoulder, and other cuts and bruises, Robeson spent ten days recovering. He talked of quitting school, but his father urged him to stay, pointing out that Robeson represented the aspirations of black students who wanted to play college football.

Robeson went out for another scrimmage and found the same attitude. "I made a tackle and was on the ground, my right hand palm down on the ground," Robeson said. "A boy came over and stepped, hard, on my hand. He meant to break the bones. The bones held, but his cleats took every single one of the fingernails off my right hand. Every fingernail off my right hand! That's when I knew rage!

"The next play came around my end, the whole first string backfield came at me. I swept out my arms—and the three men running interference went down, they just went down. The ball carrier was a first-class back named Kelly. I wanted to kill him, and I meant to kill him.

"I got Kelly in my two hands—and I got him up over my head. I was going to smash him so hard to the ground that I'd break him right in two, and I could have done it. But just then the coach yelled the first thing that came to his mind. He yelled, 'Robey, you're on the varsity!' That brought me around."

Robeson played offensive and defensive end at Rutgers for the next four years and won 15 varsity letters in football, basketball, baseball, and track. It was football that earned Robeson his reputation as the greatest athlete in the school's history and made his name familiar to readers of the nation's sports pages. Walter Camp, premier sportswriter of the day, called Robeson the finest end "both in attack and defense" that he had ever seen. Robeson was named first-team All-American in 1917 and 1918.

Off the field, Robeson was elected to Phi Beta Kappa his junior year, was valedictorian of his class, and was a debating champion. He was a member of the student council and was tapped for Cap and Skull, the senior honorary. Despite his interest in singing he wasn't asked to join the college glee club. One of his classmates recalled, "Tradition declares that he never made the glee club because he never tried, a partial truth. Glee club concerts in those days were followed by dances, and Robeson understood the unwritten rules."

Robeson moved to Harlem after graduation, and attended Columbia University Law School. He spent autumn weekends playing end in the fledgling National Football League, starring for the Akron Steels in 1920 and 1921, and then the Milwaukee Badgers in 1922, when professional football was a tough, no-holds-barred game with few player benefits. There were no $400,000 quarterbacks or middle linebackers. In fact, there were few salaried players. Although Robeson was one of the biggest names in pro football, earning as much as $1,000 a game, he hung up his uniform after graduating from law school.

Robeson briefly considered becoming a heavyweight boxer. He was promised an incredible—for those days—one million dollar financial package to meet Jack Dempsey for the world's championship. Robeson turned it down.

Instead, he joined a large New York law firm. By then, he was married to Eslanda Cardozo Goode, an attractive, intelligent chemist at the Columbia Medical Center. He resigned from the law firm, disillusioned, after its partners restricted his work to menial tasks.

His wife suggested that he consider a theatrical career. At Columbia he had performed in an amateur production; Eugene O'Neill had been in the audience and had later asked Robeson to play the leading role in "Emperor Jones."

Robeson refused the O'Neill role. He chose instead to play opposite Margaret Wycherly, an English actress, in "Taboo," a Broadway drama of Africa, the South, and race. The play flopped after being torn apart by New York's critics.

But Alexander Woollcott, the crusty sage of the Algonquin round table and the most influential New York critic, was impressed by Robeson's performance: "I think I felt at the time that I had just crossed the path of someone touched by destiny. He was a young man on his way. He did not know where he was going, but I never in my life saw anyone so quietly sure, by some inner knowledge, that he was going somewhere."

Robeson decided to reconsider O'Neill's offer. O'Neill, the only American playwright to win the Nobel Prize, alternated Robeson in "All God's Chillun Got Wings" and "Emperor Jones."

"Chillun" was O'Neill's daring critique of American racism. Robeson, as the heroic Jim Harris, received rave reviews. George Jean Nathan of the *American Mercury* said, "Robeson, with relatively little experience and with no training to speak of, is one of the most thoroughly eloquent, impressive, and convincing actors that I have looked at and listened to in almost twenty years of professional theater-going."

"The Emperor Jones" was another artistic triumph. Robeson played Brutus Jones, the proudly defiant Pullman porter who murders a man over a crap game, kills a white guard on a chain gang, and escapes to a Caribbean island where he makes himself emperor.

It was in "The Emperor Jones" that Robeson, almost by accident, first made his reputation as a singer. A jungle scene called for Robeson to whistle a Negro spiritual. Robeson, unable to whistle on opening night, sang instead. The audience liked his rich, powerful baritone voice.

Friends encouraged Robeson to give a concert. Assisted by Lawrence Brown, his accompanist for four decades, Robeson sang "Swing Low, Sweet Chariot," "Go Down Moses," "Every Time I Feel The Spirit," and other spirituals at the Greenwich Village Theater. The *New York World*'s music critic wrote, "All those who listened last night to the first concert in this country made entirely of Negro music . . . may have been present at a turning point, one of those thin points of time in which a star is born and not yet visible . . ."

In 1930, Robeson became the first black man to portray Shakespeare's "Othello" on the London stage. He had strong reservations about doing the play. London critic Hannen Swaffer raised the question of how the British public would view a black actor "making love" to a white woman on stage.

"Now most people, that didn't bother a bit," Robeson later recalled. "But it sure bothered me. For the first two weeks I played in every scene with Desdemona, that girl couldn't get near me. I was backing away from her all the time. I was like a plantation hand in the parlor, that clumsy."

There were twenty curtain calls on opening night and London's drama critics called Robeson's Othello a milestone in British theatrical history. Robeson's success in "Othello" prompted Jed Harris, a leading American producer, to talk about bringing him back to New York for a Broadway production with Lillian Gish as Desdemona. But Harris, faced with strong opposition from newspapers and civic leaders, backed down. The United States, it seemed, was not ready to accept the black-white love scenes of Shakespeare's classic play. Robeson would have to wait.

Robeson, for the first time, talked publicly of American racism when he returned to New York. "I have twice left this country determined not to return," he said. "I feel that the Negro is patronized too much here. If he has half a voice they call him a marvel. If he is literate, they call him a genius. Why, I had to go abroad to find out whether I could really sing or not."

As he became involved in the civil rights movement, Robeson took up other causes. He gave concerts for Jewish refugees from Nazism. He traveled to Spain to sing to Loyalist soldiers as they fought Franco's Fascist armies. He identified with such future Third World leaders as Jomo Kenyatta, Kwame Nkrumah, and Jawaharlal Nehru.

When he visited Russia at the invitation of film director Sergei Eisenstein, Robeson was given a hero's welcome. He was so impressed that he left his son there to attend school. Robeson would later describe the Soviet Union as his "second motherland," recalling that, "There I walked the earth for the first time with complete dignity." After World War II, Congressional witch-hunters used those remarks to smear Robeson as a traitor.

"Americans will swear that Dad spent a great deal of his life in Russia," Paul Robeson, Jr. says. "But when you add it all up, you find that he spent less than a year of his life in the Soviet Union."

He cut short his motion picture career in 1939, denouncing Hollywood and London studios for typecasting black actors as savages and Uncle Toms. "I thought I could do something for the Negro race in films," Robeson said, "show the truth about them and about other people too. I used to do my part and go away feeling satisfied, thought everything was OK. Well, it wasn't. The industry is not prepared to permit me to portray the life or express the living interests, hopes, and aspirations of the struggling people from whom I come . . . You bet they will never let me play a part in a film in which a Negro is on top."

To escape the Stepin Fetchit–Bill "Bojangles" Robinson stereotype, he went to England where he was promised more challenging roles. He accepted the role of Bosambo, an African tribal chief, in "Sanders of the River," with assurances that the film would truthfully portray African life. Film crews went to Africa to record native songs and chants for the sound track. African workers were cast. Robeson was enthusiastic about the film when it was completed.

But when he returned to London after a short vacation, Robeson learned that the producers were filming an unusually large number of retakes.

Robeson, according to Marie Seton, one of his biographers, "realized that he had lent his talents and his name to a film which in effect justified British colonial rule. A number of new scenes had been written into the scenario which glorified British imperialism. And he had signed a contract with no provision giving him the right to approve the finished film."

He attended the film's premiere at London's Leicester Square Theater. But when he was asked to make a speech at the end of the film, Robeson walked out in protest. His next film, "Song of Freedom," was another African melodrama, but there was a difference. Robeson had veto power over the final version. He said, shortly before the picture's release, "I believe this is the first film to give a true picture of many aspects of the life of the colored man in the West. Hitherto on the screen he has been caricatured or presented only as a comedy character."

But Robeson's other film roles brought more disappointments. In "King Solomon's Mines," he played Umbopas, an African chief, who, after editing and retakes, was portrayed as little more than a black servant. In "Proud Valley," Robeson gives his life serving white men.

Even so, Robeson's popularity was enormous. He appeared in CBS

Radio's "Pursuit of Happiness" program in November, 1939, to intro-
duce Earl Robinson's "Ballad for Americans," which avowed that
whites cannot be free if blacks are enslaved.

The studio audience—more than 600 people—gave Robeson a rous-
ing ovation that continued 15 minutes.

Robeson returned to Broadway in the winter of 1940, playing the
lead in "John Henry," a musical about the legendary black strongman.

He followed that triumph with the role he had spent years waiting
for—Shakespeare's "Othello." Although Robeson's earlier English portrayal of Othello had been successful, there was reason to believe that
it might be a disaster in New York—simply because Shakespeare's tragedy had never caused much of a stir on the American stage.

The skeptics were wrong.

Robeson's "Othello" ran 296 performances, setting an all-time
record for a Shakespearean play in New York. Burton Rascoe of the
New York World Telegram summarized critical acclaim, calling it "one
of the most memorable events in the history of the theatre . . . there
has never been and never will be a finer rendition of this particular
tragedy. It is unbelievably magnificent."

In the meantime, Robeson was becoming involved in the affairs of
Black America and the Third World, explaining that "I couldn't live
with my own conscience, feeling I was getting the gravy." Despite his
celebrity status, he was forced to travel in segregated railroad cars,
ride in freight elevators at private clubs, and, in Boston, was unable to
get a hotel room. He never asked for preferential treatment, only for
an end to Jim Crow laws. But American's sensitivity toward race in
the early 1940s was exemplified by the *Saturday Evening Post* which
ran a cartoon series called "Ambitious Ambrose," about a dimwitted
black grocery clerk. Even the liberal *New Republic* implied that American blacks were going to undermine the war effort.

Instead, during World War II, Robeson gave no less than 25 free
concerts for American troops; according to USO officials, they were
better received than any others.

After the war, Robeson led picket lines at the White House, declaring that "Jim Crow Must Go." He testified before Congressional committees on civil rights legislation. He urged Congress to open major
league baseball to black athletes. He formed the American Crusade to
End Lynching.

President Harry S. Truman met with Robeson and other anti-
lynching leaders at the White House in September, 1946. Robeson

urged Truman to issue a statement endorsing "a definite legislative and educational program to end the disgrace of mob violence." Truman promised such an action "when the timing was right," adding that the U.S. and Great Britain were the "last refuge" of freedom in the world. Robeson cut Truman short, retorting that "The British Empire is one of the great enslavers of human beings."

Robeson was suspicious of Truman's civil rights program, perceiving him, perhaps unfairly, as a Southern reactionary. When Henry A. Wallace launched his third-party campaign against Truman, Robeson became one of that movement's most prominent supporters. The Wallace campaign was viewed, at the time, as a major third-party effort. As Franklin Roosevelt's vice-president, Wallace had become the country's leading spokesman for social liberalism. Like George McGovern, Wallace campaigned on a platform of peace, civil rights, and reform of the capitalist system.

Robeson and many other black leaders believed in Wallace's programs. So did trade unionists, intellectuals, and college students. The Communist Party openly supported Wallace, and, during the campaign the former vice president was denounced as a Communist dupe. Some of Wallace's more outspoken supporters, sensitive about the Communist issue, withdrew from the campaign. Robeson held firm, spending most of the year campaigning for Wallace. He was seriously mentioned as a potential running-mate on Wallace's Progressive ticket, but Robeson insisted he had no interest. It was just as well, too, for Wallace, in the November election, failed to carry a single state.

It was during this supercharged period that Robeson began running into right-wing opposition. He couldn't give a concert without interruptions from superpatriots: "Go Back to Russia!" chanted flag-waving American Legion members. Sometimes veterans' organizations provoked violent confrontations. During the summer of 1949, two Robeson concerts turned into riots. The anti-Robeson violence, said the *New York Times*, was reminiscent of "a lynch mob in darkest Georgia."

"I'm a radical and I'm going to stay one," Robeson told one cheering audience. The House UnAmerican Activities Committee replied that Robeson was "invariably found supporting the Communist party and its front organizations." Robeson, meanwhile, refused to say whether he was a Communist. He wasn't, but he considered the question a violation of his civil rights. And he made no effort to disassociate himself from "many dear friends" who were active Communists.

His independence exacted a price. The State Department revoked his passport in 1950, citing his support of African revolutionaries as one of its reasons. His refusal to sign an affidavit stating whether he was or had been a Communist was, of course, another reason.

Orthodox black leaders, like the NAACP's Walter White, took pains to isolate Robeson: "We do not feel that Mr. Robeson voices the opinion of the majority of Negro Americans."

Sterling Stuckey, a Northwestern University black historian, strongly criticizes the black leadership of the era:

"Preventing Robeson from reaching his people during the 1950s, together with the NAACP's forcing W. E. B. Du Bois to leave its ranks for the second and last time in 1948, had an effect on the freedom struggle so shattering that Afro-Americans are still reeling from it," says Stuckey. "With Robeson and Du Bois effectively isolated, their people for the first time in history were led by men with no interest whatever in Africa."

Nevertheless, Robeson fought his attackers during the 1950s. He told HUAC members, "I am not being tried for whether I am a Communist; I am being tried for fighting for the rights of my people who are still second-class citizens." Asked if he had made a pro-Stalin speech in Moscow, Robeson snapped back, "You are responsible and your forebears for sixty million to one hundred million black people dying in the slave ships and on the plantations, and don't you ask me about anybody please."

When a Congressman suggested that Robeson might be happier in Russia, he fired back, "My father was a slave, and my people died to build this country, and I am going to stay and have a piece of it just like you. And no fascist-minded people will drive me from it. Is that clear?"

Robeson, although he acted in England and made concert appearances in Soviet bloc countries, was an old man by the time he was able to travel again. The magnificent voice was gone. In 1961, stricken with what was called a "circulatory ailment," he retired from singing. He left East Germany to return to the United States in December, 1963. He made no more public appearances, with the exception of a testimonial dinner in New York in April, 1965. That, for many friends, was the last time they saw Robeson.

Robeson's health, from all reports, has deteriorated. He was found lying in a clump of weeds in a vacant New York lot in October, 1965.

His wife, who had reported him missing, said he was suffering from dizzy spells and loss of balance.

Mrs. Robeson died in December, 1965, and it was shortly afterward that Paul Robeson moved to Philadelphia. He stays with his sister, Mrs. Marion Forsythe, a retired school teacher. Letters from friends go unanswered. His phone number is unavailable—he never did care for telephones. And his family refuses to make any exceptions to Robeson's request for privacy.

For the record, however, Robeson taped a public statement that was played at the Carnegie Hall birthday celebration. "I want you to know that I am the same Paul," he said, "dedicated as ever to the world-wide cause of humanity for freedom, peace, and brotherhood . . . Though ill health has compelled my retirement, you can be sure that in my heart I go on singing:

" 'But I keeps laughing
Instead of crying,
I must keep fighting
Until I'm dying,
And Ol' Man River
He just keeps rolling along!' "

Gwendolyn Brooks
Chicago Sun-Times, 6/23/97

She is a poet of the people.

Illinois poet laureate Gwendolyn Brooks, who celebrated her 80th birthday this month, is a master of American verse in the tradition of Bessie Smith and Langston Hughes. It has been nearly a half-century since she became the first African American to win a Pulitzer Prize. But the author of more than 20 books has never been content to rest on her laurels. A new book of her poetry will be published this fall.

"My poem is life, and it will never be finished," Brooks recently told a student audience at West Leyden High School. "People always want to know: Where do I get my ideas? They're everywhere. I'm inspired by people and things around me."

Brooks, who sparks with a life force, is still very active. Today, she is presenting awards to the winners of her 28th state-wide poet laureate's competition. Twenty-seven high school and elementary school students will read their works during the ceremony at the University of Chicago.

Since 1990, she has held the Gwendolyn Brooks Chair in Black Literature and Creative Writing at Chicago State University. In addition to teaching, she has organized writing workshops, poetry festivals and other cultural events.

"I'm always anxious to learn, and I have learned a great deal from young people," Brooks said.

Few major writers have had more staying power. The theme of social justice that runs through her work is ageless. She also has written illuminating satire. "The Lovers of the Poor" is a devastating portrait of North Shore socialites slumming in the city. Her signature poem, "We Real Cool," describes seven inner-city youths who play hooky from school and lose their souls.

Her first published collection, *A Street in Bronzeville* (1954), vividly portrayed life on the South Side. She wrote of Satin-Legs Smith, who "has not a flower to his name. Except a feather one for his lapel," and DeWitt Williams, who "drank his liquid joy" under the L at 47th Street.

"They are hard and real, right out of the central core of Black Belt life in urban areas," Richard Wright wrote of the first Brooks collection. "There is no self-pity here, nor a striving for effects. She takes hold of reality as it is and renders it faithfully."

Brooks describes her poetry as "a life distilled." Like other great writers, she is a keen observer. "In my 20s, when I wrote a good deal of my better-known poetry, I lived on 63rd Street—at 623 E. 63rd St.—and there was a good deal of life in the raw all around me," she told historian Paul M. Angle in 1967. "I wrote about what I saw and heard in the street. I lived in a small second-floor apartment at the corner, and I could look first on one side and then on the other. That was my material."

Brooks is among America's more versatile poets. One of the reasons that her work is so fresh and compelling is that she is always discovering new forms. She has written free verse, sonnets, couplets, quatrains, blues poems, a novel and an autobiography. "Her craftsmanship is careful. [She] belongs to the school of writers who do not believe in wasting a single word," writer Blyden Jackson has written. "Selection and significance—one can divine in her diction how she has brooded over them, how every word has been chosen with due regard for the several functions it may be called upon to perform."

She is genuine in her commitment to black economic and political empowerment. For three decades, she was published by Harper & Row, an old New York publishing house. But she switched to the black-owned Broadside Press in 1969 and in 1974 to Third World Press.

Brooks was named our poet laureate in 1968. Her predecessor was Carl Sandburg. In a tribute to her friend Robert Frost, Brooks shows her own warm humanity in verse that also applies to her:

He is splendid. With a place to stand.
Some glowing in the common blood.
Some specialness within.

Cesar Chavez
Chicago Sun-Times, 4/27/93

He was the last icon.

Cesar Chavez, who died Friday, was the last of '60s movement leaders and the most influential U. S. labor organizer since World War II. Robert F. Kennedy called him "one of the heroic figures of our time," which he was.

When Chavez launched his farm workers' movement more than 30 years ago, his efforts weren't taken seriously. Hundreds of previous attempts had failed. But Chavez, who was a skilled organizer, was a man of faith and hope. He believed in the justice of his cause.

"If an organizer comes looking for appreciation, he might just as well stay home," Chavez said then. "He's not going to get any, especially out of a group that's never been organized or had any power before."

The farm workers needed help. Many lived in tarpaper shacks with dirt floors and were drinking impure water. The growers used toxic pesticides that caused illnesses. Workers were being paid $1.10 an hour. Conditions hadn't improved since John Steinbeck had written *The Grapes of Wrath*.

Chavez organized the farm workers and launched the most successful boycott in American history against California grape growers. Chavez's mentor, Chicagoan Saul Alinsky, had warned that middle-class Americans wouldn't stop eating grapes. But Chavez thought otherwise. With quiet eloquence, he rallied public opinion to his struggle.

"The boycotts are predicated on faith in the compassion of people," he said. "We are convinced that when consumers are faced with a direct appeal from the poor struggling against great odds, they will react positively. The American people still yearn for justice. It is to that viewpoint and that yearning we appeal. . . . When you sacrifice, you force others to do the same. It is a powerful weapon. When you work and sacrifice more than anyone around you, others feel the need to do at least a little bit more than they were doing before."

In an age of racial polarization, Chavez forged alliances among all ethnic groups. His union included Latinos, Asian Americans, blacks and whites. "Our belief is to help everybody, not just one race," he said. "Humanity is our belief."

Even so Chavez had powerful enemies. At a 1968 campaign rally, Richard M. Nixon ate California grapes in defiance of the boycott and called for "new moral leadership." Then California Gov. Ronald Reagan denounced the farm-worker strike as "immoral" and referred to Chavez allies as "noisy barbarians." Chavez later achieved a historic breakthrough in 1975 when California enacted the nation's first collective-bargaining law for farm workers.

More than any other U.S. labor leader, Chavez sacrificed. In the spring of 1968, he fasted for 25 days, yielding a fifth of his flesh, 35 pounds, for the movement. "My heart was filled with grief when I saw the pain and suffering of the workers," said Chavez. He ended his fast at an open-air mass with Sen. Robert F. Kennedy taking communion with him. Chavez was too weak to speak.

Dr. Martin Luther King Jr. sent Chavez a telegram: "I am deeply moved by your courage in fasting as your personal sacrifice for justice through nonviolence. Your past and present commitment is eloquent testimony to the constructive power of nonviolent action and the destructive impotence of violent reprisal. Your stand is a living example of the Gandhian tradition with its great force for social progress and its healing spiritual powers." Chavez, with Dr. King, now belongs to the ages.

Jesse L. Jackson

Chicago Sun-Times, 10/9/91

If the Rev. Jesse L. Jackson had listened to the conventional wisdom, he never would have run for the presidency of the United States.

Eight years ago, Jackson was warned by the Democratic Party's establishment, including African-American leaders, that a black presidential candidacy would be divisive and futile. Jackson wouldn't be deterred. He surprised nearly everyone by gaining more than 3 million votes in the Democratic primaries.

Four years ago, Jackson was urged by old allies not to become a two-time loser. But Jackson, never afraid to challenge the odds, mobilized an even more successful presidential campaign. He forged a coalition of blacks, Hispanics and working-class whites, winning more than 7 million Democratic votes in the process.

Now, as Jackson weighs a third campaign for the presidency, he is hearing the same arguments against his candidacy from the Democratic establishment, and also from former supporters. Jackson has been bluntly told that his candidacy could further split the Democratic Party and that he could be tagged as a perennial also-ran.

Jackson, who celebrated his 50th birthday on Tuesday, said in an interview that he is "giving serious consideration" to a '92 Democratic presidential bid and will decide within a month. "We would start from the base of our accumulated work over the years," said Jackson, who said that there are more reasons to run than not.

Even Jackson's critics have acknowledged that he has made an enormous contribution to American politics over the last decade. More than anyone else, Jackson was responsible for mobilizing the new voters that elected Harold Washington as mayor of Chicago in 1983, elected a Democratic U.S. Senate in 1986 as black voters ousted four Republican incumbents in the South and elected David N. Dinkins as mayor of New York in 1989. If Jackson had listened to the doubters, these significant victories might not have been achieved.

"Nothing will ever again be what it was before," writer James Baldwin said after Jackson's first campaign. "It changes the way the boy in the street and the boy on Death Row and his mother and father and his sweetheart and sister think about themselves. It indicates that one is not entirely at the mercy of the assumptions of this republic to what they have said you are."

In an era when some prominent Democrats moved toward the political right, Jackson has promoted affordable housing, fair prices for farmers, an increase in the minimum wage, pay equity for women and minorities and national health care. "My constituency is the damned, the disinherited, the disrespected and the despised," Jackson once said. "America is not like a blanket, one piece of unbroken cloth—the same color, the same texture, the same size. It is more like a quilt—many patches, many pieces, many colors, many sizes, all woven and held together by a common thread."

Since the tragic deaths of Robert F. Kennedy and Martin Luther King, Jr. in 1968, no one has fought harder for the dispossessed and powerless.

Presidents

Franklin D. Roosevelt

Philadelphia Inquirer, 4/14/91

Franklin D. Roosevelt was arguably the best spin doctor in American history. Despite the opposition of powerful media barons, FDR shaped his own image through the working press and also through the newly important medium of radio, which he understood better than any of his political contemporaries.

Betty Houchin Winfield, University of Missouri journalism professor, has written a balanced, readable and insightful study of FDR's relationship with the news media. She is particularly effective at showing how Roosevelt became a dominant political force through his mastery of radio. Like John F. Kennedy and Ronald Reagan in the television age, FDR made straight men out of his political opponents.

In the age of radio, nobody could seriously compete with Roosevelt's rich voice. Winfield discloses that Roosevelt added a false tooth for his radio speeches. "With the separation between his front two lower teeth he would whistle slightly on certain words, a most noticeable broadcast sound," Winfield writes. "Grace Tully [one of his secretaries] recalled that when he would occasionally forget to bring down the removable bridge there would be a last-minute dash to rescue the tooth in its little silver box on his bedside table."

After taking office in 1933, FDR got off to a good start with White House reporters by getting rid of the written-question requirement for news conferences. Roosevelt held twice-weekly news conferences in the Oval Office, which were off-the-record. He also hosted reporters on Sunday nights for dinner and private screenings of Hollywood films. Winfield writes that Roosevelt gave reporters the full diplomatic treatment.

Herbert Hoover, Roosevelt's predecessor, went months without news conferences and sought to avoid reporters, which contributed to his image as an aloof, out-of-touch chief executive. Roosevelt learned from Hoover's mistakes.

Roosevelt, who briefly wrote a newspaper column in the 1920s, liked most of the reporters who chronicled his presidency, and they liked him. At Harvard, Roosevelt had been the president of the *Crimson*, and he never lost his enthusiasm for attempting to manipulate the news. His wife, Eleanor, became one of the nation's best read columnists during the New Deal, and their daughter Anna became a newspaper executive. She married John Boettiger, the *Chicago Tribune*'s White House correspondent, and they later ran a Seattle newspaper.

White House correspondents described Roosevelt as the best managing editor in the history of the presidency. FDR, this volume shows, wasn't above suggesting leads for news reports about himself. He also had a keen sense of timing, knowing when to break news with maximum impact.

"Instead of using it right now, jot your notes down and let me give you a hint," Roosevelt once told reporters. "Let me dig that up for you. Don't use it today—use it for a Sunday or Monday story. Wait until you know more about it." Roosevelt would also suggest adverbs and adjectives: "In regard to the [Budget] Message, I suppose if I were writing your stories for you, I would say it is the most brutally frank Budget Message ever sent in."

According to Winfield, White House press secretary Stephen Early put friendly reporters in the front row at FDR's news conferences to ask planted questions. This technique was still in use a half-century later during the Reagan years when White House press spokesman Larry Speakes assigned front-row seating to "known friendlies," who could be counted on to throw softballs at a moment's notice.

Winfield says that Arthur Krock, bureau chief for the *New York Times* in the Roosevelt era, didn't attend the White House news conferences, making the argument that it was better to maintain distance between himself and the engaging FDR.

During World War II, FDR imposed the toughest censorship of his administration. Winfield reports that Roosevelt held 89 news conferences in 1941 but only 55 in 1944. Instead of having two news conferences a week, the wartime president would go for as long as three weeks without meeting reporters. But in contrast with President Bush's news management during Operation Desert Storm, Roosevelt was accessibility itself.

Roosevelt's handlers prohibited photographs of the president in a wheelchair or on crutches. The White House press office asked that all pictures of Roosevelt that suggested he was crippled be voluntarily withheld and destroyed. Some Republican publications, including *Life* magazine, *Look*, the *New York Herald Tribune* and the *Chicago Tribune*, sometimes broke Roosevelt's rules about using such photographs. But most publications only showed Roosevelt in heroic poses. Even Henry Luce, *Life*'s publisher, found that Roosevelt's handsome, well-chiseled face sold magazines.

There are some surprising gaps in Winfield's history of FDR's press relations. War correspondent Quentin Reynolds, who seconded Roosevelt's nomination for the presidency at the 1944 Democratic National Convention, isn't mentioned. Influential columnists Walter Lippmann and Dorothy Thompson are given short shrift. Westbrook Pegler, Roosevelt's most persistent and acerbic critic, is overlooked completely.

Winfield discusses Roosevelt's relationships with publishers William Randolph Hearst and Col. Robert McCormick but doesn't mention that FDR persuaded Marshall Field to launch the *Chicago Sun* in 1941 as a liberal counterpoint to Hearst and McCormick. There is almost no mention of the late David Stern, whose *Philadelphia Record* was Roosevelt's most stalwart defender.

Moses Annenberg, the anti-Roosevelt publisher of the *Philadelphia Inquirer*, is also curiously omitted. Annenberg was a target of Roosevelt's IRS and went to jail.

Though this study could have been more comprehensive, Winfield has made a valuable contribution to the Roosevelt literature.

Harry S. Truman

Chicago Sun-Times, 8/8/95

It was the most controversial decision of World War II.

A half-century later, President Harry S. Truman's decision to drop atomic bombs on Hiroshima and Nagasaki is under attack.

In a recent 90-minute special that was aired on ABC and narrated by Peter Jennings, the revisionist historians said that Truman was wrong. Their argument was that Japan had already been defeated and that Truman dropped the bombs to scare the Soviet Union.

Many Americans now question whether Truman should have used the lethal weapon. A recent Gallup Poll reported that only 44 percent of the American public supported Truman's decision.

Was it necessary for Truman to have dropped the bombs?

His goal was to end the war.

Truman had been reluctant to use the bomb. But he and his top military advisers had concluded that it was necessary to use the ultimate weapon to end the war.

"I realize the tragic significance of the atomic bomb," Truman said in a radio address on Aug. 9, 1945, which is quoted in David McCullough's 1992 Truman biography. "Its production and its use were not lightly undertaken by this government. But we knew that our enemies were on the search for it.

"We won the race of discovery against the Germans.

"Having found the bomb, we have used it. We have used it against those who attacked us without warning at Pearl Harbor, against those who have starved and beaten and executed American prisoners of war, against those who have abandoned all pretense of obeying international laws of warfare. We have used it to shorten the agony of war, in order to save the lives of thousands and thousands of young Americans.

"We shall continue to use it until we completely destroy Japan's power to make war. Only a Japanese surrender will stop us."

The revisionist historians are wrong that Japan was ready to surrender. Truman had repeatedly asked Imperial Japan to surrender. His pleas were rejected. The Japanese fought to the finish on Iwo Jima and on Okinawa. Truman persisted in seeking peace. Finally, he gave the Japanese an ultimatum. It was ignored.

Truman had authorized an invasion of Japan. According to U.S. military estimates, the invasion could have resulted in between 250,000 and 500,000 American casualties. Truman later asserted that the revisionist historians were distorting the facts for political purposes.

"It was a question of saving hundreds of thousands of American lives," Truman said in 1965. "You don't feel normal when you have to plan hundreds of thousands of deaths of American boys who are alive and joking and having fun while you're doing your planning. You break your heart and your head trying to figure out a way to save one life. . . . I couldn't worry about what history would say about my personal morality. I made the only decision I ever knew how to make. I did what I thought was right."

If Japan or Germany had invented the atomic bomb, there is little doubt that they would have deployed it with ruthlessness. Neither Tojo nor Hitler was troubled by the slaughter of innocents. Truman ended the war that they started.

Truman did what he had to do.

"Although many Americans have expressed contrition over exploding the first atomic bombs, it is difficult to see how the Pacific war could otherwise have been concluded, except by a long and bitter invasion of Japan," said the late Adm. Samuel Eliot Morison. Truman's decision saved lives.

Dwight D. Eisenhower
American Heritage, 12/85

Shortly after Dwight D. Eisenhower left office, a poll of leading American historians judged him to be among our worst Presidents. Thirty years later, historians have come around to the opinion most of their fellow Americans held right along.

Early in 1952, Gen. Dwight David Eisenhower confided to a friendly Republican politician why he was reluctant to seek the Presidency: "I think I pretty well hit my peak in history when I accepted the German surrender."

Emerging from World War II as the organizer of the Allied victory, Eisenhower was America's most celebrated hero. "You have made history, great history, for the good of mankind, and you have stood for all we hope for and admire in an officer of the United States Army," wrote Gen. George C. Marshall. Both major political parties sought to nominate him for the Presidency. And when Ike decided to risk his historical reputation, he captured the 1952 Republican presidential nomination and ended twenty years of Democratic rule. Ronald Reagan was among the millions of Democrats who crossed party lines to support the Republican general. Afterward, the badly beaten Democratic candidate, Adlai E. Stevenson, asked his friend Alistair Cooke: "Who did I think I was, running against George Washington?"

Not only did Eisenhower win two terms by margins of historic proportions, but he maintained his popularity throughout his Presidency.

He left office in 1961 still revered by two-thirds of his countrymen, and the American public never stopped liking Ike.

But however much historians and political scholars may have liked Ike, respect was something else. Until recently it seemed that Eisenhower had lost his gamble with history. Like Ulysses S. Grant and Zachary Taylor, Eisenhower was frequently portrayed as a military hero who turned out to be a mediocre Chief Executive. Soon after Ike left the White House, a poll of leading scholars ranked him among the nation's ten worst Presidents.

Since then, however, Eisenhower's historical image has been dramatically rehabilitated. In 1982 a similar poll of prominent historians and political scholars rated him near the top of the list of Presidents. Eisenhower is gaining recognition as one of the large figures of the twentieth century, not just for his role as Supreme Allied Commander in World War II, but also for his eight years as President of the United States.

Which measure is more accurate? How could Eisenhower command such affection from the American public without winning similar respect from scholars and political commentators? Why is his historical reputation suddenly being revived? And is the revisionism justified?

One of the reasons for Eisenhower's comeback is nostalgia for an enormously popular President after an era of assassinations, political scandals, military defeat, and economic turmoil. Another factor in the reassessment is Eisenhower's record of eight years of peace and prosperity, which is unique among twentieth-century Presidents.

Eisenhower, a man of war, conducted his foreign policy with restraint and moderation. During the most turbulent era of the Cold War, he ended the Korean War, blocked British and French efforts to crush Arab nationalism, opposed military intervention in Southeast Asia, opened a new dialogue with the Soviet Union, and alerted the nation to the dangers of the expanding military-industrial complex. He was criticized for being too passive by the Cold Warriors Henry Kissinger and Gen. Maxwell Taylor, and the same critics berated him for a missile gap that turned out to be nonexistent. In retirement, Eisenhower said his most notable presidential achievement was that "the United States never lost a soldier or a foot of ground in my administration. We kept the peace."

In domestic affairs, Eisenhower also strove to maintain a peaceful equilibrium in handling such explosive issues as McCarthyism and segregation. While critics charged that Ike was spineless in his refusal to openly fight Sen. Joseph McCarthy, the President worked behind the scenes to reduce McCarthy's influence. Despite private doubts about a Supreme Court decision that outlawed segregation, he sent the 101st Airborne into Little Rock, Arkansas, when the state's governor defied the law. He also pushed through the first federal civil rights law since Reconstruction and established the United States Commission on Civil Rights.

Although Eisenhower's memoir of his first term was entitled *Mandate for Change*, his most notable achievement in domestic policy was the continuance of New Deal reforms. For nearly a generation, congressional Republicans had been pledging to dismantle FDR's social programs. But Eisenhower had other ideas. "Should any political party attempt to abolish Social Security, unemployment insurance, and eliminate labor laws and farm programs, you would not hear of that party again in our political history," he wrote to his brother Edgar, an outspoken conservative. During the Eisenhower era the number of Americans covered by Social Security doubled, and benefits were increased. The Department of Health, Education, and Welfare was established as a domestic Pentagon. Eisenhower also launched the largest public-works project in American history by building the federal highway system, which turned out to be almost as important as the transcontinental railroad. Barry Goldwater denounced the Eisenhower administration as a "dime-store New Deal," and another conservative critic, William F. Buckley, characterized Eisenhower's record as "measured socialism." But the Republican President's acceptance of the Roosevelt legacy effectively ended debate over the New Deal and meant that the reforms would endure.

The prosperity of the Eisenhower years was no accident. He produced three balanced budgets; the gross national product grew by over 25 percent; and inflation averaged 1.4 percent. To hold the line on inflation, Eisenhower made the tough political choice to accept three recessions. The AFL-CIO president George Meany, who frequently criticized Ike's policies, nonetheless said that the American worker had "never had it so good."

Although he continued Roosevelt's social programs, Eisenhower's concept of presidential leadership was very different from FDR's. Ike's style was managerial with an orderly staff system and a strong cabinet. FDR was an activist who encouraged chaos and creative tension among his hyperactive staff and cabinet. Most political scholars shared

Roosevelt's philosophy of government and viewed Eisenhower as an ineffectual board chairman. There were jokes about the Eisenhower doll; you wound it up and it did nothing for eight years. A memorable Herblock cartoon showed Ike asking his cabinet, "What shall we refrain from doing now?"

The early Eisenhower literature consisted of affectionate memoirs by World War II associates and adoring biographies by war correspondents. But as Chief Executive, Ike suddenly found a more independent panel of observers judging him by new and different standards.

Many of Ike's critics were Democratic partisans. A large factor in his low rating among scholars and liberal commentators was the extraordinary popularity among intellectuals of his major political rival, Adlai Stevenson. Stevenson's admirers were bitter that Eisenhower had twice routed their champion. In *Anti-Intellectualism in American Life*, the renowned historian Richard Hofstadter described Stevenson as a "politician of uncommon mind and style" and Eisenhower as "conventional in mind, relatively inarticulate."

Arthur Larson, the University of Pittsburgh law dean who became an Eisenhower speech writer, recalled: "It was one of the paradoxes of my position in those days that the people I was most at home with, intellectually and ideologically, were more often than not bitterly critical of Eisenhower, if not downright contemptuous of him."

Eisenhower did not improve his image in the academic community by flippantly remarking that an intellectual was someone "who takes more words than are necessary to tell more than he knows." As for the syndicated columnists, he declared that "anyone who has time to listen to commentators or read columnists obviously doesn't have enough work to do."

Eisenhower's poor showing in the poll taken shortly after he left office, in which Arthur M. Schlesinger, Sr., got seventy-five historians to rate Ike's Presidency should not have been surprising: the participants included two of Stevenson's speech writers, a leader of the 1952 "Draft Stevenson" movement, and other Democratic partisans. Malcolm Moos, a political scholar and former Eisenhower speech writer, declined to participate in the survey, which he believed was stacked against Ike.

In the poll, Eisenhower finished twenty second out of thirty-one Presidents, which placed him just between the White House mediocrities Chester Alan Arthur and Andrew Johnson. John F. Kennedy reportedly chuckled over Ike's low score in the Schlesinger survey. Eisenhower's associates were concerned that the negative rating might have staying power. "I'm very distressed at this tendency of academics to look down their noses at the Eisenhower administration," the former White House chief of staff Sherman Adams acknowledged years later. "It's a common sort of thing with the intelligentsia. It's just typical. Look at Mr. Roosevelt. He's a great favorite with the academics, and he's probably a great man. But he lost a lot of battles, didn't he? . . . Well, we may not have done as much, may not have been as spectacular in terms of our willingness to break with the past, but we didn't lose a lot of battles either. A lot of our most important accomplishments were negative—things we avoided. We maintained a peaceful front and adjudicated a lot of issues that seemed ominous and threatening at the time."

Had Eisenhower served just one term, it is unlikely that his historical stock would have dropped so much. Near the end of his first term, his reputation looked fairly secure. A respected journalist, Robert J. Donovan, had written an authoritative history of Eisenhower's first term, which in many ways remains the best study of a sitting President, and which showed Ike firmly in charge. The Pulitzer Prize-winning historian Merlo Pusey had written a friendly treatment of the Eisenhower administration and predicted that Ike would be remembered as a great President, while the political scholar Clinton Rossiter wrote in *The American Presidency* (1956) that Eisenhower "already stands above Polk and Cleveland, and he has a reasonable chance to move up to Jefferson and Theodore Roosevelt."

But like most second terms, Eisenhower's last four years were less productive than his first. The nation was jolted when the Soviet Union launched Sputnik in 1957, and it took months to rebuild American confidence. The recession of 1958 marked the worst economic slide since the Great Depression; more than five million workers were jobless before the recovery began. Ike's 1957 stroke, his third major illness in three years, reinforced doubts about his health and capability to govern. His chief aide, Sherman Adams, became entwined in a political scandal and was forced to resign in 1958. Although Ike had hoped to build a new Republican majority, his efforts were minimal and his party was thoroughly trounced in the 1958 midterm elections.

Eisenhower's 1960 Paris summit with Soviet premier Nikita Khrushchev and leaders of the Western alliance was ruined when an American reconnaissance aircraft, the U-2, was shot down over Central Russia and the pilot, Francis Gary Powers, was captured. Khrushchev stormed out of the summit, withdrawing his invitation for the President's scheduled June visit to the Soviet Union. Had Eisenhower followed his instincts, the U-2 fiasco might have been avoided. A year earlier, he had suggested that the spy flights be halted, but he relented when his National Security Council advisers objected. Later he personally approved Powers's flight. In suggesting that Eisenhower might not have known of the secret mission over the Soviet Union, Khrushchev provided Ike with an alibi that might have salvaged the summit. Indeed, Sen. J. William Fulbright had urged Ike to disclaim responsibility. But Eisenhower told associates that denials would have been ineffectual because of the overpowering evidence. Furthermore, Eisenhower did not want to give credibility to the charges made by his detractors that he was not in control of his own administration.

In his critical 1958 portrait, *Eisenhower: Captive Hero*, the journalist Marquis Childs suggested that Ike was in the wrong job. "If his public record had ended with his military career, it seems safe to assume that a high place would be secure for him," Childs wrote. "But Eisenhower's performance in the presidency will count much more heavily in the final summing up." Childs offered the interpretation that Eisenhower had been a weak and ineffective President, "a prisoner of his office, a captive of his own indecisiveness," another James Buchanan.

Striking a similar theme, the Harvard political scholar Richard Neustadt, in his 1960 study, *Presidential Power*, depicted Eisenhower as a passive, detached Chief Executive. According to Neustadt, Eisenhower became too isolated from his staff and should have been more involved in discussing policy options. "The less he was bothered," Neustadt quoted a White House observer, "the less he knew, and the less he knew, the less confidence he felt in his own judgment. He let himself grow stale."

In a revised 1960 edition of *The American Presidency*, Rossiter concluded that Eisenhower had been a disappointment. "He will be remembered, I fear, as the unadventurous president who held on one term too long in the new age of adventure." Without directly attacking Eisenhower, Kennedy suggested in his 1960 presidential campaign that the Republican incumbent was a tired old man, whose lack of leadership had weakened America's prestige in the world. Following his election, Kennedy privately acknowledged that he was struck by Eisenhower's vitality and ruddy health.

Eisenhower's own history of his Presidency was more authoritative but less provocative than those written by his critics, and it had little immediate impact on his reputation. Until the era of six-figure book advances, most American Presidents had left the interpretation of their administrations to others. But during the Eisenhower years, Herbert Hoover and Harry Truman had both published their own White House memoirs, and John Eisenhower had persuaded his father to undertake a similar project after he left office. John, who would later become a military historian, was then serving as a presidential aide. During the final weeks of his father's Presidency, the younger Eisenhower organized White House files and arranged for their transfer to Gettysburg. On leaving Washington, the Eisenhowers devoted much of the next four years to the memoirs. The first volume, *Mandate for Change*, was published in late 1963, and *Waging Peace*, the second installment, came out two years later.

The former President's refusal to disclose his unvarnished opinions of political contemporaries or admit mistakes helped set a bland tone for both volumes. In *Mandate*, Eisenhower described a secret meeting at the Pentagon with a prominent Republican senator in the winter of 1951, without revealing the other man's identity. At the meeting Ike offered to renounce all political ambitions if the senator would make a public commitment to economic and military aid to Western Europe and American participation in the North Atlantic Treaty Organization. When the senator declined, Eisenhower began thinking much more seriously about running for the Presidency.

This meeting had been a turning point in modern American history because the senator Eisenhower neglected to identify in his memoirs was Robert A. Taft, the leading conservative contender for the 1952 Republican presidential nomination. Ike's memoirs would have been much more compelling reading if he had written what he told associates—that in the wake of their meeting he considered Taft a very stupid man. Had the Ohio senator accepted Eisenhower's offer at the Pentagon, it is more than likely that he would have been nominated for the Presidency and Eisenhower would have remained a soldier.

When Johns Hopkins University Press issued the first five volumes of Ike's papers in 1970, the former President's historical image received a boost almost overnight. John Kenneth Galbraith, who had been Stevenson's adviser and had once described the Eisenhower administration as "the bland leading the bland," wrote in the *Washington Post* that Ike's private writings demonstrated that he had been an "exceedingly vigorous, articulate, and clearheaded administrator, who shows himself throughout to have been also a very conscientious and sensible man."

With the opening of Eisenhower's private correspondence and other key documents of his administration to scholars in the seventies, scholars were soon focusing attention on the primary source material, and a major reassessment of the Eisenhower Presidency was inevitable. Herbert S. Parmet, one of the first historians to make extensive use of newly declassified papers, made the argument in *Eisenhower and the American Crusades* (1972) that those who rated presidential greatness had overlooked Ike's importance in restoring the confidence and building a national consensus in postwar America. To many erstwhile critics, Eisenhower's restrained style of leadership looked better in retrospect during the Vietnam War. At a time when thousands of Americans were dying in a long, bloody, fruitless struggle in Southeast Asia, there were new interpretations of the Eisenhower foreign policy. Murray Kempton's "The Underestimation of Dwight D. Eisenhower," which appeared in the September 1967 issue of *Esquire*, described how Ike had rejected the advice of Cold Warriors to seek military adventure in Vietnam. "He is revealed best, if only occasionally, in the vast and dreary acreage of his memoirs of the White House years," wrote Kempton. "The Eisenhower who emerges here . . . is the President most superbly equipped for truly consequential decision we may ever have had, a mind neither rash nor hesitant, free of the slightest concern for how things might look, indifferent to any sentiment, as calm when he was demonstrating the wisdom of leaving a bad situation alone as when he was moving to meet it on those occasions when he absolutely had to."

Other influential political analysts later expanded the same theme. I. F. Stone noted that Eisenhower, because of his confidence in his own military judgment, was not intimidated into rash action by the Pentagon.

Eisenhower's most enduring and prescient speech was his 1961 farewell address warning of the potential dangers of the military-industrial complex. "In the councils of government," he declared, "we must guard against the acquisition of unwarranted influence, whether sought or unsought, by the military-industrial complex. The potential for the disastrous rise of misplaced power exists and will persist."

Eisenhower's correspondence effectively demonstrates that his farewell address was an accurate reflection of his political philosophy. In an October 1951 letter to the General Motors executive Charles E. Wilson, Eisenhower wrote: "Any person who doesn't clearly understand that national security and national solvency are mutually dependent, and that permanent maintenance of a crushing weight of military power would eventually produce dictatorship, should not be entrusted with any kind of responsibility in our country." The White House press secretary James Hagerty wrote in his diary that Ike had confided, "You know, if you're in the military and you know about these terrible destructive weapons, it tends to make you more pacifistic than you normally have been."

Stephen E. Ambrose, a former editor of the Eisenhower papers and author of the most comprehensive Eisenhower biography, shows how Ike slowed the arms race and exerted firm leadership in rejecting the Gaither Commission's call for sharp increases in defense spending. "Eisenhower's calm, common-sense, deliberate response to [the Soviets launching of Sputnik] may have been his finest gift to the nation," wrote Ambrose, "if only because he was the only man who could have given it." Because of his military background, Eisenhower spoke with more authority about the arms race than his critics. In a 1956 letter to Richard L. Simon, president of Simon and Schuster, who had written him and enclosed a column urging a crash program for nuclear missiles, Eisenhower replied, "When we get to the point, as we one day will, that both sides know that in any outbreak of general hostilities, regardless of the element of surprise, destruction will be both reciprocal and complete, possibly we will have sense enough to meet at the conference table with the understanding that the era of armaments has ended and the human race must conform its actions to this truth or die."

But while many recent historians have portrayed Eisenhower as a dove, a pioneer of detente, there are dissenters. Peter Lyon argued in his 1974 Eisenhower biography that the President's 1953 inaugural address was a "clarion" that "called to war," and that the general was a hawkish militarist. In her 1981 study *The Declassified Eisenhower*, Blanche Wiesen Cook said that Eisenhower used the CIA to launch a "thorough and ambitious anti-Communist crusade" that toppled governments on three continents.

Arthur Schlesinger, Jr., who had previously described Eisenhower as a weak, passive, and politically naive executive, asserted in his 1973 book *The Imperial Presidency* that Ike went overboard in his use of presidential powers by introducing claims for "executive privilege" in denying government documents to Sen. Joseph McCarthy and by also approving the buildup of the CIA. Even so, Schlesinger now ranks Eisenhower with Truman and his former White House boss John F. Kennedy as the successful Presidents of the postwar era.

Another Eisenhower critic, William Leuchtenburg, insists that Ike was not so different from his more obviously hawkish successors. He points to Eisenhower's covert intervention in Iran and Guatemala, his threats to use nuclear weapons in Korea, and his war of words with China over the islands of Quemoy and Ma-tsu. Leuchtenburg also blames Eisenhower for neglecting major public issues, especially in the field of civil rights, "at a considerable cost." Even so, Schlesinger and Leuchtenburg both concede that Eisenhower was much more of a hands-on executive that was realized during his administration.

The records of the Eisenhower administration have ended the myth that the old soldier left foreign policy to his influential secretary of state, John Foster Dulles. A leading Eisenhower revisionist, Fred I. Greenstein, reported in his 1982 study *The Hidden-Hand Presidency* that Ike made the decisions and Dulles carried them out. Greenstein said that it was Eisenhower's international political strategy to be the champion of peace in his public statements, while his secretary of state acted as a Cold Warrior. Dulles once claimed that he, as secretary of state, had ended the Korean War by threatening the use of atomic weapons. But the diplomatic historian Robert A. Divine wrote in *Eisenhower and the Cold War* (1981) that Dulles had exaggerated his role. "It was Eisenhower, in his own characteristically quiet and effective way, who had used the threat of American nuclear power to compel China to end its intervention in the Korean conflict. Perhaps the best testimony to the shrewdness of the President's policy is the impossibility of telling even now whether or not he was bluffing."

Eisenhower's decision not to intervene militarily in Vietnam is described by some revisionists as his finest hour. Nine years later Eisenhower explained in a private memorandum that he had not wanted to tarnish the image of the United States as the world's foremost anticolonial power. "It is essential to our position of leadership in a world wherein the majority of the nations have at some time or another felt the yoke of colonialism. Thus it is that the moral position of the United States was more to be guarded than the Tonkin Delta, indeed that all of Indochina."

Largely because of his White House staff structure and the authority that he delegated to ranking subordinates, Eisenhower was often characterized as a disengaged President. His chief of staff, Sherman Adams, wielded more power than any White House adviser since FDR's Harry Hopkins, and a popular joke of the fifties had the punch line: "What if Sherman Adams died and Ike became President?" But the memoirs of Adams, Richard M. Nixon, Henry Cabot Lodge, Hagerty, Emmet John Hughes, Milton, and John Eisenhower have shown that Ike was firmly in command.

Eisenhower's uneasy relationship with Nixon has also been distorted by some revisionist scholars. While Ike and Nixon were never close, some historians have demonstrated political naivete in accepting Eisenhower's private criticism of his Vice President at face value. If Eisenhower held such strong reservations about Nixon as they have suggested, it is unlikely that he would have retained him on the ticket in 1956 and supported him for the Presidency in 1960 and 1968. Eisenhower did not share Nixon's zest for Republican partisanship, but he considered him a loyal and capable Vice-President. Had one of Ike's personal favorites, such as his bother Milton or Treasury Secretary Robert Anderson, emerged as a potential heir, there is evidence that Eisenhower might have supported them over Nixon. But Ike definitely preferred his Vice-President over his leading rivals Nelson Rockefeller and Barry Goldwater.

Nothing damaged Eisenhower's standing with intellectuals more than his vague position on McCarthyism. Eisenhower historians are sharply divided over the President's role in ending the Wisconsin senator's reign of fear. Ambrose criticizes Eisenhower's "muddled leadership" and unwillingness to publicly condemn McCarthy and his abusive tactics. But Greenstein and William Bragg Ewald have made a strong argument that Eisenhower's behind-the-scenes efforts set the stage for McCarthy's censure by the Senate and destroyed his political influence. Eisenhower loathed McCarthy but believed that a direct presidential attack on him would enhance the senator's credibility among his right-wing followers. The President's papers indicate that he never doubted his strategy against McCarthy, and in the end he felt vindicated.

Eisenhower is also still criticized for not showing sufficient boldness in the field of civil rights. The President was not pleased with the 1954 Supreme Court decision that overturned the "separate but equal" doctrine in public education, and he privately observed that the firestorm touched off by the *Brown v. Board of Education* decision had set back racial progress fifteen years. Despite his misgivings, Eisenhower never considered defying the Court, as his successors Gerald Ford and Ronald Reagan would do, over the volatile issue of school desegregation. Eisenhower enforced the Court's decision in sending federal troops into Little Rock, and he went on to establish a civil rights division in the Justice Department in 1957 that committed the federal government to defend the rights of minorities and provided momentum to the civil rights movement.

As a national hero, Eisenhower's popular appeal transcended his political party. According to a 1955 Gallup Poll, 57 percent of the nation's voters considered Eisenhower a political independent, which may have been why Eisenhower was unable to transfer his enormous popularity to the Republican party. Between 1932 and 1968, he was the only Republican elected to the White House. Ironically the GOP-controlled Eightieth Congress may have shortened the Eisenhower era five years before it began by adopting the Twenty-second Amendment, prohibiting any future President from serving more than two terms. Without the constitutional limit, John Eisenhower said his father would have run for a third term in 1960. Even Truman acknowledged that Eisenhower would have been reelected in another landslide.

Eisenhower restored confidence in the Presidency as an institution and set the agenda for the economic growth of the next decade. He understood public opinion as well as Roosevelt had, and he had a keener sense of military problems than any President since George Washington. As the failings of his successors became apparent, Eisenhower's Presidency grew in historical stature. A 1982 *Chicago Tribune* survey of forty-nine scholars ranked him as the ninth best President in history, just behind Truman and ahead of James K. Polk.

With the renewed appreciation of Eisenhower's achievements, Ambrose predicts that Ike may eventually be ranked ahead of Truman and Theodore Roosevelt, and just behind Washington, Jefferson, Jackson, Lincoln, Wilson, and FDR. "I'd put Ike rather high," the historian Robert Ferrell says, "because when he came into office at the head of an only superficially united party . . . he had to organize that heterogeneous group, and get it to cooperate, which he did admirably with all those keen political instincts of his."

"Whatever his failings," Robert J. Donovan wrote of Eisenhower in 1984, "he was a sensible, outstanding American, determined to do what he believed was right. He was a dedicated peacemaker, a president beloved by millions of people . . . and, clearly, a good man to depend on in a crisis. Of his high rank on the list of presidents there can be little doubt."

Henry Steele Commager, who was among Eisenhower's most thoughtful critics during his Presidency, said recently that he would now rank him about tenth from the top. Though Commager faults Eisenhower for not showing leadership against McCarthysim and on behalf of civil rights, he gives Ike high marks in foreign policy for not intervening in Vietnam and "having the sense to say 'no' to the Joint Chiefs of Staff."

Commager says that Eisenhower's election was the decisive factor in ending the Korean War. "Only a general with enormous prestige could have made peace with Korea. An outsider couldn't have done it." Even Adlai Stevenson told a reporter that the election of Eisenhower in 1952 had been good for the country. (He did not, however, feel the same way about Ike's second term.)

William Appleman Williams, the dean of revisionist historians, says that Eisenhower was far more perceptive in international politics than his predecessor or those who followed him. "He clearly understood that crusading imperial police actions were extremely dangerous," Williams notes, and he was determined to avoid World War III.

In the final months of his Presidency, Eisenhower made this private assessment of his managerial style: "In war and peace I've had no respect for the desk-pounder, and have despised the loud and slick talker. If my own ideas and practices in this matter have sprung from weakness, I do not know. But they were and are deliberate or, rather, natural to me. They are not accidental."

John F. Kennedy

Chicago Sun-Times, 9/22/89

Of all the Irish-American politicians who returned to Ireland as Mayor Daley has this week, John F. Kennedy is the one that they still talk about.

The Daleys of Chicago, former President Reagan, House Speakers Tom Foley and Tip O'Neill, former Democratic National Chairman James A. Farley, Supreme Court Justices William Brennan and Sandra Day O'Connor, and Sens. Ted Kennedy and Daniel Patrick Moynihan are among the more popular Irish-American politicians in the land of their ancestors. But JFK has become nothing less than an Irish legend.

Contrary to popular legend, Kennedy wasn't the first president of the United States of Irish ancestry. Nine of his predecessors, including fellow Democrats Andrew Jackson, James Buchanan, and Woodrow Wilson were of Scotch-Irish descent. But in Ireland, where the Catholic Church is a dominant influence, Kennedy's 1960 election carried special meaning in shattering the myth that a Catholic couldn't win the presidency of the United States.

Less than three years later, Kennedy became the first American president to make an official trip to Ireland. From the cheering throngs in the streets of Dublin to the hushed silence of the crowd at the New Ross docks where his great-grandfather had boarded a ship for the United States, Kennedy was received as a conquering hero.

"In a sense all who visit Ireland come home," Kennedy declared, noting that Americans feel at home in Ireland because of its independence. He made no reference to the British-occupied northern counties.

JFK's speech to the combined houses of the Irish parliament was the first event in the Dail's legislative chamber ever televised, and he was the first outsider to address a joint assembly. Kennedy's remarks were sprinkled with quotes from the masters of Irish literature—George Bernard Shaw, William Butler Yeats and James Joyce. Before JFK's speech, the only reference to Joyce in the Irish parliament had been in argument over censorship. Kennedy, a Joyce aficionado, had visited most of the Joyce landmarks in Dublin on his only previous visit to Ireland, in 1947.

Kennedy told the Irish legislators that if his ancestors had never left Ireland, "I might be fortunate enough to be sitting here with you." Then, referring to Ireland's American-born president Eamon De

Valera, who was sitting at JFK's side, Kennedy quipped, "Of course if your own president had never left Brooklyn, then he might be standing here instead of me."

When Kennedy left the Dail, he commented on the political skills of the Irish to longtime sidekick Kenny O'Donnell and noted that the two best politicians in the U.S. were Mayor Daley of Chicago and Senate Majority Leader Mike Mansfield.

As Kennedy departed from Ireland at Shannon Airport, he said that he wished his trip could have lasted another month and then recited the lyrics of the plaintive old song, "Come back to Erin." As someone in the crowd held up a sign that said, "Johnny, I hardly knew ye," Kennedy pledged to "come back in the springtime."

In just four months he was gone. But he will never be forgotten.

Lyndon B. Johnson

Chicago Sun-Times, 10/31/97

In the turbulent summer of 1964, Lyndon B. Johnson was worried.

Mayor Richard J. Daley of Chicago, the Democratic Party's most influential big-city boss, hadn't followed through on his promise to call after a meeting with Robert F. Kennedy, who was angling for the vice presidential nomination.

At an Oval Office meeting with Texas Gov. John B. Connally, Johnson confided that he feared an alliance between Daley and RFK. "An extremely reliable and perceptive observer reports 'the consensus among the Cook County organization is that Daley favors the attorney general [Kennedy] for vice president but might not press the matter openly against the president's wishes,'" Johnson told Connally.

"I have about come to the conclusion that it is just as positive as we're sitting here that he [Daley] is going to force a roll call on his name for this place or the other place [the presidency or the vice presidency]," Johnson lamented.

For three days after Daley's visit with Kennedy, Johnson grew more restless by the hour waiting for the mayor's call. Finally, LBJ couldn't take it anymore and telephoned Daley. "I thought I was going to hear from you," Johnson began.

Johnson's relationship with Daley is chronicled in *Taking Charge: The Johnson White House Tapes, 1963–1964*, a new book edited by Michael R. Beschloss (Simon & Schuster, $30). It is an extraordinary study of one of the more extraordinary characters in American history. Johnson the man is brought vividly to life in *Taking Charge* with thoughtful analysis by Beschloss.

"I was going to call you yesterday, and then I thought I'd call you Monday," Daley responded when LBJ pressed him for details about RFK.

Johnson asked Daley if Kennedy felt that he was entitled to the vice presidency, or did he want to fight for it?

"Not the latter," Daley said.

"Did he give you an indication that he knew the trend of my thinking?" Johnson asked.

"He didn't say that," Daley replied. "He kept saying . . . how everyone was depending on some of the fellows to speak out, including myself." Beschloss writes that RFK wanted Daley and other Democratic leaders to demand that LBJ put him on the ticket.

In another conversation with Johnson, Daley warned that Kennedy could quit the Cabinet and make a floor fight for the vice presidential nomination. "It's different if you're an old-timer in the ranks, like yourself and myself. But realizing he's not, then you never know what's going to be the consequence of that," Daley said.

Johnson told Daley that he wanted to be president in his own right without a Kennedy on the ticket. "I think—my people think—they [the Kennedys] are relying primarily on emotionalism. They think that most of these delegates that go there will be delegates that were there in '60 and will be people that like the name and were friendly, and that they'll have a demonstration and they'll say, 'Now this man [JFK] didn't get to finish his job, and he's got a lot of friends, and we need this name, and we just ought to go ahead and give him a vote.'"

Johnson later called Daley and told him of his selection. "Is it all right with you if I go along with [Hubert] Humphrey?" Johnson said with a chuckle.

"Why, it is," Daley said. "I've told you a hundred times! Anything you want, I'm with you 100 percent, and he's a good man. . . . I love him and think he'll do a good job. Just as you did in '60 when the man [John F. Kennedy] talked to me, like you are. He said, 'What do you think of him?' I said, 'If you can get him, it's the greatest choice you can make.'"

Johnson won Daley's support for the War on Poverty by pledging more federal aid. "We love everything you're doing. You're doing great. We're very proud of you out here," Daley told LBJ.

Johnson accepted Daley's invitation to speak at a fund-raising dinner. "I'm a Dick Daley man. We'll be there," LBJ said.

Daley then asked Johnson to appoint Edward Hanrahan as U.S. attorney. "He's a great Democrat. He ran for Congress. He was defeated. He's a graduate of Notre Dame. But more than that, Mr. President, let me say with great honor and pride, he's a precinct captain!"

"Do you want him?" asked Johnson.

"We surely do," said Daley.

"You got him," said Johnson.

"You're doing a great job, and don't let them tell you any differently. And the people are with you—the fellow on the bottom rung—and the people that elect presidents are with you," Daley said.

"Will you call me when I need to know otherwise?" Johnson asked.

"I surely will," said Daley. "You know that."

Richard M. Nixon

Chicago Sun-Times, 4/27/94

Richard M. Nixon greeted us at the door.

It had been 10 years since he had resigned the presidency of the United States to avoid impeachment.

But Nixon was coming out of the political wilderness.

I was among a group of political reporters who had been invited to dinner at Nixon's home in Saddle River, N.J. Except for writing sidebars about the Watergate era, none of us had covered Nixon's political career. Political consultant Roger Stone, who had made arrangements for the dinner, said that Nixon wanted to meet younger reporters.

Nixon was embarking on his campaign for elder statesman. The evening was carefully planned. As Nixon escorted us into his den, he settled into a comfortable chair and began talking about his views on the future of American politics, the direction of U.S. foreign policy and Ronald Reagan's place in history.

When Nixon talked, a hush came over the room. In one of the few mistakes in his three-volume biography of Nixon, the historian Stephen Ambrose reported that Nixon reminisced with reporters at Saddle River about world leaders he had known and about his past. Nixon, who was always looking ahead, made few references to the history he had made. He was more interested in having an impact on

39

American politics. Nixon came across as tougher and smarter than most national political figures.

Nixon was more insightful about political trends than personalities. He predicted the outcome of the 1984 presidential election almost to the decimal point. Because of his closeness to Sen. Bob Dole (R-Kan.) and former Secretary of State Alexander Haig, Nixon overestimated their appeal to voters in the 1988 Republican presidential primaries. But Nixon showed prescience in predicting that Democrats would regain the White House with a ticket headed by Southern white males with a centrist message that would recapture Reagan Democrats.

Strobe Talbott, a reporter from *Time* magazine who had written several books about U.S.-Soviet arms talks, seemed dazzled that night by Nixon's knowledge of global political forces. Talbott would later interview Nixon for a *Time* magazine cover story about the former president's rehabilitation.

When the cocktail hour arrived, Nixon said that he mixed a good martini. Howell Raines of the *New York Times*, who wrote the novel *Whiskey Man* and is a connoisseur of Southern bourbons, sampled one of Nixon's see-throughs that night. Nixon said later that he collected wines from significant dates in his life. He served a Bordeaux from 1966, the year that Nixon's campaigning helped to produce a GOP victory in the midterm elections that set the stage for his election to the presidency in 1968.

I gave Nixon a copy of my biography of Wendell L. Wilkie, the 1940 Republican presidential nominee. Nixon recalled campaigning for Willkie in 1940 and said that Willkie's vision of One World had been fulfilled. Several days later, I received a handwritten note from Nixon with more comments about the book. He sent me inscribed copies of several of his own books.

After hosting reporters for dinner, Nixon would frequently share his thoughts on the current political scene through correspondence. Those memos are going to be missed.

Gerald Ford

Chicago Sun-Times, 10/27/89

Gerald R. Ford, the 38th president of the United States, is quietly confident about his place in history.

"You can't help but miss the presidency. I could never understand those who didn't like it," Ford told an audience of scholars last week during a seminar sponsored jointly by his presidential library and the Herbert Hoover Library in West Branch, Iowa.

Ford, who served as the nation's chief executive from August of 1974 through January of 1977, is retired but far from unemployed. He has written a best-selling memoir and is now collaborating with an official biographer.

Like all former presidents, he is making his case for the history books. As a former president, he has delivered more than 700 lectures at 170 universities. He is actively involved in his presidential library at the University of Michigan and his presidential museum at Grand Rapids.

He has few complaints about his treatment by historians. He is widely recognized as a competent, intelligent chief executive if not among the presidential greats, "a Ford, not a Lincoln," in his own words. When a survey of nationally prominent historians rating the nation's presidents was conducted in the early 1980s, Ford scored significantly higher than his predecessor Richard M. Nixon and his successor Jimmy Carter. Ford got high marks for his character and for his political skills.

His presidency was one of the more unusual in American history because of how he got the job; and also because of his plain-spoken Midwestern style in an era of imperial presidents. "My fellow Americans, our long national nightmare is over," Ford declared after taking the presidential oath. Ford inherited the job when Nixon resigned to avoid impeachment for his role in the Watergate coverup.

"I did not seek out the office of president. My political ambition— Speaker of the House. Even as vice president, I did not expect to become president until only a few days before Richard Nixon's resignation in August, 1974. The truth is, I wish there had never been a need for Spiro Agnew to resign and never been a Watergate. Although I was the beneficiary, Betty and I would have been very happy with the life we had laid out after my planned retirement from the House at the end of 1976," Ford said.

Ford ended the Watergate era by granting Nixon a pardon. He knew that the pardon would be unpopular, but Ford believed it was necessary for the healing to begin. Ford, a Navy veteran of World War II, also sought to heal the wounds of the Vietnam era by offering amnesty to draft resisters and deserters. More than 22,000 persons applied for Ford's amnesty program.

There were substantial accomplishments during his brief term. Ford cut government spending, reduced personal and corporate taxes to boost the nation's economy and reduced the unemployment rate. He jawboned U.S. automobile manufacturers into trimming a planned price increase.

He negotiated a treaty with the Soviet Union that limited strategic weapons systems; signed the Helsinki agreement with Leonid Brezhnev to protect human rights in 33 other nations; improved ties with China; mediated the Greek-Turkish dispute over Cyprus and broke the deadlock over the Sinai between Israel and Egypt.

His historical reputation has gotten better when he is measured against his successors. Bush's inaction during the recent coup attempt in Panama that he had encouraged is drawing unfavorable comparisons with Ford's decisive action in May of 1975, when he took personal command of the U.S. recovery of an American cargo ship that had been seized by the Cambodians. "We had more time and also better intelligence information than Bush did in Panama," Ford said.

Ford, the only person ever to defeat Ronald Reagan (for the 1976 Republican presidential nomination), nearly overcame a 33-point deficit in the polls in the general election, but fell short to Carter. "I was disappointed to lose. It's the only election I've ever lost in politics, and naturally I thought that the best man with the best policies had lost," Ford said. "But I reconciled myself to the fact that we had run a good campaign." Reagan offered him the vice presidency in 1980, but Ford turned it down after concluding that their partnership probably wouldn't last.

His major regret, Ford confides, is that he did not make more of an effort to persuade his vice president, Nelson A. Rockefeller, to run for re-election with him in 1976. Rockefeller jumped off the ticket when the GOP's right-wing threatened to block Ford's renomination. "We should have taken them on," Ford said. His later choice for a running mate was Sen. Bob Dole. "I've always believed that the vice president should be someone who is ready to serve as president if the time comes," said Ford. He was "dumbfounded" by President Bush's selection of Dan Quayle as his vice president. "I had hoped that he would have chosen [Sen.] Alan Simpson," Ford said.

Few presidents have moved into the White House with more political experience than Ford, who had spent a quarter-century as a congressman and a decade as the GOP minority leader. He was renowned for his candor, small-town values, and fundamental decency. U.S. Rep. Dan Rostenkowski described Ford as "a Republican Harry Truman." President Bush, who served with Ford in the House, wrote in his memoirs that he never knew anyone with a better grasp of legislative detail than the former president.

Even out of power, Ford has maintained political influence. Some of his former advisers have landed in high places. Consider the following:

Bush, a former congressional colleague, was named by Ford as U.S. envoy to China and, later, as CIA director. Secretary of State James A. Baker III was Ford's 1976 campaign manager; Secretary of Defense Dick Cheney was Ford's White House chief of staff; Attorney General Dick Thornburgh was head of the criminal division in Ford's Justice department; and National Security Adviser Brent Scowcroft had the same job under Ford.

Ford was disappointed, though, that Bush brushed aside the recommendations made jointly with former President Carter about reducing the federal deficit. "President Bush listened. But my sense was that his staff opposed our report," said Ford.

In retirement, Ford has become a close friend of Carter, his erstwhile opponent; and they often work together in promoting governmental reforms and foreign-policy initiatives. Not since Hoover and Harry Truman have two former presidents worked more closely. "When we travel, we never have to search for things to talk about," Ford said. "We talk about our kids and our grandchildren, about our presidencies, and about the issues that face us all."

At the Hoover Library, Ford rejected a suggestion that the nation's former presidents should participate in televised forums. "I don't think it would be a very popular show," said Ford. "I didn't find all those debates in the presidential primaries very stimulating. I found them boring."

Jimmy Carter

Chicago Sun-Times, 9/20/94

Hail to the former chief.

Since leaving the White House in January, 1981, Jimmy Carter has quietly redefined the standard for former presidents of the United States. There have been 32 ex-presidents since George Washington retired to his farm. None has made a larger contribution than the man from Plains, Ga. He's the most productive former president in American history.

In negotiating the 11th-hour agreement with Haiti's military leaders on Sunday night that averted a U.S. invasion, Carter showed why he's still a valuable player on the world stage. Though it was hinted that the Clinton administration had serious doubts about Carter's role in Haiti, President Clinton deserves credit for accepting the former president's offer to serve as a special envoy. Carter's diplomacy gave peace a chance.

Only three months ago, Carter played an important role in attempting to resolve a conflict between the United States and North Korea over nuclear development. Carter, who disagreed with the Clinton administration's plan to impose sanctions against North Korea, eased tensions between the two countries and gave Clinton a chance for a diplomatic resolution to the crisis.

As he left the presidency, Carter pledged to dedicate the rest of his life to promoting the peaceful resolution of conflict. His first mission after leaving office was to embark for Wiesbaden, West Germany, where he welcomed back to freedom the 52 Americans who had been held hostage in Iran for the last 444 days of his presidency. Carter had never stopped working for their return.

The establishment of the Carter Presidential Center in Atlanta showed why Carter is different from other ex-presidents. Instead of building a monument to himself, Carter developed the center at Emory University as an institution dedicated to human rights, resolving regional conflicts around the globe, and fighting disease and improving agricultural productivity in underdeveloped countries. Though his goals were ambitious, Carter has been indefatigable and remarkably successful in carrying out his good works.

Until Carter launched his International Negotiating Network as a program of the Carter Center, there wasn't an established organization that mediated disputes within nations. Under their charters, the United Nations and Organization of American States lacked the authority to intervene in such conflicts. But Carter, who knew that 90 percent of the world's conflicts were internal, is filling the void.

As an international mediator, Carter has negotiated in Ethiopia, the Middle East, the Sudan, Somalia, and the former Yugoslavia. He also has monitored the election process in Panama, Nicaragua and Haiti. He frequently has taken risks and shown grace under pressure. Last weekend, he was jeered by supporters of the Haitian military regime as he rode in a motorcade. While monitoring the 1989 election in Panama, he found a polling station that had been shut down by armed troops. The former president confronted the soldiers and demanded access to the polling booth. Carter got what he wanted.

As Carter has grown in stature, his presidency looks better. The historian Garry Wills has written of Carter: "He will be perceived, in time, as the prophet of a broader vision of history, one who laid the foundation for better ties with the Third World, and whose emphasis on human rights was worthy of a great nation."

Ronald Reagan
Philadelphia Inquirer, 11/18/90

If Ronald Reagan had been a song-and-dance man, he might never have left Hollywood for the big screen of American politics. In *An American Life*, Reagan confides that he went on the speaking circuit during his movie career because he didn't sing or dance.

He soon learned that he could give a speech like nobody else, and he rose to power and prominence through his eloquence, delivering a message that was simple, yet powerful.

Though derided at first by political opponents for his show-business background, Reagan nearly always had the last laugh. In the video age, he turned out to be the only professional in a trade dominated by amateurs. From former California governor Pat Brown through Walter F. Mondale, Reagan's rivals became his straight men.

He became one of the more important and popular presidents of the 20th century. More than any president since Franklin D. Roosevelt, he moved the country's political center. Ending an era of failed presidencies, Reagan, first elected in 1980, revived the prestige and authority of the nation's highest office. The old Cold Warrior achieved historic arms agreements with the Soviet Union and encouraged freedom movements within the Soviet bloc.

But there were times during his two terms when he seemed asleep at the wheel. His inattentiveness to detail contributed to the Iran-contra fiasco and the S&L debacle. As for his place in history, the jury is still out.

Like other former presidents, Reagan is determined to fix his image for posterity. *An American Life* is his brief for the court of history. But few ex-presidents are capable of standing back and taking a hard look at their administrations, and Reagan is no exception.

Such flamboyant personalities as Lyndon B. Johnson and Harry S. Truman took out all the salt from their presidential memoirs. By the time they finished their self portraits, they seemed more like striped-pants British diplomats than rip-snorting democratic populists. *An American Life* is no less disappointing.

It is surprising how little Reagan chooses to add to what is already known about his life. His formative years are covered in far more detail in his 1965 autobiography, *Where's the Rest of Me?*

In this new volume, Reagan tells about getting into fistfights as a youngster because he was from an Irish-Catholic family in a Protestant town in downstate Illinois. But Reagan doesn't explain how his family was religiously divided and why he chose to follow his mother's Protestant faith. For those interested in Reagan's religious views, Garry Wills provides a fresh and compelling account in his 1987 biography, *Reagan's America*.

Though the breakup of Reagan's first marriage, to actress Jane Wyman, was among the major traumas of his life, it is mentioned here only in passing. Reagan offers no clues about how the divorce changed his life.

If Reagan had taken more time to reflect on his White House years, this book might have been an important contribution to American history. But it appears to have been rushed into print like other as-told-to celebrity books, in time for the holiday season.

There are some fascinating glimpses at his White House diaries, including his disclosure that his "only disagreement" with Secretary of State Alexander Haig "was over whether I made policy or the secretary of state did." Reagan said that was why he accepted Haig's resignation in 1982.

Reagan is less than truthful in claiming in this book to have writ-ten all of his own speeches until he became president. Among Reagan's ghostwriters were such gifted wordsmiths as George Will, Peggy Noonan, Ken Khachigian, Tony Dolan and Peter Hannaford. None of them is mentioned in this volume, which itself was mostly ghost-writ-ten by former *New York Times* reporter Robert Lindsey.

Reagan isn't the first major political figure to stretch his claims of authorship. Former Illinois Gov. Adlai E. Stevenson annoyed his speechwriters by taking all the credit for their words.

The book also stretches the truth when Reagan claims to have de-flected the age issue in the 1980 presidential campaign by running the legs off younger reporters. In truth, it was obvious that his appear-ances were carefully paced. His daily schedule was padded with events such as "breakfast in suite" and "staff time" each afternoon.

Reagan's handlers knew what they were doing. Network correspon-dents needed just one good visual for the nightly news. And the tanned, well-rested Reagan always looked fresher and more vigorous than his younger rivals who campaigned around the clock.

Reagan isn't above rewriting history about others in his book, ei-ther. The former president recalls that Gen. Douglas MacArthur warned in the early 1950s that American troops would have to fight another war "in a place called Vietnam" if MacArthur wasn't allowed to win the Korean war.

Forty years ago, though, there wasn't a Vietnam; it was French Indochina. And MacArthur was among the first prominent American military strategists to warn against U.S. intervention in what became Vietnam.

For some reason, Reagan now claims that he was never a serious candidate for the 1968 Republican presidential nomination. All I know is that when I interviewed him in his Sacramento office in March 1968, he talked hopefully about his White House chances that year. Later he formally declared his candidacy for the nomination and came close to stopping Richard Nixon on the first ballot.

A decade later, Reagan told me that he wasn't ready to be president in 1968. And now, he apparently believes that he wasn't even a real candidate that year.

An American Life is padded with the texts of speeches that have al-ready been published by the government printing office as part of Reagan's public papers. If included at all in this volume, they belonged in an appendix rather than cluttering the main text. And that's not all.

More than 25 pages of correspondence from Soviet Leader Mikhail S. Gorbachev are also included in the book's main text, with nearly 10 pages of Reagan's responses. Though historically significant, the letters should have been placed in the appendix or at least edited. Pen pal Ron also includes his letters to three other Soviet leaders. Reading *Crime and Punishment* is less strenuous.

On the domestic front, Reagan is proudest of cutting taxes and inflation, which set the stage for an era of economic growth and large budget deficits. Like Roosevelt and John F. Kennedy, Reagan knew the importance of symbolism and seldom failed to convey hope and optimism.

There are no revelations in these pages about the Iran-contra affair. Reagan says he doesn't know exactly what happened, but perhaps he should have pressed Lt. Col. Oliver North or national security adviser John Poindexter for more details.

Among the book's chief shortcomings is that it has no sense of proportion. What can you say about a presidential memoir that omits numerous major players in his administration, but includes references to Sophie Tucker, Gene Autry, Tom Mix, Fred Astaire and Pat O'Brien (who co-starred with him in the movie in which he portrayed Notre Dame's George Gipp, "the Gipper" whose nickname he appropriated).

White House Chief of Staff James A. Baker III, who also served as Reagan's treasury secretary, is mentioned seven times, once more than actor James Cagney. Pennsylvania Gov. Dick Thornburgh is overlooked. So incredibly, is former U.S. Sen. Richard S. Schweiker, a Republican from Pennsylvania who was Reagan's surprise choice for vice president in a losing effort to wrest the party nomination from President Gerald Ford in 1976. Later, Schweiker was Reagan's first secretary of health and human services.

The book is dedicated to Reagan's wife Nancy, and it springs to life as he discusses their relationship. The Reagans have one of the more genuine romances in the history of the presidency, and it showed. Reporters who have followed Reagan have noticed that his speeches are more forceful and his demeanor more upbeat when she is with him.

He movingly describes his emotions about his wife during their courtship, political controversies, and her surgery for breast cancer. Reagan acknowledges that her judgment about personnel was often better than his own. If Reagan was lucky in his movie and political careers, he was also fortunate in his marriage to the former Nancy Davis.

An American Life is likely to have little impact on Reagan's historical reputation. One of his more notable predecessors, Thomas Jefferson, said that he was reluctant to write his memoirs because historians would make their own judgments. "To become my own biographer is the last thing in the world I would undertake," said Jefferson. "If there has been anything in my course worth the public attention, they [historians] are better judges of it than I can ever be myself."

Bill Clinton
Chicago Sun-Times, 7/31/98

Is this a presidency or a National Lampoon movie?

William Jefferson Clinton, who will be 52 next month, is the world's oldest teenager. When confronted with allegations about his relationship with former White House intern Monica Lewinsky that threatened his presidency last winter, he gave evasive answers and plotted damage control with a sitcom producer.

In the short run, the strategy worked. By stalling the independent counsel and asserting that he wanted to get on with the business of the country, Clinton improved his ratings in the polls. But at what cost?

Even though Clinton was successful in depicting special prosecutors as morality cops, he might also have defined himself for future generations by making his private life the subject of public debate and late-night television humor.

Only 29 percent of the American people believe Clinton's denials about a sexual relationship with Lewinsky. His double-talk and evasiveness have cost him support and credibility. But he'll always have Geraldo.

Clinton is among the few presidents whose smiling image makes us laugh. When a clip of a sword duel in *The Mask of Zorro* was recently featured on *The Tonight Show*, it showed Zorro (Antonio Banderas) cutting off the blouse of Catherine Zeta-Jones. But when Zorro was unmasked as a Clinton look-alike, it brought down the house.

The program's host, Jay Leno, noted in his monologue that NBC had an intern program. Leno then showed himself interviewing a young woman who listed her credentials as communications major at UCLA, cheerleader and gymnast. The camera then panned to the Clinton look-alike, who sighed, "Oh, yeah."

Another night, Leno made reference in his monologue to the actress Jodie Foster, who won't tell who the father of her baby is. Leno then showed Clinton making his famous declaration at the White House: "I did not have sex[ual relations] with that woman."

Clinton isn't the only president of the United States to have multiple affairs. John F. Kennedy and Lyndon B. Johnson were notorious womanizers. But Clinton's relationships have gotten much more scrutiny. Early in his 1992 campaign, Clinton survived the Gennifer Flowers controversy by being less than candid with the American people. He struck a bargain with the voters that if elected he would govern like a grown-up.

Once elected, Clinton might have become even more reckless in his personal conduct. His relationship with a 21-year-old White House intern must be considered in a different category than the extramarital dalliances of his predecessors. Clinton took advantage of a college intern working in his office. He then lied about it when asked under oath last winter about their relationship. Clinton might be more candid next month when he is questioned by the independent counsel.

Clinton's affair with Lewinsky is reminiscent of the congressional page scandal of the early 1980s. An investigation by the House Ethics Committee determined that Representatives Gerry Studds (D-Mass.) and Dan Crane (R-Ill.) had sexual relationships with teenage pages. Like Clinton, Studds and Crane exploited young people for their personal gratification. The congressmen were both censured by their colleagues in 1983. "In no way did I violate my oath of office," Crane said then. "I know I did wrong. I made a mistake and I am sorry."

There are also parallels between Clinton's relationship with Lewinsky and the Washington state grade-school teacher Mary Kay Letourneau, whose affair with her student became a national scandal. Some of Letourneau's friends have alleged that the boy, who just turned 15, was the aggressor in the relationship. A few of Clinton's apologists have accused Lewinsky of coming on to Clinton.

Hillary Rodham Clinton is her husband's most credible defender. She is also the cover subject for the August issue of *Psychology Today* under the headline "After Infidelity." That's another historic first for the Clinton administration.

Mayors of Chicago

Richard J. Daley

Chicago Sun-Times, 1/23/96

He deserved better.

The late Mayor Richard J. Daley was back in prime time Monday night as the subject of a two-hour documentary, "The Last Boss." It was this week's chapter in "The American Experience," the acclaimed PBS series.

Daley is in elite company. Among the other notable Americans whose lives have been chronicled on the PBS series are Franklin D. Roosevelt, Richard M. Nixon, Lyndon B. Johnson, Malcolm X and Charles A. Lindbergh. But the Daley program wasn't up to the standard of previous documentaries in the series.

The Daley portrait is distorted. Though he was among the more enduringly successful figures in American politics, he is portrayed as out of touch. He made mistakes. But he learned from them. Daley, a complicated man, is depicted as one-dimensional.

In his introduction to the Daley program, historian David McCullough said that Daley was "cut from the familiar mold" of big-city bosses. Others listed by McCullough included 19th century boss William Marcy Tweed of New York's Tammany Hall and Tom Pendergast of Kansas City. Tweed and Pendergast were looters of the public domain and, as McCullough notes, "wound up behind bars." By putting Daley in the same category, McCullough implies that Daley also was corrupt. He wasn't.

Daley's major accomplishments are trivialized by producer Barak Goodman.

Much of the program focuses on how Daley dealt with the civil rights and anti-war movements of the 1960s. "His problem, his tragedy, the tragedy for Chicago and for the country, was that he'd been overtaken by change, and he couldn't change," McCullough says. "By the 1960s he was the wrong man for the times."

Wait a minute.

If time passed him by, then why was Daley re-elected to a fifth term in 1971 and to a sixth term in 1975 by landslides? House Minority Leader Michael J. Madigan (D-Chicago), who learned much about politics from watching Daley, once said that Daley's political genius was his ability to adapt. Madigan, who is among the shrewdest observers of the local political scene, wasn't interviewed for the Daley program.

"I think Daley was caught between a rock and a hard place," said Andrew Young, who was the Rev. Martin Luther King, Jr.'s lieutenant in his 1966 Chicago campaign for open housing and one of the more thoughtful interviews in the documentary. "He needed the white neighborhoods that we were marching in to get elected and run Chicago, but he also needed the black neighborhoods. And there's no question that we made his job very difficult."

Daley's "shoot to kill" comment during the riots that followed King's assassination is given prominent play in the PBS special. That's part of Daley's legacy. But the late mayor—as a teenager—is unfairly linked to the 1919 race riots without evidence. That's not history. It's character assassination.

Though Daley is the patriarch of one of the more successful dynasties in American politics, there wasn't much about Daley's family in the PBS program. He didn't talk family values. He lived them. He and his wife Eleanor made certain that their children were well educated. Three of their daughters became teachers and three of their sons became lawyers. A fourth son is an insurance broker.

If the late mayor was so out of step with his times, one might wonder why his eldest son went on to win three terms as mayor of Chicago. Oddly enough, the current Mayor Daley wasn't interviewed for this program. Daley's critics got most of the air time.

Michael A. Bilandic

Chicago Sun-Times, 12/29/93

Michael Anthony Bilandic, the next chief justice of the Illinois Supreme Court, is the first mayor of Chicago since the late Edward F. Dunne to have a public life after leaving City Hall. Dunne, who served as mayor from 1905 to 1907, was governor from 1913–1917. Since then, the mayor's office has been a political dead end. But Mike Bilandic has staying power.

It has been nearly a quarter-century since the low-key, soft-spoken Bilandic won his first public office as alderman of the Southwest Side's 11th Ward. Bilandic was the personal choice of the late Mayor Richard J. Daley, Bilandic's mentor and Bridgeport neighbor. He became Daley's floor leader and chairman of the Finance Committee.

It was 17 years ago this week that Bilandic was chosen by the Chicago City Council as Daley's successor. He easily won the 1977 special election to fill the remainder of Daley's unexpired term. Bilandic defeated the late Harold Washington and Roman C. Pucinski in the Democratic mayoral primary. "Bilandic is a civilized, cultured human being," Washington said of his erstwhile rival. "He's not phony. He may be described as dry, but he's genuine."

Bilandic, who had been the favorite to win a full term in 1979, fell casualty to one of the city's worst blizzards. When city workers faltered in removing the snow, angry voters took out their frustration on Bilandic. He was edged out in the February primary by Jane M. Byrne.

After losing the mayor's office, Bilandic returned to private law practice. He was elected in 1984 as a justice of the Illinois Appellate Court. The scholarly Bilandic was elected to the Illinois Supreme Court in 1990. Bilandic won a 10-year term on the bench with 69 percent of the vote and a plurality of 443,646 votes.

Justice Bilandic is disciplined, hard-working, and collegial in his deliberations with judicial brethren. "I've never been a table pounder, a shouter or a screamer," Bilandic once said of his low-key style. "I've basically been an achiever. In order to do that, you don't need to be boisterous."

As mayor, Bilandic had a tough if not impossible act to follow. Bilandic found it impossible to escape Daley's shadow. He had some substantial accomplishments, including contributions to the city's economic development and opening more opportunities for minorities in city government. Bilandic negotiated an agreement with then-Gov. James R. Thompson for the construction of new mass-transit lines and for rebuilding of roads.

His wife, Heather Morgan Bilandic, the first executive director of the Chicago Council on Fine Arts, also made a difference.

Justice Bilandic, who is the son of Croatian immigrants, is the product of an ethnically diverse, working-class neighborhood that produced five mayors of Chicago. He served as a lieutenant in the Marine Corps during World War II. Before running for public office, he was a master in chancery for the Circuit Court of Cook County and also served as a special assistant attorney general of Illinois.

Bilandic, who still jogs daily and has participated in numerous marathons, is also a long-distance runner in his public career.

Jane M. Byrne

Chicago Sun-Times, 2/23/87

She refuses to quit.

The comeback kid of Chicago politics is betting that the wise guys are wrong again. When you're Jane Byrne, nothing is impossible. She became one of the nation's best known political leaders by playing a long shot and winning.

Despite polls reporting that she is trailing Mayor Washington by a wide margin and a Las Vegas line that rates her as an 8-to-5 underdog, Byrne is confident about her status as the city's once and future mayor.

"I feel very good about it," she said on the campaign's final weekend. Some of her top supporters are more subdued about her prospects.

Washington's camp, however, isn't writing her off.

"Nobody should underestimate Jane Byrne," said David Axelrod, Mayor Washington's political consultant who designed the negative TV blitz against Byrne. "She's a fierce competitor, and, if she gets a few breaks, she's certainly in the ballgame."

Byrne acknowledges that Axelrod's video handiwork hasn't been helpful to her comeback chances, but she still thinks that her record will by judged favorably by a majority of Democratic primary voters when compared with Washington's.

Overcoming what Byrne describes as her "negatives," the political scars of her four-year reign, has been the biggest problem of Byrne's 1987 campaign.

For all the controversies of her revolving-door administration, Byrne has gotten higher marks for her job performance than her critics have acknowledged. A recent University of Illinois at Chicago survey of more than 40 leading Chicago scholars and journalists ranked Byrne second in accomplishments only to the late Richard J. Daley among mayors in the last 40 years. In other categories, Washington got slightly higher marks than Byrne for leadership and political skills.

Though Byrne was often petty and vindictive in her dealings with political rivals, few people have accused her of thinking small in terms of programs. As mayor, she did things on a grand scale, whether lining up President Reagan's support for the 1992 Chicago World's Fair, or building the Columbus Avenue bridge, the city's largest in a half century.

When a department store threatened to abandon State Street, Byrne kept it in town by responding that she would cut off the owner's highly profitable business at the airport. During her current campaign, Byrne has vowed to revive the world's fair and to increase city revenues by pushing for a Loop-sized commercial area at O'Hare Airport.

In her four-year bid for a City Hall return, Byrne has often demonstrated keen political instincts and has made relatively few mistakes. She reached out to former political enemies and enlisted them as allies.

The former mayor studied Spanish to help her communicate more effectively in Hispanic neighborhoods. Byrne managed to put Washington on the defensive by criticizing the administration's record on taxes, crime and economic development.

Some observers thought she was guilty of overkill in airing a commercial that seemed to blame Washington for racial polarization, but the so-called watchdog group that asked her to pull the ad wasn't exactly an unbiased party. One of the group's members even appeared in a television spot endorsing Washington, and others were Washington political contributors. So it wasn't surprising that the group didn't object when Washington likened Byrne to Nazi war criminals Adolf Hitler and Joseph Goebbels.

Although Byrne is comparing this week's election to her 1979 insurgency that toppled former Mayor Michael Bilandic, there's one notable difference. At the time, she was a fresh face, a new personality. It's more difficult to campaign as an outsider if a candidate has already held the office being sought.

Few defeated officeholders are given a second chance by the voters. Only one president of the United States and one governor of Illinois have made successful comebacks, both in the 19th century. And a Chicago mayor hasn't pulled such a stunt since William Hale Thompson back in 1927.

Byrne, whose name is already in the political record books as the city's first woman mayor and the first independent candidate to win a Democratic nomination in more than a half century, has built a political career out of breaking historical precedents rather than following them.

When she worked for John F. Kennedy in 1960, more experienced political professionals told Byrne that a Catholic couldn't be elected to the presidency. Byrne didn't believe them and turned out to be right.

It's no accident that two of Byrne's biographers are also novelists. As much as anyone in recent Chicago history, she has managed to defy reality. And, in tomorrow's election, Byrne is trying to beat the odds for one last time.

Harold Washington
Chicago Sun-Times, 11/30/87

He was a man of distinction.

Harold Washington was no ordinary political figure but a social phenomenon. Which is why hundreds of thousands of Chicago residents stood in the rain over the weekend to pay final homage to their fallen mayor, and why his portrait is displayed in more Chicago homes than any politician since John F. Kennedy.

Washington became the rare political figure to step into the history books during his lifetime. The Rev. Jesse L. Jackson says that Washington's election as mayor of Chicago in 1983 will be long remembered as a milestone in the civil rights movement. Washington created his own political movement in Chicago.

Washington understood that national prominence was less important than his standing in his hometown. He was a product of the South Side and a lifelong resident of its neighborhoods. One secret of his enduring popularity was that he never forgot his roots. After winning election as mayor, Washington retained his old phone number so that his pals and constituents might keep in touch.

Early in his 1983 mayoral campaign, Washington was ridiculed by television commentators for making what they termed a "homecoming" visit to Cook County Jail, where he had served a monthlong term for not filing tax returns. Washington noted that he had been visiting the inmates during the Christmas season for many years.

Even though it would have been politically pragmatic to have skipped this gesture of good will in December of 1982, Washington didn't bow to expediency. He went and accepted the criticism.

Washington was a scholar of politics who could speak in private conversation of the writings of Thomas Jefferson, Machiavelli or W. E. B. Du Bois.

But when asked to write an article about his favorite literary subjects, Washington declined on grounds that he didn't want to be depicted as an intellectual "egghead."

He was proud of his political skills and wasn't afraid of losing an election. One of the reasons for his self-confidence was that Washington had broken with the Machine of Mayor Richard J. Daley and had won. Nothing was ever handed to Washington. He won a congressional seat by trouncing a Democratic incumbent.

And in a remarkable upset, he became mayor of Chicago by edging out Mayor Jane M. Byrne.

At City Hall, Washington's priorities were much different than those of his recent predecessors. He wasn't a believer in the longtime practice of funneling public funding into the Loop at the expense of the neighborhoods.

Washington pushed through a massive citywide public works program. He viewed the 1992 World's Fair as a boondoggle and he killed it.

Washington, a former prep champion hurdler, was the city's No. 1 sports fan. He strived to keep his beloved White Sox from moving to the Sun Belt, and worked to come up with a plan for a new stadium to save the franchise. Washington cringed at the prospect of the Sox moving to Du Page County.

As a lifelong fan, Washington understood the damage to civic pride that would result from the loss of a major professional sports franchise. He lobbied hard and successfully at discouraging the Cubs and the Bears from fleeing to the suburbs.

Washington, a former middleweight boxer, vowed to restore Chicago's eminence as a fight town. And he appeared to be succeeding.

Last summer, he landed the city's first title bout in 25 years, for the lightweight championship, and he had cultivated friendships with heavyweight champion Mike Tyson and promoter Don King, seeking to bring other fights to Chicago.

In his fighting days, Washington said that he was never knocked down. Nor was he as a politician. At the end of his career, Washington was a winner and still champion.

Eugene Sawyer
Chicago Sun-Times, 3/2/89

He tried.

During his brief term as the city's chief executive, Eugene Sawyer strived to fulfill the legacy of former Mayor Harold Washington. To a remarkable degree, he succeeded in carrying out the programs that Washington had championed but not enacted.

Sawyer may have lost his bid for renomination on Tuesday, but he is still viewed with respect and affection by most Chicagoans. According to a *Chicago Sun-Times*/Channel 7 poll taken last month, more than two-thirds of Chicago voters have a favorable opinion of Sawyer.

Illinois Comptroller Roland Burris, a longtime associate, says that Sawyer "is the greatest city official in this city." Few persons would question that Sawyer is among the more knowledgable, decent and humane mayors in the city's history. Even Sawyer's political opponents concede that he's a class act.

The Rev. Jesse L. Jackson said that Sawyer should be remembered as a healer. Following an era of confrontational politics and racial strife, Sawyer did much to ease racial tensions and to improve the city's image nationally. During the recent mayoral campaign, Sawyer was unfairly criticized by some political observers for not repudiating some of his more overzealous supporters.

In conceding defeat to Richard M. Daley Tuesday night, Sawyer said he had worked "to make Chicago one city, one people, working together. I reached out to all people in this city, black, brown, yellow and white."

"Our struggle for fairness, justice and equality must continue," Sawyer said. "We must continue to work to rid this city of racial divisiveness—any thought of sexism, anti-Semitism, any form of hatred has to be removed from this city. We must come together as a people who love each other, who work together in brotherhood."

If Sawyer is to be judged on his political skills and accomplishments, he will be remembered as one of the more effective mayors of the post–World War II era. "I can't think of many mayors who have compiled a better record that Gene Sawyer," said City Treasurer Cecil A. Partee, a Sawyer ally. "Washington was a charismatic leader. But Sawyer was more effective governmentally, just as President Johnson got more programs through than President Kennedy."

The Sawyer administration will be well remembered. Sawyer was the first mayor in a decade to pass a city budget without a major tax hike. After 15 years of stalled efforts, Sawyer managed to push through the human rights ordinance. Sawyer was at the forefront of the effort to push for meaningful school reform.

Labor and industry both prospered during Sawyer's term. Sawyer has been more effective in promoting economic development than any mayor in the past decade. He also was responsible for a four-year labor agreement with every major unit of city workers except the police that has assured a measure of stability at City Hall. Bob Healey, president of the Chicago Federation of Labor, says that Sawyer has been among the city's more pro-labor mayors.

Like former mayor Ed Kelly, Sawyer showed leadership in the area of affordable housing. Sawyer was responsible for the most significant reforms at the Chicago Housing Authority since World War II. He also took the lead in reclaiming neighborhoods by rehabbing housing units and renovating YMCAs into public housing.

An avid sports fan, Sawyer deserves much of the credit for retaining Chicago's status as one of only three Major League cities with rival baseball teams. Working closely with Gov. Thompson, Sawyer managed to keep the White Sox from moving to Florida by backing a new ballpark. He also kept the Cubs in town by allowing night baseball at Wrigley Field.

In conceding defeat, Sawyer assured a cheering ballroom of supporters at the McCormick Inn that he planned to remain politically active. Former Mayor Washington often referred to Sawyer as the best ward committeeman in the city. Given his successful term as acting mayor and his considerable citywide popularity, Sawyer is still a force to be reckoned with.

Richard M. Daley

Chicago Sun-Times, 8/5/94

They still haven't been seen together.

So the mystery continues.

Is Mayor Daley really Forrest Gump?

The publication of a new book makes the question even more perplexing. At a bookstore near City Hall, a clerk pulled me aside and showed me a fresh stack of *Gumpisms: The Wit and Wisdom of Forrest Gump.* There are so many similarities between Gumpism and Daleyism that it's almost eerie. Daley is as Daley does.

"Curiosity killed a cat" is Daley's response when he doesn't want to know about something. A similar quote is in Gump's book. Are they splitting the royalties?

"Don't expect anybody else to help you. If they do, fine. If they don't, file it away," according to Gump. Or was it Daley on Gov. Edgar, House Speaker Mike Madigan, and Senate President James "Pate" Philip?

"Try not to screw up. This will satisfy a few people and amaze everybody else," Gump said. Or was it the mayor after looking at his approval ratings? The best and the brightest are the ones who often commit the monumental blunders. Daley and Gump quietly get the job done.

"Don't trust nothin' except your instinct," which sounds like Daley but is actually Gump. Both are loners.

"Do not wear T-shirts that advertise somebody else's products," Gump said. But it's also Daley's philosophy.

Gump or Daley: "What do you want me to do, drop my pants?" That's easy—Gump in the famous scene with Lyndon B. Johnson. Sorry, folks, it was Daley's response to a question about his lukewarm support of a Democratic candidate.

Was it Daley or Gump who quipped that he couldn't have jumped ship because he didn't have one to jump off? Gump jumped off his fishing boat when he saw a friend on the shore, abandoning the driverless boat to crash into the dock. But it was Daley who issued the denial that he had abandoned ship on riverboat casinos. "What am I supposed to do, swim down the River?" asked Daley. Or was it Gump?

"Honesty is the best policy unless you're a crook" is Gump, though it could have been Daley complaining about the Capone museum.

"When you celebrate something in America, you break a window and grab something" was Daley venting his frustration, though it might have been Gump.

Daley and Gump are brighter than their test scores. "I'll be very frank. Some people can't take an exam the first time, but they learn from the first time and take the exam the second time," said Daley, speaking of his own experience. Gump and Daley are often underestimated.

Both Daley and Gump are resentful when their character is questioned. "Oh, I'm moral all right. Moral authority? I mean, we're going above morals. Let's get above them. Let's go to God. Let's be serious," Daley responded Wednesday when asked about a controversial city contract to a gang-linked organization.

Who said this? "Be very suspicious if somebody says they want to make a movie of your life story." It sounds more like Daley. Actually it was Gump, who doesn't always follow his own advice. But then neither does Daley. Daley is as Daley does. But who's the guy on the park bench?

Chicago Sun-Times, 1/4/99

Is he mayor for life?

As Richard M. Daley seeks re-election to a fourth term, he is an overwhelming favorite. Daley, 56, who has held office for nearly a decade, is more popular now than when he won the 1989 special election to fill the remainder of the late Harold Washington's unexpired term.

If Daley goes on to defeat Rep. Bobby L. Rush in next month's election, he will become only the second person to win four mayoral terms in the 20th century. His father, the late Richard J. Daley, won a record six terms and served for 21 years until his death in December, 1976.

Daley has passed up several opportunities to run for governor and is more than comfortable in the office he holds. He was just 13 years old when his father took office in his first term at City Hall and was 34 when the first Mayor Daley died in office.

Sources close to Daley said he is looking to break his father's record for mayoral longevity. Daley has said he will leave only when he no longer has enthusiasm for the job and "the fire in the belly."

From all indications, the spark still glows.

When Daley first won the mayor's office, it was largely because of his famous name. But he has twice won re-election because of his job performance. When an incumbent goes before the voters, the election is a referendum on how he or she is doing. Three of Daley's four predecessors were defeated in their bids for second terms. Daley won his second term in 1991 with 70.7 percent, and got 60 percent in 1995. Based on his past showing and recent polls, Daley's vote will probably fall within this range next month.

Daley is succeeding because he has responded with ideas and creativity to the problems of the city. The crime rate has dropped by more than 25 percent since 1991. The city's bond and credit ratings have been upgraded.

Before Daley took office, former U.S. Education Secretary William Bennett had referred to Chicago's public schools as the worst in the nation. Under Daley's leadership, Chicago has set national standards for school reform. Test scores in reading and math have improved for the last three years in elementary schools and for the last two years in high schools.

More than $4.5 billion in capital improvements have been invested during Daley's tenure. This includes a dozen new schools and 27 annexes, more than 120 acres of new parkland and 50 new or renovated branch libraries.

Although Rush has accused Daley of cronyism and favoritism, the mayor is generally viewed as fair and inclusive. It is a measure of Daley's broad political base that his 1999 budget was approved 48–1 by the City Council.

In recognition of the city's diversity, Daley has sought to bring more minorities into the work force and has been even-handed in the distribution of public works money. The Rev. Jesse L. Jackson, who is supporting Rush, gives Daley credit for reaching out to all communities.

But the mayor's determination to hire more minorities has deeply angered many white policemen and firefighters who view themselves as the victims of Daley's political agenda. It's doubtful that this disappointment with Daley will translate into votes for Rush.

Daley has also had his setbacks. He failed to win legislative approval in Springfield for a new regional airport at Lake Calumet or a land-based casino gaming center. But Daley got public funding for the renovation of Navy Pier and expansion of McCormick Place.

As he prepares to face the voters, most of them seem to like the job he is doing. More than four out of five voters on the Northwest and Southwest sides and on the city's northern lakefront approve of Daley's performance, according to a benchmark poll of 800 Chicago voters that was taken for Daley's campaign by Greenberg Quinlan Research.

The poll indicated that Daley is rated favorably by a 3–2 margin on the predominantly black West Side and by more than half of the voters in Rush's South Side political base. Rush will still win the bulk of this vote. But Daley, who launched his '99 campaign in Lawndale, is forging a rainbow coalition. By reaching out to all of Chicago, Daley can probably hold the mayor's office as long as he wants it.

Illinois Governors

Adlai E. Stevenson

Chicago Sun-Times, 7/8/90

He was a man for all seasons.

For a generation, Adlai E. Stevenson of Illinois was the conscience of American politics, a symbol of decency and integrity. The witty, urbane Stevenson, who died 25 years ago this weekend, spoke with eloquence but not piety.

Twice in the 1950s he won the Democratic presidential nomination but lost both elections to World War II hero Dwight D. Eisenhower. He was drafted against his will by the 1952 Democratic National Convention.

"He brought to American politics a quality of ideas, of thinking, of excitement as if somehow one could have a reasonable discourse with people about the future," presidential historian Theodore H. White wrote of Stevenson. "No man left a larger legacy."

When Stevenson died July 14, 1965, the world mourned. He was so admired in the emerging nations of the Third World, where he was a more visible presence than any other American politician, that Stevenson often quipped he ran for president on the wrong continent.

Stevenson was often prophetic. Thirty-one years ago, Stevenson told Soviet Premier Nikita Khrushchev that the Eastern Europeans under Soviet domination would choose freedom if given a choice. "Communism has had its way in Europe only by force and conspiracy," Stevenson said. He would have been richly vindicated by the breakup of Soviet Europe.

In the quarter-century since his death, Stevenson has grown in historic stature. More biographies have been written about him than any presidential also-ran of the 20th century. The publication of his private papers, which are available in most of the nation's libraries, has further enhanced Stevenson's reputation as a man of intelligence and humanity.

Stevenson is still the subject of political debates. The conservative columnist George F. Will recently devoted a full-page column in Newsweek to an attack on Stevenson, blaming him for the Democratic Party's decline in the 1970s, while not giving him credit for Democratic victories of the 1960s.

Cartoonist Garry Trudeau, who often lampoons President Bush and such New Right Republicans as Newt Gingrich in his "Doonesbury" comic strip, has contrasted Stevenson with today's Republicans. "If something happens to me," Doonesbury said to his wife, "you must tell our son about Adlai Stevenson."

Stevenson, who served as governor of Illinois from 1949 through 1953, was rated as one of the 10 best American governors in a survey of political scholars taken by Harvard University's John F. Kennedy School of Government.

"What he left behind was something more splendid, in a public man, than a record of power," said the journalist Alistair Cooke. "It was simply an impression of goodness."

Sen. Paul Simon (D-Ill.), who launched his own political career in the 1950s as a Stevenson supporter, said that Stevenson had "a shyness and sensitivity that are seldom encountered in politics."

When Stevenson accepted the presidential nomination in 1952 at the International Amphitheater, he told the delegates that he would have preferred "a better man than myself."

But millions of Americans were mad for Adlai. He inspired thousands of men and women to become actively involved in Democratic politics and in progressive causes.

It was former President Harry Truman who elevated Stevenson to national prominence by touting him as a possible successor. Eleanor Roosevelt admired Stevenson more than any other American political figure. Former Sen. Wayne L. Morse quit the Republican Party to become a Democrat because of his enthusiasm for Stevenson.

In his time, Stevenson wasn't afraid to take unpopular stands. He was the first major American political figure to urge a ban on the testing of nuclear weapons. He was among the first American leaders to urge U.S. recognition of the People's Republic of China.

During the tranquility of the 1950s, Stevenson focused the nation's attention on the struggle for black equality, the problems of poverty amid affluence, and the threat to the nation's environment.

"We must have affirmative values and clear-cut objectives," Stevenson said. "The challenge to all of us is to prove that a free society can remain free, humane, and creative; that it can combat poverty, injustice, and intolerance in its own midst, even while resisting monstrous foreign despotism; and that it can mean a glimpse of serenity and hope, even while calling on them for sacrifice."

Stevenson lived to see many of his ideas become political reality. His political platforms of the 1950s were the foundations for the 1960s Democratic administrations of Presidents John F. Kennedy and Lyndon B. Johnson. Stevenson served both as U.S. ambassador to the United Nations.

It was Stevenson's bad luck to twice be matched in presidential elections against the unbeatable Eisenhower.

Oddly enough, Eisenhower might never have run for the presidency if he had known that Stevenson would be the Democratic nominee in 1952. Eisenhower flatly told his son John that he would not have run against Stevenson. Eisenhower would have been more than satisfied if Stevenson had defeated GOP Sen. Robert A. Taft, an isolationist.

Stevenson was born into one of the Midwest's more durable political dynasties. He was the grandson and namesake of a former vice president of the United States, who also served as a congressman and ran unsuccessfully for governor of Illinois. Lewis Stevenson, the future governor's father, served a term as Illinois secretary of state. Five years after Gov. Stevenson's death, his son and namesake, Adlai E. Stevenson III, was elected to the U.S. Senate. But Sen. Stevenson lost two attempts to win the governorship in the 1980s.

Though he fought hard in each of his political campaigns, Stevenson believed in fair play. He was among the few major politicians with the courage to denounce Sen. Joseph R. McCarthy at the peak of his influence. "Hard-hitting factual debate is the essence of democracy," Stevenson said. "Innuendo, smear, and slander are not. . . . The English language can take a lot, especially in an election year, but there are limits to the burden of deceit and infamy which it should be asked to bear."

In 1960, there were thousands of Democrats who wanted Stevenson to seek the presidency a third time. But Stevenson didn't want to risk a third loss, even though some his allies thought that he could win the nomination and the election. A movement to draft him at the Democratic National Convention touched off such an emotional demonstration that Kennedy's strategists were determined to prevent a second ballot on which Stevenson might have prevailed. But Stevenson had waited too long.

In the 25 years since his death, two-time losers Richard M. Nixon and Ronald Reagan went on to capture the White House. If Stevenson had made a third attempt to win the presidency, he just might have made it.

William G. Stratton
Chicago Sun-Times, 2/14/97

He is the oldest and youngest of 20th century Illinois governors.

William G. Stratton, who will celebrate his 84th birthday Feb. 26, is still active. The Republican former governor is co-chairing a task force on campaign finance reform with former Sen. Paul Simon (D-Ill.). The panel recommended contribution limits and more disclosure.

"We don't want to discourage people from contributing to political candidates and taking part in the process," said Stratton. "But I think it's useful to have some limits and full disclosure."

He supports Gov. Edgar's effort to change the way schools are funded. "I think a case could be made for shifting the tax burden," he said.

Stratton, who was governor from 1953 to 1961, was among the state's more accomplished chief executives. He transformed Illinois by building 7,057 miles of new roads, including 187 miles of expressways in the Chicago area. He pushed through the first legislative reapportionment since 1901, which gave Chicago and the suburbs more power in Springfield. He also is credited with major expansion of the state's universities.

When the 38-year-old Stratton became the state's 32nd governor in January, 1953, he was the youngest governor since 35-year-old John Marshall Hamilton took the oath in 1883. Now white-haired, Stratton has lived longer than any Illinois governor since Civil War veteran Joseph Wilson Fifer (1889–1893), who died at 97 in 1938.

"He was an activist governor. And he was a governor who was really on top of details," recalled Simon, a state representative in the Stratton years.

Stratton wrote the state budgets in pencil on white legal pads. "I was a hands-on executive. I knew the government inside and out. I had definite ideas about what I wanted to do. I'd stay up all night writing the budget," he said.

"He was an effective manager of state government. He is an unassuming, decent man who gives good advice," said Gov. Edgar.

Former Gov. James R. Thompson said that Stratton is often underestimated. "If you look at his accomplishments, they're extraordinary," said Thompson.

Stratton, who won 14 of 18 statewide primary and general elections, is the son of a former secretary of state. It was because of his well-known name that Stratton was elected in 1940 as the nation's youngest congressman.

As governor, Stratton named the first woman and the first African American to Cabinet positions. He was more accessible to the public, holding regular open houses "to know what's going on." Stratton never lost touch with constituents.

Stratton had a close relationship with the late Mayor Richard J. Daley. Working together, they built O'Hare International Airport, McCormick Place and the University of Illinois at Chicago. "It was to his advantage and mine to have a good relationship," he said.

President Dwight D. Eisenhower, who rated Stratton among the nation's top governors, also touted him as a potential vice-presidential candidate in 1960. But Stratton was defeated for re-election to a third term that year.

Stratton won a legal battle over his use of campaign funds. He was cleared of wrongdoing. "In this game, sometimes a curve ball comes your way," he said. "If you can't hit a curve ball, you don't belong in the big leagues."

Richard B. Ogilvie

Chicago Sun-Times, 5/13/88

He was always out in front.

Whether it was leading his tank unit against the Nazis along the Maginot Line in World War II, or sacrificing his political career by pushing through the state's income tax, Dick Ogilvie wasn't troubled by the probable consequences.

In an age of prepackaged politicians, Ogilvie was a political rarity, a leader who wasn't afraid to lead. He was tough, direct, blunt and decisive. Although Ogilvie could have been governor for a long time if he had played it safe and not enacted the income tax, he was the rare political figure who believed that there are things more important than winning elections.

When Gov. Ogilvie imposed the income tax in 1969, he was jeered at the state fair, shunned by politicians of his own Republican Party and subjected to death threats. Ogilvie, though, knew that he was right. If he didn't rescue the state from impending bankruptcy, there wasn't anybody else to make the tough call.

Like Harry Truman, Ogilvie knew where the buck stopped. There was a lot of Truman in Dick Ogilvie, who was born within shouting distance of Truman's hometown and died the day after Truman's birthday. Both Midwesterners were unpopular when they left public office, but won vindication during their lifetimes as honest, gutsy leaders who were missed.

Just as Truman's leadership qualities were shaped in World War I, Ogilvie's were formed in World War II. When Ogilvie was a student at Yale, he sought to enlist in the Marines after the Japanese attack on Pearl Harbor but was turned down because of faulty eyesight. Later, he enlisted in the Army Reserve Corps and qualified for Officer Candidate School.

Ogilvie drew a safe assignment, far from the war, as a small-arms instructor at Fort Knox. Other successful politicians, such as Lyndon Johnson and "Tail-Gunner Joe" McCarthy, would later embellish their war records. But Ogilvie was among those who got restless when he was away from the action. He worked out a transfer to a tank battalion as a gunner and got shipped to France in 1944.

On the morning of Dec. 13, 1944, Ogilvie's unit was involved in heavy fighting in the Alsace-Lorraine region, along the Maginot Line. When Ogilvie's tank came under heavy German tank and mortar fire, he was hit by a high-explosive shell that shattered his jaw and ripped his face. Ogilvie said later that it was like getting hit with a sledgehammer.

The German shell may have knocked Ogilvie out of the war. But it also helped launch his political career. Like John F. Kennedy of the PT-109 and Bob Dole of the 85th Mountain Infantry, Ogilvie was among the war heroes who came back and played a major role in the shaping of postwar America.

For Ogilvie, World War II was the major influence in his leadership style. He didn't make threats or read public opinion polls before answering questions about controversial issues.

Ogilvie once told former *Chicago Sun-Times* Springfield Bureau Chief Mike Lawrence that he learned an important lesson from a grizzled old sergeant.

"He was instructing us all as to what our duties were and we were all issued a .45 automatic. He explained how it would work and said, 'Now don't take this thing out unless you're going to shoot somebody, and if you take it out, shoot him.' That stuck with me. If you're going to do it, then make up your mind and do it," Ogilvie told Lawrence.

When Dick Ogilvie gave his word, there were no hidden agendas. Illinois never had a better governor.

James R. Thompson

Chicago Sun-Times, 5/8/96

He isn't ready to write his memoirs.

"I'm too busy," said former Gov. James R. Thompson, chairman of the Loop law firm of Winston & Strawn. "My calendar is worse than when I was governor. I'm going to different places. But I'm on airplanes just as much."

Thompson, who is celebrating his 60th birthday today, still casts a large shadow on the state's political scene even though he has been out of office for more than five years. He has remained a player in Republican politics and is among Sen. Bob Dole's allies. "He has to bring focus to his campaign," said Thompson. "His campaign hasn't gotten rolling yet."

Though he never realized his boyhood dream of winning the presidency, Thompson had an extraordinary political career. He retired undefeated as the only four-term Illinois governor, and he said Tuesday that he will never run for another office. It has been 20 years since the newly elected Thompson was touted nationally as the GOP's "new superstar."

He had even larger ambitions. When I first interviewed Thompson in November, 1976, he was the fresh new face at a Washington, D.C., meeting of the Republican Governors Association. Thompson talked about his future with confidence. "Ever since I was 11 years old, I've said I wanted to be president of the United States," he said then. "I think that's an honorable position to aspire to."

Former New York Gov. Nelson A. Rockefeller listed Thompson in late '76 as the GOP's best hope of regaining the White House. But at the GOP governors' conference, Thompson showed that he was more liberal than his party. He cast the only dissenting vote against a resolution that endorsed the conservative Republican platform. Like Rockefeller, Thompson's rise to the leadership of the moderate wing of the GOP came at a time when conservatives were gaining control.

Thompson said he has no regrets that his national ambitions were unfulfilled. "While the presidency is a lot of people's boyhood dream, it gets tempered with reality as you grow older. It was a combination of really liking my job as governor and understanding that maybe I wasn't as conservative as a lot of people in my party. That would have made it difficult at the national convention. I didn't have to be president to be happy."

His support of abortion rights would have made Thompson vulnerable in GOP presidential primaries. "I still believe that a reasonable pro-choice position is not only right but is a majority view of my party," he said. "But it's not the majority view of the people who control my party."

At the state level, the political style and policies that made Thompson unacceptable as a national GOP candidate made him remarkably successful. He promoted jobs and economic development. By reaching out to organized labor and other Democratic constituencies, he won a record four terms. Thompson said "stamina and luck" also worked in his favor.

Thompson was a builder on a grand scale, but not without controversy. He built more highways and prisons than any governor. He persuaded the General Assembly to expand McCormick Place, develop Navy Pier and build the $173 million glass palace in the Loop that now bears his name as the James R. Thompson State of Illinois Center.

But among the reasons Thompson's legacy has endured is that his former associates have risen to positions of influence. They include Gov. Edgar, Sen. Carol Moseley-Braun (D-Ill), U.S. Attorney Jim Burns, DuPage County Board Chairman Gayle M. Franzen and Commonwealth Edison President Samuel K. Skinner. Thompson predicted that Edgar will seek a third term. "I don't know why he wouldn't. He's enjoying the job and has found his own rhythm," Thompson said.

Jim Edgar

Chicago Sun-Times, 8/21/97

Gov. Edgar, who is in his 17th year in statewide executive office, is the longest-serving constitutional officer in state history.

Few of the state's 38 chief executives have had a keener understanding of state government than Edgar. He was the first statewide constitutional officer elected to the governorship since 1952 and the only former legislator elected to the state's top political office in the second half of the 20th century.

Edgar, who grew up in Charleston in Downstate Coles County, took his first election when he won a class office in the second grade. From then on, he said he was hooked on politics.

He recalled on the eve of his retirement that he had wanted to be governor since he was a youngster in 1956 and watched Gov. William G. Stratton campaigning for re-election. Edgar, who puts Stratton on the short list of the state's better governors, also said that Stratton made a mistake when he sought a third term in 1960.

Another Illinois governor who was among Edgar's role models was the late Gov. Richard B. Ogilvie, who served from 1969 to 1973 and lost his re-election bid after pushing through the state's income tax. As a young legislative aide, Edgar worked for passage of the tax.

Edgar's biggest disappointment as governor was his failure to win approval of an income tax increase last spring to provide a more reliable funding source for schools.

In pondering whether to seek a third term, Edgar told associates that he had watched other top elected officials stay in office too long. Edgar worried about possible burnout in a third term.

Because of his low-key style, Edgar often was underestimated. But he is among the more enduringly popular politicians in Illinois history. Edgar won four statewide elections, for secretary of state in 1982 and 1986 and governor in 1990 and 1994. He received 63.87 percent of the vote in his '94 re-election over Democrat Dawn Clark Netsch. His approval rating seldom has dropped below 60 percent in more than six years.

One reason for his popularity is the state's economic boom. He noted Wednesday that more than 600,000 jobs had been created during his administration.

Edgar, who presented a $34.6 billion budget this year, listed welfare reform, property tax caps and school reform initiatives as among the major accomplishments of his administration.

But his greatest success may have been in putting the state's fiscal house in order.

By reducing the size of state government and holding the line on spending, Edgar took advantage of a favorable economy during the 1990s and trimmed a $1.3 billion Medicaid debt that had lowered the state's bond rating.

Edgar's image as a fiscal watchdog was tarnished somewhat during the recent bribery trial involving Management Services of Illinois, a major campaign contributor that bilked the state out of $7 million. Edgar, who was not accused of wrongdoing, testified that he couldn't recall specifics about a dinner in which MSI officials had pledged $40,000 to his 1994 campaign. He did not look forward to a campaign in which the MSI case figured to be a central issue.

Democratic and Republican strategists said Wednesday that Edgar probably would have won a third term despite the scandal.

Though accused by critics of being excessively cautious, Edgar showed political courage in 1990 when he called for making permanent a temporary surcharge on the state income tax for schools. His Democratic rival, Neil F. Hartigan, attacked Edgar for proposing the largest tax increase in state history. Edgar was urged by GOP politicians to back away from his risky position on the tax. But Edgar wouldn't bow to expediency and narrowly won the election.

Edgar often was frustrated by his own party's legislative leadership. He did not get along with Senate President James "Pate" Philip (R-Wood Dale) or House Minority Leader Lee A. Daniels (R-Elmhurst), who joined forces in 1996 and again last spring to help kill Edgar's $1.9 billion school-funding reform proposal.

In announcing his retirement, Edgar renewed a plea for his school-funding program, which would increase the income tax, provide property tax relief and reduce the funding gap between rich and poor school districts.

Edgar fell short in another ambitious proposal—to build a new regional airport at Peotone in rural Will County. Though he had strong support in the south suburbs, the opposition of major airlines, Mayor Daley and a Democratic administration in Washington, D.C., doomed his plan.

Edgar's relationship with Mayor Daley often was strained. Though

Edgar gave Daley important support in 1992 for the expansion of McCormick Place, neither trusted the other. Daley thought Edgar was unreliable because he couldn't deliver the support of the Republican legislative leadership. Edgar endorsed Daley's proposal for a new regional airport at Lake Calumet, but it was killed by Philip. Edgar vetoed Daley's 1992 proposal for land-based gambling in Chicago and this year won a power struggle with Daley to reopen Meigs Field.

Edgar has had a passion for state government since he went to Springfield while a student at Eastern Illinois University as a legislative intern. He began his public career in 1968 as an aide to former Senate President W. Russell Arrington of Evanston and worked for former House Speaker W. Robert Blair of Park Forest. He later served on the staff of the National Conference of State Legislatures in Denver.

In 1974, Edgar ran for the Illinois House but lost in the primary. He won on his second try in 1976 and was re-elected in 1978. Gov. James R. Thompson, who viewed Edgar as one of the rising stars of the General Assembly, hired him as his legislative lobbyist in 1979. A year later, Thompson put Edgar on the path to the governorship by appointing him secretary of state to succeed Democrat Alan J. Dixon, who had just been elected to the U.S. Senate.

As secretary of state, Edgar took an office that long had been a dumping ground for hacks and made it into an instrument of good government. He led a crackdown on drunken driving by replacing one of the nation's weakest drunken-driving laws with one of the toughest. He won legislative approval for mandatory auto insurance.

Edgar was tempted to run for the U.S. Senate next year, in part so he could have become the first sitting Illinois governor elected senator by popular vote. But in weighing his political legacy, he decided that 30 years in politics and government was enough.

Illinois Senators

Paul H. Douglas
Chicago Sun-Times, 4/5/92

He was among the last of the giants.

In the U.S. Senate of the 20th century, Paul H. Douglas of Illinois left an indelible mark on the American life. With his white hair and craggy features, he was born for the role.

Douglas, who represented Illinois in the Senate from 1949 through 1967, was a transplanted New Englander. The senator, who was born 100 years ago last week in Salem, Mass., grew up in a log cabin in the Maine woods. "This may help to explain some of the weaknesses and the strengths of my character," he wrote in his memoirs. He shared the values and flinty independence of his regional brethren Robert Frost and Henry David Thoreau.

He moved to his adopted state in 1920 when he became a professor of economics at the University of Chicago. Douglas soon emerged as one of the more outspoken critics of utility mogul Samuel Insull. After the Great Crash, Douglas was frequently consulted by politicians, including New York Gov. Franklin D. Roosevelt, about how to deal with unemployment. When Roosevelt became president, Douglas was among the architects of the Social Security system.

Douglas, a fighting Marine, wouldn't have much use for Vice President Dan Quayle, who used family connections to avoid serving in the Vietnam War, though Quayle was an outspoken hawk. Douglas might have had more sympathy with Democratic presidential candidate Bill Clinton, who opposed the Vietnam War but put his name into the draft because he thought it would look good politically. Douglas was a genuine war hero. In 1942, at the age of 50, he pulled strings to join the Marines, not to help him politically but because he thought it was the right thing to do. He received two Purple Hearts and a Bronze Star in the Pacific. Douglas, who was then a major, didn't want special treatment. He told medics that he was a private. Douglas lived the role that John Wayne played in "The Sands of Iwo Jima."

The late Col. Jacob M. Arvey, then chairman of the Cook County Democratic Central Committee, slated Douglas for the Senate in 1948 to challenge Republican Sen. Wayland Brooks. Arvey also tapped Adlai E. Stevenson II for governor. Douglas and Stevenson proved to be such attractive candidates that they overwhelmed the Republican incumbents and helped Harry Truman narrowly win Illinois and the presidential election.

In looking back on this century's notable senators, Douglas ranks high on the short list, just below Robert M. La Follette Sr. of Wisconsin and George W. Norris of Nebraska, about even with Hubert H. Humphrey of Minnesota and above Robert A. Taft of Ohio, J. William Fulbright of Arkansas, Wayne L. Morse of Oregon, Lyndon B. Johnson of Texas and Jacob K. Javits of New York.

"There is no member of the Senate who has stamped his name on more major issues, major bills and major legislation than Paul Douglas," Humphrey said, describing his colleague as "a giant of a man and a giant of a senator."

Douglas led the fight for the passage of the first civil rights legislation since Reconstruction in 1957, then, later, for the historic 1964 civil rights bill. He was among the first prominent senators to stand up to Sen. Joseph R. McCarthy in the early 1950s for his abuse of civil liberties.

He was an environmentalist long before there was such a word. Through the force of his personality, he saved the Indiana Dunes, sponsoring the legislation that made it a national shoreline.

Douglas wrote the legislation that increased the minimum wage to a dollar an hour and the law that required disclosure of union and management pension funds. "Back in the days when they had almost no chance of enactment," Humphrey recalled, "Paul Douglas was a sponsor or co-sponsor of medicare, federal aid to elementary education and aid to higher education."

He would probably have been a great president. But like Webster, Calhoun and Clay, Paul H. Douglas showed that some legislators can leave a more enduring mark than mediocre presidents.

Everett M. Dirksen

Chicago Sun-Times, 9/7/89

When he spoke, the world listened.

His colleagues in the United States Senate snapped to attention and took their seats when Everett McKinley Dirksen of Illinois stood to speak. The half-empty galleries were suddenly over-crowded. As Dirksen took the floor, the marble corridors of the Capitol turned so quiet that you could hear the tinkling of the crystal chandeliers.

With his tousled white hair, his lined cornfield face, and his rugged and big-boned physique, Dirksen was an imposing presence. But it was his golden voice and Shakespearean manner that set Dirksen apart from political mortals. Some of his critics suggested that he marinated his tonsils in honey and that he was born with the multivolume *Oxford English Dictionary* in his mouth. Nicknamed "The Wizard of Ooze," Dirksen was an American artifact.

With a Barrymore flair, Dirksen was the undisputed master of old-fashioned American oratory. But for all his style, Dirksen was also a man of considerable substance, perhaps the most influential legislator of his time. Former Sen. Prescott Bush of Connecticut, President Bush's late father, observed that Dirksen was among the few senators who could actually change the votes of his colleagues through his eloquence.

On June 10, 1964, Dirksen rose before his colleagues and declared, "The time has come for equality of opportunity in sharing in government, in education, and in employment. It will not be stayed or denied. It is here. America grows. America changes. And on the civil rights issue, we must rise with the occasion. That calls for cloture and for the enactment of the civil rights bill."

In no small part because of Dirksen's leadership, President Lyndon B. Johnson managed to push through the most sweeping civil rights legislation in American history.

Dirksen was accustomed to working with presidents. In 1947, he helped Harry Truman gain approval for the Marshall Plan to rebuild Europe. In the 1950s, he was Ike's chief legislative ally. In 1963, John F. Kennedy relied on his old friend Dirksen to gain passage of the nuclear test ban treaty. The Democratic Kennedy covertly supported Dirksen's re-election to the Senate in 1962 because of his special relationship with the Illinois Republican.

"Dirksen could play politics as well as any man, but I knew something else about him," Johnson later wrote in his presidential memoirs. "When the nation's interests were at stake, he could climb the heights and take the long view without regard to party. I based a great deal of my strategy on this understanding of Dirksen's deep-rooted patriotism."

In the 20 years since his death on Sept. 7, 1969, Dirksen has grown into a legend, one of the more notable American political figures of the 20th century. Within the Senate, he is seen as one of the most gifted and influential legislators in history. Dirksen lost a 1944 GOP White House bid, but managed to leave a far richer legacy than many of the nation's chief executives.

"He was a teacher and an example and an inspiration," said Sen. Edward M. Kennedy of Massachusetts. "He tutored us just by being himself, in the art of eloquence, the skill of advocacy, the science of compromise, and the power of persistence."

"He had a magnificent sense of drama, loved the center stage, enjoyed the sound of his mellifluous, some said unctuous, voice filling the Senate chamber. He loved the legislative game, manipulating language, cadging a vote for an amendment. Laws to him were organic, growing, flowering like the marigolds on which he lavished such care and affection in his yard," the late Sen. Hubert H. Humphrey (D-Minn.) recalled of Dirksen. "But mostly, when you scraped away everything else, he had a sense of history and his place in it."

As the son of German immigrants, Dirksen had great faith in the American dream. He grew up in the central Illinois town of Pekin, graduating from the local high school with honors and starring on the football and debate teams. After working his way through the University of Minnesota, Dirksen enlisted in the Army to serve in World War I.

Before entering politics, Dirksen had failed in his attempt to run a washing-machine factory and as a writer. He turned out scores of short stories and several novels, all of which were rejected by publishers. Dirksen made a comfortable living as the owner of a wholesale bakery in Pekin.

Political office was never handed to Dirksen. He got elected to Congress in 1932 by successfully challenging the Republican incumbent in a bitter primary contest. He retired from Congress in 1948, suffering from a severe eye ailment. But when he recovered the next year,

Dirksen took on the Democratic majority leader of the U.S. Senate, Scott Lucas, and scored one of the more dramatic upsets in Illinois political history.

Although Dirksen was politically conservative, he wasn't an ideologue. A 1950 *Chicago Sun-Times* survey found that he had changed his position 31 times on national defense issues; 62 times on foreign policy; and 70 times on farm policy. "I am a man of principle," Dirksen declared, "and one of my basic principles is flexibility."

"I'm just an old-fashioned garden variety of Republican who believes in the Constitution, the Declaration of Independence, in Abraham Lincoln, who accepts the challenges as they arise from time to time," Dirksen said once in defining his political philosophy. "I never close any doors. There are no absolutes in this world."

Charles H. Percy
Chicago Sun-Times, 11/18/96

He is the last Republican senator from Illinois.

It was 30 years ago this month that Charles H. Percy defeated Democratic Sen. Paul H. Douglas. With his right hand raised in victory, Percy was featured on the cover of *Time* magazine. He was 47 years old and touted by Dwight D. Eisenhower and others as a future president of the United States.

He never came close to winning the White House because he is more liberal than his party. But during his 18 years in the Senate, he gained recognition as a high-minded and skillful legislator. He was chairman of the Senate Foreign Relations Committee from 1981 to 1985. Despite some differences with Percy, President Ronald Reagan lauded him as "a major American statesman."

Percy is also among the more successful politicians in Illinois history. He and the late Everett M. Dirksen were the only Republicans since 1950 elected to the Senate from Illinois. Six Democrats have been elected during this same period. After losing the last six Senate elections, Illinois Republicans ought to be looking for another moderate like Percy. When he was elected as "a strong new voice for Illinois," Percy showed that a centrist also can be a force for change. Recent GOP candidates have been too extreme for Illinois voters.

"I wouldn't presume to give [Illinois Republicans] advice since I lost my last election," Percy said when asked about the GOP losing streak. After his 1984 loss to Paul Simon, he remained in Washington, D.C.

Percy, 77, is still trim and athletic. He easily could pass for 20 years younger. He swims regularly and plays singles tennis. "You don't get enough exercise playing doubles," he said. A Christian Scientist, he always has shunned liquor and tobacco.

During a recent visit to Chicago, Percy said he had no regrets about not winning the presidency. He was a favorite-son presidential candidate at the 1968 GOP national convention. But that was Richard M. Nixon's year. "I didn't run because I wasn't ready," Percy said.

Percy recalled that Gerald R. Ford, as Nixon's vice president, urged him to seek the GOP presidential nomination in 1976. "Jerry Ford pledged to support me. I set up an exploratory committee," he said. "But when Ford became president, I went to see him and he said that the pledge wasn't binding because it was made when he was vice president.

"He never expected to be president," Percy said. "When he got in office, he liked the job and decided that he wanted to run for a full term. I gave him my support and recommended my political consultants, who were then hired by the Ford campaign."

In looking back at his Senate career, Percy said his proudest accomplishment was an amendment he sponsored that provided equal opportunity for women in the federal government.

Percy got more attention for his leadership in foreign affairs. He was among the early Republican opponents of the Vietnam War and among the first to urge U.S. recognition of China. During the Reagan years, he pushed for arms-reduction talks with the Soviet Union. Percy helped Reagan win Senate approval for the sale of AWACS planes to Saudi Arabia. Despite Israeli opposition, Percy said that Israel is more secure because of the surveillance flights.

Percy is still active in the Mideast and is developing a technology park in Lebanon.

Perhaps his most enduring contribution was improving the quality of federal judges in Illinois. Previous senators often named their cronies. Percy looked for the best-qualified candidates. His nominees included John Paul Stevens, Prentice Marshall and Joel Flaum. He set a standard for excellence.

Alan J. Dixon
Chicago Tribune, 12/15/83

For most of his first three years in the U.S. Senate, Alan J. Dixon maintained a low-key profile as he studied the subtleties and nuances of Capitol Hill. The 1984 *Almanac of American Politics* says that the Illinois Democrat "has not been a major legislative actor."

Such a verdict may have been premature.

In recent months, Dixon has become more assertive on a wide range of issues. Following the attack on U.S. Marine headquarters in Beirut, he co-sponsored a resolution calling for a troop pullout within three months. Dixon contends that the U.S. presence in Lebanon isn't helping the peacekeeping process and may well be further polarizing the embattled region. Last week, he outlined his views in a discussion with veteran diplomat George Ball on the nationally televised "Phil Donahue Show." Dixon, who has made a career out of keeping his ear close the ground, thinks the Reagan administration is courting disaster in Lebanon.

On the home front, Dixon has emerged as the chief Democratic advocate of a constitutional amendment which would give line-item veto authority to the president on appropriations bills. Because of the looming $200 billion federal deficit, Dixon says that the president should have this additional power to cut the growth of federal spending. Unlike the Illinois amendatory veto which Gov. James R. Thompson has used to rewrite bills in other areas, Dixon's proposal is confined to federal spending measures.

In the 1984 Democratic presidential race, he was among the first U.S. senators and among the first prominent Illinois Democrats to endorse his old buddy Walter Mondale. The former vice president hasn't forgotten that Dixon's endorsement came at a time when Mondale had dipped in the polls and that it gave his campaign a major boost in Illinois.

Dixon's opposition to the cable TV industry's efforts to remove local governmental controls made him the most quoted member of Congress during last summer's annual meeting of the U.S. Conference of Mayors. Dixon got interested in this cause when his office began receiving mail from local officials who were upset that local programming would be squeezed out if the cable industry had its way. While the bill favored by the industry passed the Senate, Dixon has carried his fight to the Democratic House.

Although Dixon has never had much trouble raising campaign funds, he is appealing to the Common Cause crowd by sponsoring a bill which would provide for public financing of U.S. Senate elections. If next year's North Carolina senate race turns out to be a $20 million spectacle, there could be powerful sentiment for such legislation.

He is chairman of the Northeast-Midwest Senate Coalition, a group of senators who have been trying to do something about reversing the flow of federal dollars to the Sunbelt and reviving industry in their home region. Dixon has also been instrumental in getting the 24-member Illinois delegation to work together much more effectively. It was Dixon who set the ground rule that only senators and congressmen—not staff members—could attend the meetings. When Republican Sen. Charles Percy announced his candidacy for re-election, he paid special tribute to Dixon for his efforts.

By his own design, Dixon's legislative style is much different from that of Percy or his predecessor, Adlai E. Stevenson III, who were often more identified in the public mind with national and international issues than with their home state. After 30 years in Illinois politics, Dixon's slogan in his successful 1980 Senate bid was "A Senator From Illinois. For Illinois." While Percy is chairman of the more prestigious Foreign Relations Committee, Dixon opted for a spot on the Agriculture Committee, which he considered more relevant to Illinois problems.

In the tradition of former Illinois Senators Scott Lucas, who served as majority leader during the Truman administration, and Everett McKinley Dirksen, whose term as minority leader spanned four administrations, Dixon would like to move into his party's floor leadership. Regardless of which party controls the Senate after the 1984 elections, it is considered likely that Democrats will make some changes in their leadership. Sen. Robert Byrd (D., W.Va.), the lackluster minority leader, could be vulnerable to a possible challenge from a more articulate and appealing figure such as Dale Bumpers of Arkansas. If that happens, Dixon might well be in a position to make a challenge for one of the other leadership positions.

Paul Simon

Chicago Sun-Times, 11/17/95

Nobody cared.

In the fall of 1991, Anita Hill had been ignored. Judge Clarence Thomas was about to be confirmed to the U.S. Supreme Court. According to the national polls, Thomas was a popular choice.

Hill, a former Thomas aide, had raised serious questions about the judge's character and past conduct. She alleged in an interview with the FBI that Thomas had sexually harassed her. The Democratic chairman of the Senate Judiciary Committee sought to avoid dealing with Hill's charges.

Finally, Hill turned to Sen. Paul Simon (D-Makanda). Through a friend, Hill contacted a Simon aide. The few senators who knew of Hill's allegations had been fearful of the political fallout from the explosive charges.

Simon was different.

As the only non-lawyer on the Judiciary Committee, Simon had a reputation for fairness. Hill got a fair hearing from the Illinois Democrat. Other senators had shunned her. Simon heard her voice.

Simon found Hill to be credible.

The rest is history. In no small part because of Simon, Hill was afforded the opportunity to make her case. Though Thomas narrowly won his battle for confirmation, Hill made the nation more aware of sexual harassment. Simon was there when it counted.

In a political career that spans 40 years, Simon has given voice to the voiceless. He is a fearless and indefatigable defender of constitutional rights. He also is the conscience of the U.S. Senate.

It is in recognition of these efforts that Simon is receiving the Bill of Rights in Action Award tonight from the Constitutional Rights Foundation of Chicago. More than any Illinois political figure since Gov. John Peter Altgeld, Simon has championed the Bill of Rights.

He is opposed to the death penalty. Most Americans are in favor of capital punishment. The two convictions of Rolando Cruz and the death sentence against him are a powerful reminder that Simon may be right. Innocent people have been executed. At his third trial earlier this month, Cruz was found not guilty. The police had manufactured evidence against him. Simon's opposition to the death penalty isn't popular. But a democracy without voices like his would be a political wasteland.

Simon has sought to reduce violent crime by going after one of its causes. He believes that excessive violence in television programs is a factor in the rising crime rate. Studies have indicated that he is right. Young people who are exposed to massive amounts of television violence are more likely to commit crimes. Instead of just giving speeches about his view, Simon went to work. He got an agreement from the networks to show less violence.

As the son of Lutheran missionaries, he inherited his idealism. "I don't know that they gave me that much advice in the way of admonition by word. I think what my parents did give me was the example of working hard, of being honest, of being square with people. My father was a pretty good preacher, but the great sermons he preached were not from a pulpit," he once told David Frost.

"My father stood up when they took the Japanese Americans away from the West Coast at the beginning of World War II. He took a very unpopular stand. And I can remember that I was embarrassed at the time. . . . I wished he hadn't done it. But now, as I look back on it, it is one of the things that I am proudest of my father for. And it taught me a great lesson. If you believe something, stand up. If a few more people had stood up for the rights of Japanese Americans, we wouldn't have perpetrated this horrible deed against them."

Carol Moseley-Braun

Chicago Sun-Times, 2/3/92

In the three-way Democratic primary for the U.S. Senate, Cook County Recorder of Deeds Carol Moseley Braun is the non-packaged candidate.

Braun, 44, former assistant majority leader of the Illinois House and a former assistant U.S. attorney, is attempting to show that ideas are more relevant to the voters than multimillion-dollar television blitzes. The African American lawyer doesn't have the financial resources to compete with Sen. Alan J. Dixon (D-Ill.) and lawyer Albert Hofeld in the video wars. But Braun has something that her opponents both lack: a well-defined philosophy.

She was drafted to challenge Dixon by a coalition of feminists, black activists and lakefront independents after Dixon's controversial vote to confirm Supreme Court Justice Clarence Thomas. In accepting their draft, Braun passed up certain re-election as county recorder. The liberal Braun has since been endorsed for the Senate by the Independent Voters of Illinois/Independent Precinct Organization and also by the National Women's Political Caucus.

Last week, Braun showed up at a Senate hearing to confront Dixon on his recent conversion to a national health-care plan. She is supporting the more comprehensive national health insurance legislation sponsored by Rep. Martin A. Russo (D-Ill).

Braun is urging political newcomer Hofeld to withdraw from the primary, which would give her a one-on-one race with Dixon. Polls taken for Dixon and Hofeld have shown Braun as the runner-up. A McKeon Associates poll of Cook County Democratic voters taken for Ald. Patrick J. O'Connor (40th) showed that Braun is running a strong second to Dixon, with Hofeld a distant third. The poll showed Braun getting a fifth of the white vote.

If Braun somehow wins an upset victory and is the first black woman U.S. senator, what kind of a legislator would she be?

Braun, who served in the Illinois House of Representatives from 1979 through 1988, was among the more skillful legislators of this period. She filed and won a historic reapportionment lawsuit in 1981 that increased the number of blacks and resulted in the election of the first Hispanics in the Illinois General Assembly. Braun, a key Springfield ally for Mayors Harold Washington and Eugene Sawyer, was a leader in the battle for school reform and co-authored legislation providing for the election of local school boards.

Four years ago, Braun was elected county recorder and moved quickly to professionalize an office long dominated by party hacks. She named a commission headed by former U.S. Attorney Thomas Sullivan that recommended sweeping changes in the office. Braun removed politics from the office, which drew criticism from Democratic ward bosses but won acclaim elsewhere. Braun is among the few countywide executives to make a positive difference in a single term at the County Building.

Braun, who is among the county's top vote-getters, could have had an open-ended lease at the County Building. But jolted by the Senate's treatment of Professor Anita Hill in the Thomas hearings, Braun chose to put her career on the line and challenge Dixon. "I'd like to bring a healthy dose of democracy to the Senate," says Braun.

Richard J. Durbin

Chicago Sun-Times, 7/21/97

It was the flight that led to smokeless skies.

In the early summer of 1987, then-Rep. Richard J. Durbin (D-Ill.) couldn't get a seat in the no-smoking section on a United Airlines flight from Phoenix to Chicago.

"I was late to the terminal and late in checking in at the airline's desk," Durbin recalls. "When I asked to be seated in no-smoking, the ticket agent told me that the only available seat was in the middle of the smoking section."

Durbin tried to get another seat assignment. "Isn't there anything you can do about this?" he asked the ticket agent.

"No. But there's something you can do about it," she responded, noting Durbin's clout as a member of the U.S. House.

During the three-hour flight, Durbin's eyes burned as he sat between two chain-smokers. "I kept turning the air vent to deflect their smoke. But it didn't help much," Durbin said. "Although this second-hand smoke was uncomfortable for me, it was very unhealthy for elderly passengers and for mothers traveling with small children."

He decided to fight back. Durbin introduced legislation to ban smoking on U.S. airline flights.

The odds were against him. House Speaker Jim Wright (D-Texas) sent out letters opposing Durbin's amendment. Cigarette manufacturers, tobacco growers and lobbyists for their industry had thwarted all previous attempts to restrict smoking. Tobacco is grown in 51 congressional districts and dominates the local economy in 27. Durbin made enemies with his legislation. Some colleagues from tobacco states are still upset with him.

But public opinion and scientific evidence were on Durbin's side. The National Academy of Sciences had warned in 1985 about the toxic threat of secondhand smoke to airline passengers. Flight attendants, who were inhaling the equivalent of a pack a day, rallied behind Durbin's proposal.

Durbin said airline executives quietly backed his amendment but were hesitant to speak out because they didn't want to offend their smoking customers.

The tar from airline smoke clogged plane valves and air filters. "When maintenance crews wanted to check the seal on the door of the plane, they would look for evidence of tar coming out of the plane from the cigarette smoke," Durbin said. "The tar would stain the seal."

Two senior members of the House Appropriations Committee from tobacco states shot down Durbin's first proposal that would have banned smoking on all domestic flights. He amended his measure to a ban on flights of less than two hours.

Durbin gained the support of the legendary Rep. Claude Pepper (D-Fla.), the last of the Franklin D. Roosevelt New Deal-era liberals and a populist on health-care issues. Pepper, who chaired the Rules Committee, sent Durbin's amendment to the floor without a committee vote. "The tobacco lobby has always been crafty in avoiding confrontations. They always kept legislation tied up in committee. The vote in the Rules Committee would have been against us. But Pepper gaveled it through," Durbin said.

After a long and emotional debate on the House floor, Durbin's measure passed by a vote of 198–193 on July 13, 1987. It was the first legislative setback for the tobacco lobby. A similar measure passed in the Senate, and President Ronald Reagan signed it into law. It was Durbin's greatest legislative triumph. Now in the Senate, he's still turning up the heat on the tobacco lobby.

Men of the House

Tip O'Neill

Chicago Sun-Times, 2/2/94

Tip O'Neill, who died last month at age 81, was one of the better storytellers of American politics. The former speaker of the House looked and talked like a character from Edwin O'Connor's *The Last Hurrah*.

All Politics Is Local is O'Neill's parting gift, an entertaining, warmly personal political primer containing the collected wisdom of more than a half-century. Reading this book is not unlike spending an afternoon with O'Neill at Jimmy's Harborside, his hangout overlooking Boston Harbor.

"Storytelling comes easy to me because I used anecdotes to keep an audience entertained—and make a point," O'Neill writes. "It's a sad commentary on today's politics that storytelling is disappearing." So are plain-spoken political figures like him.

O'Neill tells how he lost his first race, in the 1930s, for the Cambridge City Council because he took his neighborhood for granted. His father told O'Neill afterward that he had neglected his own precinct. "All politics is local," the elder O'Neill said. "Don't forget it."

Loyalty meant something to O'Neill. He recalls how he supported a Democratic pal named Mike Neville over the young John F. Kennedy in the 1946 congressional campaign. Several times JFK asked O'Neill for his support. O'Neill explained that he had a commitment to his friend.

Though O'Neill knew Kennedy was the likely winner, he remained loyal to Neville and delivered a big vote for him in O'Neill's legislative district. After the election, Kennedy told O'Neill: "I can see that when you're with a friend, you're with him all the way." O'Neill and Kennedy then became longtime allies.

A lifetime of public service, O'Neill avers, shouldn't make one rich—a philosophy not shared by some of Chicago's more prominent political figures. In the early 1950s, O'Neill earned about $9,000 a year as speaker of the Massachusetts House and brought in another $25,000 as an insurance broker.

When he rose to national prominence as House Democratic whip in 1971, he was still making money from his insurance business. Common Cause blew the whistle on O'Neill for selling insurance on the side. O'Neill did the right thing and got out of the business.

In O'Neill's world, politicians didn't succeed by climbing on the backs of their colleagues. When he was choosing members for the House Ethics Committee, O'Neill recalls, the father of a new congressman flew to Washington and asked O'Neill to name his son to the panel. "If he can get on the Ethics Committee, he can become president of the United States," the father told O'Neill. The speaker immediately scratched the new congressman from his list.

O'Neill's book, though containing only 190 pages, is long on political wisdom. For instance, he writes, it's easier to run for office than to run the office. O'Neill, who retired as speaker in 1987, says public officials should know when to quit. "I think if you get frustrated over a long period of time or find yourself getting cynical or find yourself hiding from your voters or your colleagues, it's time to get out," he observes. Sen. Bob Packwood should take O'Neill's advice.

O'Neill, who was an avid fan, advises politicians not to get introduced at sporting events. Once O'Neill attended a middleweight championship fight in Massachusetts and asked not to be introduced. But the ring announcer ignored O'Neill's plea. He was roundly booed. "People go to sports events to enjoy the action. They feel intruded upon if some outsider imposes on what they paid good money for," O'Neill writes.

His checklist of maxims should be required reading for anyone who cares about politics.

"You can accomplish anything if you're willing to let someone else take the credit."

"Never speak of yourself in the third person."

"Tell the truth the first time and you don't have to remember what you said."

"Vote your conscience, your country, your district, the leadership in that order."

Tip O'Neill's values are enduring. His book is a delight.

Sidney R. Yates

Chicago Sun-Times, 11/6/96

Rep. Sidney R. Yates is the last of the New Deal liberals.

Yates, 87, the oldest and longest-serving congressman, ended his final campaign Tuesday. First elected in 1948, he still is a tough competitor. Joe Walsh, Yates' 34-year-old Republican rival, sought to make age the issue. With a twinkle in his eye, Yates quipped that he wouldn't make an issue of Walsh's youth and inexperience.

In a career of almost a half-century, Yates said, he had never called a news conference. Nor has he had a press secretary. Yates preferred to go directly to the voters. He declined invitations to appear with his opponent on television interview programs. Yates didn't want to forfeit his advantage in name recognition.

There never was any doubt about where Yates stood on the issues. In contrast with so many of today's politicians, Yates isn't a captive of focus groups. He is a staunch liberal who never has wavered in his convictions. Yates has a 100 percent rating from the liberal Americans for Democratic Action in the current edition of the Almanac of American Politics. Yates is more forthright on the issues than most public officials. He believes that voters would rather hear straight talk than smooth talk.

Yates, who looks more than a decade younger than his years, once described himself as "a champion of lost causes." But for more than four decades, he has had a quiet but major influence as a member of the powerful House Appropriations committee. For 20 years, he was among the subcommittee chairmen known as "the College of Cardinals." He controlled more than $10 billion in annual spending on management of public lands, parks, forests and wildlife preserves. He was responsible for the protection of about one-third of the nation's land. The Sierra Club broke a 97-year tradition of nonpartisanship in 1982 and gave Yates its first endorsement.

He obtained federal funding to prevent further erosion of the Lake Michigan shoreline and provided financial aid to such institutions as the Art Institute of Chicago, the Chicago Historical Society and the establishment of a Chicago laboratory to fight water pollution. Yates also helped obtain funding for the construction of new federal buildings in the South Loop and for the Harold Washington Library.

Former Rep. Dan Rostenkowski (D-Chicago), who chaired the Ways and Means Committee from 1981 to 1994, said Yates was the real power in the Illinois delegation. When the GOP won the House in 1994, Yates lost his subcommittee chairmanship.

In his long career, Yates has watched many of his colleagues go on to higher office. He is the only member of the House who served during Harry Truman's administration. Five of his former House colleagues later moved up to the presidency: John F. Kennedy, Lyndon B. Johnson, Richard M. Nixon, Gerald R. Ford and George Bush. "Sid is among the real gentlemen in Congress," Ford said in a recent interview. "He and I were elected together in 1948 and are good friends, though we have different political views."

Yates also tried for higher office. In 1962, he gave up his House seniority and ran against Sen. Everett M. Dirksen (R-Ill.), who was Senate minority leader. Yates made a strong race but lost. For the next two years, Yates served as an ambassador at the United Nations. He was re-elected to the House in 1964.

Among his more notable accomplishments was saving the U.S. atomic submarine program in the 1950s. Adm. Hyman G. Rickover said that Yates was his key ally. Yates also thwarted Interior Secretary James Watt's effort to give away public lands to private interests in the 1980s, and he was a driving force in the creation of the Holocaust Museum in Washington, D.C. It is a 48-year legacy of doing good.

Dan Rostenkowski
Chicago Sun-Times, 4/9/96

He had it all.

Dan Rostenkowski wasn't just the most powerful congressman in the history of this town. He also was a friend and confidant of presidents from John F. Kennedy to Bill Clinton. Rostenkowski, 68, is on the very short list of very important national legislators of the last 40 years.

But Rostenkowski will be remembered more for his fate. If he accepts a plea agreement to corruption charges, Rosty will go down in history as the congressional leader who went to prison.

That's a stiff price. Former President Richard M. Nixon, Vice-President Spiro T. Agnew and House Speaker Jim Wright fell from even greater heights than Rostenkowski. But they never lost their freedom. Nixon accepted a pardon for his Watergate crimes. Agnew got probation after pleading no contest to tax evasion charges. Rostenkowski is facing stiffer penalties.

There is a lingering sadness in Chicago and in Washington, D.C., about Rostenkowski's fall. "What happened to Danny is the same thing that happened to Nixon," a former senior Republican official lamented. "The rules changed and they didn't."

There were few restrictions on congressional expenditures when Rostenkowski was first elected to the U.S. House in 1958. Many of his colleagues viewed their office stamp allowance as personal income. But when the rules were tightened in the post-Watergate era, Rostenkowski got annoyed. By ignoring the new rules, he set the stage for his eventual destruction.

The tragedy of Rostenkowski's fall is that he was among the more effective national and local legislators. He was the driving force behind Clinton's 1993 deficit-reduction package and the North American Free Trade Agreement. As chairman of the Ways and Means Committee from 1981 to 1994, Rostenkowski had a major role in the tax reform act of 1986. Clinton's health care plan was doomed when Rostenkowski was forced to relinquish his committee chairmanship after his 1994 indictment.

House Speaker Tip O'Neill said that Rostenkowski grew more into his role than anyone he had served with in Congress. Rostenkowski could have been elected House majority whip in 1981 but took the Ways and Means chairmanship at O'Neill's urging. The committee had lost influence and prestige during the previous decade. Rostenkowski brought it back. He understood the tax code and trade policy. He also drove a hard bargain.

Rostenkowski also was highly effective at bringing home federal dollars for Chicago. In his final year as committee chairman, Rostenkowski brought home about $292 million in federal aid. The projects included funds for a new science building at DePaul University, Lake Michigan shoreline protection, the Loop Circulator, AIDS research and affordable housing. Mayor Daley called him Chicago's battleship in the competition for federal dollars. In the current Republican Congress, Daley doesn't even have a lifeboat. Since Rosty's defeat in 1994, Chicago has lost federal aid.

After his indictment in 1994, Rostenkowski ran a low-profile reelection bid. If he had wanted to win, it's probable that he could have squeaked out a narrow victory. But since Rostenkowski already had been forced to yield his chairmanship, he didn't have much enthusiasm for a campaign. Rostenkowski handled his loss with the dignity of an old fighter.

He once wanted to be mayor of Chicago. But he wouldn't play racial politics to get there. When civic leaders urged him to run against Mayor Harold Washington, he declined. Rostenkowski didn't want to lead a divisive campaign against the city's first black mayor. Rostenkowski showed character in refusing to run against Washington in a race that he might have won. He also declined to push for the selection of a white-ethnic as interim mayor after Washington's death. Rostenkowski thought it was a time for healing.

Rostenkowski, who made serious mistakes, ought to be remembered for his achievements as well.

Henry J. Hyde

Chicago Sun-Times, 12/13/96

Rep. Henry J. Hyde (R-Ill.) isn't playing games.

Hyde, 72, chairman of the House Judiciary Committee, is opposed to congressional term limits. But he is planning to send a term-limits amendment to the House floor early next year.

House Speaker Newt Gingrich, who has little enthusiasm for term limits, has pledged that a term-limits measure will be among the first votes of the new Congress. Hyde is helping Gingrich to keep that commitment.

The U.S. Supreme Court ruled last year that congressional term limits can be enacted only by amending the U.S. Constitution. In nine states, voters passed term-limits amendments last month to "instruct and inform" members of Congress to propose a constitutional amendment.

In March, 1995, a term-limits amendment fell 61 votes short of the required two-thirds majority in the House. It was the first defeat of a proposal in Gingrich's 1994 Contract With America.

The contract pledged to "replace career politicians with citizen legislators." Term-limits advocates are divided over whether the tenure of House members should be limited to six or 12 years. Gingrich supported a 12-year limit. U.S. Term Limits, a lobbying group, said that six years was enough and criticized the GOP amendment as "watered-down."

Hyde, who chaired the 1996 Republican National Convention's platform committee and has been among the GOP's most influential conservative leaders of the last two decades, makes a compelling argument against term limits. In contrast with former Senate Majority Leader Bob Dole and Rep. Phil Crane, who support term limits but not for themselves, Hyde applies the same standard across the board. He believes that term limits are a dumb idea. Hyde even noted his opposition in a brief filed with the U.S. Supreme Court last year.

His eloquence helped to defeat term limits on the House Floor in '95. Thirty-nine other GOP congressmen joined him. Hyde is vowing to take the lead in opposition this winter.

"I want to tell you how unpleasant it is to take the well in militant opposition to something that is so near and dear to the hearts of so many of my colleagues and [House] members whom I revere," Hyde declared on the House floor last year. "But I just cannot be an accessory to the dumbing down of democracy. And I think that is what this is.

"I might also say . . . that it is a little amusing to see the stickers that have been worn by so many of my colleagues. It says 'term limits, yes.' It does not say 'term limits now.' "

As Hyde pointed out, the Founding Fathers wrestled with term limits and rejected them. He noted that Alexander Hamilton and James Madison argued that term limits were undemocratic. Hyde cited Robert Livingston's comment during a 1788 debate on the ratification of the Constitution. Livingston asked: "Shall we then drive experience into obscurity?"

"The unstated premise of term limits is that we are progressively corrupted the longer we stayed around here," said Hyde, who cited a long list of distinguished legislators from both parties. Hyde's productive career is a strong argument against term limits.

"Our negative campaigning, our mudslinging, our name-calling has made anger the national recreation. But that is our fault, not the system's," said Hyde, who is respected for his intellect and civility. "America needs leaders. It needs statesmen. It needs giants, and you do not get them out of the phone book."

Hyde argued that term limits aren't conservative. "It is radical distrust of democracy. It is cynical. It is pessimistic, devoid of the hope and the optimism that built this country. This corrosive attack on the consent of the governed stems from two sources. One is well meaning but misguided, and the other are those who really in their heart hate politics and despise politicians.

"I confess, I love politics and I love politicians. They invest the one commodity that can never be replaced, their time, their family life, their privacy, and their reputation. And for what? To make this a better country."

Hyde contends that Americans have a constitutional right to democracy. Term limits deprive the voters of choice. "Trust the people," said Hyde. Term-limits advocates would rather not.

William O. Lipinski
Chicago Sun-Times, 4/25/97

On the 50th anniversary of the NBA, Rep. William O. Lipinski (D-Ill.) wants the league to take care of the men who invented the league.

Lipinski, 59, a former AAU basketball coach and Chicago Park District athletic supervisor, has been an avid follower of professional basketball since he watched former DePaul All-American George Mikan lead the Chicago American Gears against the Fort Wayne Zollner Pistons at the International Amphitheatre.

In that era, the best seats in the arena cost $2.50. The players traveled by bus instead of chartered planes. Mikan, who would go on to win five NBA titles with the old Minneapolis Lakers, was the league's first superstar and earned about $12,000 a year during his pro career. The average player was paid about $4,500 a year in the late '40s. As the Bulls head into the playoffs, Michael Jordan is under a $30 million contract. Forward Juwan Howard of the Washington Bullets has a $105 million contract. Shaquille O'Neal of the Lakers, who signed as a free agent last year after leaving Orlando, got a $120 million contract for seven years.

Lipinski, who says that the NBA has much to celebrate on its golden anniversary, thinks it should be more attentive to the men who helped build the league. William M. Tosheff, who heads the pre-1995 NBA Players Association, called Lipinski's attention to the league's neglect of its oldest living players. Under the NBA's pension rules, players who entered the league after 1965 are vested for a pension if they played three seasons. But the pre-1965 players must have played five seasons to qualify.

"This decision created a double standard for eligibility in the NBA Players Pension Plan and harmed those retired players who needed the pension benefits the most," Lipinski wrote in letters to the NBA commissioner's office and to the NBA Players Association.

Lipinski noted that John Ezersky, who played for the Boston Celtics in the 1940s, works as a cab driver at 75 to pay his bills. The late Nat "Sweetwater" Clifton of DuSable, who became the first black to play in the NBA, with the Knicks, drove taxis in Chicago after his retirement.

According to Lipinski, about 60 former NBA players from its first decade have been unfairly excluded from pension benefits. "The NBA did remember its glorious past with a celebration of the Old-Timers at the All-Star Game but it must also remember those who are suffering daily under the hardships of poverty," Lipinski said in his letter to the league and players association. "I have heard the argument that the NBA is not legally obligated to provide for the pre-1965 players. I cannot accept this excuse. I feel the NBA has a moral obligation to establish a uniform requirement of three years participation for eligibility."

Former Sen. Bill Bradley (D-N.J.), a former NBA player for the Knicks, also wants NBA pensions for old-timers. If the league isn't responsive, Lipinski has drafted a congressional resolution calling for the inclusion of the game's pioneers in the NBA's pension plan. The league owes that to its founders.

Bobby L. Rush

Chicago Sun-Times, 5/13/93

Bobby Rush is the Black Panther who came in from the cold.

Once, he was a revolutionary. But he's become one of the more influential figures in American politics. Rush has traveled a long and often lonely road.

It has been a quarter-century since Rush declared war on the political establishment. "Black people have been on the defensive for all these years," Rush, then deputy minister of defense for the Illinois Black Panther Party, told the *Chicago Daily News* in 1969. "The trend now is not to wait to be attacked. We advocate offensive violence against the power structure."

Rush, who spoke in a street-tough rhetoric, talked about how the Panthers intended to deal with police brutality. "The only language the pigs understand is the language of the gun," Rush told the *Daily News.* "So we intend to teach everybody in the black community that same language. We plan to arm the total black community so when the pigs come down on us, we will be equal."

But on Dec. 4, 1969, Black Panthers Fred Hampton and Mark Clark were slain in a nighttime raid by Chicago policemen directed by then-State's Attorney Edward V. Hanrahan. The attack is among the more infamous events in Chicago history. Families of the slain Panthers were later awarded $2 million in damages by the courts. Rush talks with bitterness and sadness about the Hanrahan raid. Rush said that Hampton is among the lost leaders of the '60s generation. "He had the potential for greatness," Rush said. "I still think about him a lot."

This week, Rush was in Cape Town, South Africa for the historic inauguration of his friend, Nelson Mandela, as the nation's first black president. When Mandela launched his bid for the presidency, he sought political advice and fund-raising help from Rush. Like Mandela, Rush was once a political prisoner. He served six months in prison in 1971 on misdemeanor weapons charges. The South African president served 27 years in prison for his political activism.

Other Black Panther leaders sought to gain power. Bobby Seale, the party's national chairman in the 1960s, ran for mayor of Oakland, Calif. Eldridge Cleaver was a third-party presidential candidate. But Rush had more political skills. Since his election to Congress in 1992, Rush has gained recognition as the Black Panther with the enduring influence.

Rush, who is deputy chairman of the Illinois Democratic Party, was the first Illinois Democratic officeholder to support Bill Clinton's '92 presidential candidacy. He played a major role in John H. Stroger's victory as the first African-American Democratic nominee for Cook County Board president. Rush also influenced the nomination of state Sen. Earlean Collins for Illinois state comptroller. Rush was a key player in millionaire personal-injury lawyer Albert F. Hofeld's triumph over former Ald. Martin J. Oberman (43rd) in the Democratic primary for attorney general. Rush and Oberman were both allies of the late Mayor Harold Washington. Oberman had the support of a majority of Washington's black allies. But Rush forged an alliance with Hofeld and collected more than $60,000 in get-out-the-vote funds from the wealthy lawyer. Rush used the funds most effectively. He also taped a radio spot for Hofeld that aired on black stations.

Rush doesn't win them all. He failed to deliver for Diane Shelley, a candidate for the Metropolitan Water Reclamation District who finished fourth out of 20 candidates for three seats, and for Margaret Hall, his candidate for state representative. But Rush, who feared for his life after the Hanrahan raid 25 years ago, knows that there are worse things than losing an election.

Lane Evans

Chicago Sun-Times, 11/2/98

He is the voice of the Vietnam generation in the U.S. House.

Rep. Lane Evans (D-Ill.), who served in the Marine Corps in the Vietnam era but was never sent to Southeast Asia, has never forgotten the sacrifices of those who went.

Evans, 47, is troubled that many of the soldiers who survived Vietnam are living with the terrible legacy of Agent Orange. It was the defoliant that was sprayed from American planes to clear the forests of Vietnam into wastelands.

More than 5 million acres of Vietnam were covered with more than 12.8 million gallons of the deadly toxin. It was named Agent Orange because of the orange stripe on the huge canisters in which the toxin was stored. When the toxin was dropped from U.S. planes, there were no soldiers on the ground. But when troops moved in after the defoliation, they were exposed to the poison.

Even though the United States stopped dropping Agent Orange in 1970 because of pressure from American soldiers and the Vietnamese, the Pentagon never admitted that the spraying had put troops at risk.

As a member of the Vietnam generation, Evans has had a major impact on Capitol Hill. When Evans was elected to the U.S. House in 1982, Mississippi Democrat G. V. "Sonny" Montgomery chaired the Veterans' Affairs Committee. Montgomery, who served in World War II and in the Korean War, was unresponsive to Vietnam veterans who sought compensation for Agent Orange.

"Sonny is a good friend of mine," Evans said. "But he told me that he had been in Vietnam for eight straight Christmas tours with Bob

Hope and that he had never met anybody who had a problem with Agent Orange. Like the Veterans' Administration, Sonny was in denial."

Evans nearly ousted Montgomery as chairman of the Veterans Affairs Committee in 1993. When Democrats lost the House in 1994, Montgomery stepped down, and Evans became the ranking minority member of the Veterans' Affairs Committee.

Three years ago, Evans finally won his long fight to win medical compensation for veterans suffering from diseases linked to Agent Orange. Last year, he won approval for funding to help children born with birth defects after their fathers' exposure to Agent Orange.

"I believe that these children are as much veterans of the war as any other person that served or who was wounded during time of war," Evans told his colleagues in the fall of 1996. "Through no choice of their own, they lost their health in service to our country."

Evans, who revealed earlier this year that he has Parkinson's disease, is locked in a very tight contest for re-election against Republican Mark Baker, a former television anchorman. Baker hasn't made an issue of Evans' illness. Evans still jogs seven miles daily to keep in shape and exudes energy and enthusiasm.

National GOP leaders, including former Vice President Dan Quayle and 1996 GOP presidential nominee Bob Dole, have campaigned for Baker in recent weeks. Baker had more than twice as much cash on hand at the end of last month than Evans. But the race is still a toss-up.

It's no accident that Vietnam veterans in Illinois and across the country have rallied behind Evans. He has always been there for them.

"It was an uphill battle on Agent Orange," said Evans. "But as the veterans of other wars became involved, it made a difference. The lesson that we learned was that never again will one group of veterans turn its back on another generation. We are now all fighting for better health care for veterans. This brought us together."

To his credit, Baker acknowledges that Evans has done a good job for veterans. "My dad is a World War II veteran. I commend Lane for his efforts, but we need to do more," Baker said at a recent debate with Evans.

But no elected official in America has done more for veterans than Evans.

J. Dennis Hastert

Chicago Sun-Times, 12/21/98

If Rep. J. Dennis Hastert (R-Ill.) had allowed his name to be put forward in the House GOP Caucus last month, he would have been the consensus choice as the next majority leader.

But Hastert had pledged his support to Majority Leader Dick Armey of Texas before their party was stung by defeat in the Nov. 3 election. As a draft-Hastert movement gathered momentum, Hastert quietly sought to be released from his commitment to the beleaguered floor leader. But when Armey resisted, Hastert kept his word.

It is because of Hastert's reputation as a straight shooter and coalition builder that he became the instant favorite as the next House Speaker when Bob Livingston made his dramatic announcement on Saturday that he would not be assuming that role.

The bearlike Hastert, 56, a former Yorkville high school government teacher and wrestling coach, who has been the GOP's chief deputy whip since 1995, has steadily gained influence during the 1990s without making enemies.

Hastert is a conservative but not an ideologue. He has been the GOP's main sponsor on health-care legislation designed to give patients more control over their coverage and on anti-narcotics legislation. Hastert used his influence earlier this year to restore federal funding for bridges over the Fox River.

"Denny just engenders a feeling of trust and loyalty. That's what he's all about. Because of his unselfishness when he turned down the draft for the majority leader, he became the clear favorite for House Speaker," said Kendall County Republican chairman Dallas Ingemunson, who has known Hastert for 30 years.

"He is just an all-around good solid guy and a very skillful legislator," said Gov-Elect George H. Ryan, who was Illinois House Speaker in 1981 when Hastert began his political career as a young state legislator. "He's a down-to-earth, common sense guy who gets along with everyone and always keeps his word. Denny did so well in Springfield that it wasn't surprising that he became the go-to guy in our congressional delegation."

"Denny isn't as well known as some of the other legislative leaders. But internally, he is a unifying force," said Rep. Mark E. Souder (R-Ind.).

Former Rep. Dan Rostenkowski (D-Chicago), who chaired the

House Ways and Means Committee from 1981 until 1994, said that Hastert strengthened his position in the House by taking a pass on the majority leader's race last month. "That points out to his colleagues on both sides of the aisle what kind of a guy he is. They respect him because he's a man of his word," said Rostenkowski.

"Denny will be an effective Speaker because he knows how to bargain. He knows that he's got to give in order to get," said Rostenkowski. "This is one person who can reach over and get Democratic votes because he's a likable guy."

Mayor Daley is among Hastert's admirers. When Daley has traveled to Washington, D.C., he has worked out of Hastert's office on Capitol Hill.

Hastert lives in Yorkville where his wife Jean is a teacher. They have two sons. For many years his family owned and operated a restaurant, the Clock Tower, in Plainfield.

A native of Aurora, Hastert was a high school wrestling star in Oswego and also won wrestling honors at Wheaton College. He later coached two state championship wrestling teams at Yorkville High and served as the president of the National Wrestling Congress in the late 1970s. In that role, he worked with elected officials and became interested in politics.

His first political bid was unsuccessful. Hastert finished fourth out of five candidates (for two positions) from the 39th legislative district that included parts of DuPage, Kane, Kendall, and Will counties. But he established a political base as the leading votegetter in Kendall county.

In 1981, Hastert with the support of Ingemunson and then state Sen. John Grotberg (R-St. Charles) was appointed to the Illinois House when state Rep. Allan L. Schoeberlein resigned. Hastert eventually became the ranking GOP member of the Revenue Committee.

Hastert was chosen as the GOP's replacement nominee for the U.S. House from the 14th congressional district in 1986 when the incumbent resigned for health reasons. Hastert survived a powerful challenge from Kane County Coroner Mary Lou Kearns. Since then, Hastert has easily been re-elected.

He has a reputation for fair play. In 1992 Hastert declined to remove his Democratic opponent from the ballot for insufficient signatures. "We thought people ought to hear about the issues," Hastert said at the time.

In the U.S. House, Hastert was groomed for a future leadership role by House Minority Leader Robert H. Michel (R-Peoria), who led the GOP from 1981 until 1994. Hastert also worked closely with the late Rep. Edward Madigan (R-Lincoln), who served as Michel's chief deputy whip. Hastert was among the key strategists in Madigan's unsuccessful 1988 run against Newt Gingrich for GOP whip. Michel later named Hastert one of six deputy whips.

When the GOP won a House majority in 1994 for the first time in 40 years, Hastert managed Texas conservative Tom DeLay's election as majority whip. DeLay then appointed Hastert as chief deputy.

Hastert considered giving up his House seat to run for the U.S. Senate against vulnerable Democratic incumbent Carol Moseley-Braun. But in weighing his options, he remained in the House because his prospects for moving up in the leadership looked good.

Hardball

Jeremiah E. Joyce

Chicago Sun-Times, 3/18/94

When the television lights came on for Rep. Dan Rostenkowski's victory celebration, former state Sen. Jeremiah E. Joyce moved to the back of the room. On a night when the television networks were reporting Rostenkowski's remarkable comeback, Joyce shunned the spotlight. Taking credit isn't his thing. But more than anyone else, Joyce was responsible for Rosty's political resurrection.

Rostenkowski, who is the target of a federal probe, looked like a political goner when he asked for Joyce's help. State Sen. John J. Cullerton was coming on strong. Polling indicated that two-thirds of the 5th District's likely Democratic voters viewed Rostenkowski unfavorably.

By reaching out to Joyce, Rostenkowski signaled that he was fighting back. Until this point in his campaign, Rostenkowski had a campaign office without furniture, brochures or buttons. His Northwest Side precinct workers were alienating voters by nailing signs onto trees.

Joyce, a former 19th Ward alderman, who is also a former Chicago police officer and former assistant state's attorney, has a keen understanding of grass-roots politics. Joyce, who is tough, disciplined and organized, has built a reputation for winning elections that were considered unwinnable.

Mayor Daley and Cook County Sheriff Michael F. Sheehan have both said that Joyce was the key player in their political careers. In 1979, President Jimmy Carter was set to nominate Joyce as a member of the Commodity Futures Trading Commission. But Daley was in a difficult race for state's attorney. Joyce took a pass on the CFTC appointment and helped Daley win his toughest election.

"Jerry has never been willing to sacrifice his friends or his principles," said Loop lawyer William M. Daley, who said that Joyce built the Daley political organization in 1980. "I was called the campaign manager. The truth of the matter is that Jerry was the campaign. Without him, Rich Daley's political career may well have ended in 1980. He has been a major force and valued adviser in all of Rich Daley's campaigns. . . . It's fair to say that Rich Daley would not be mayor of Chicago if not for Jerry Joyce."

When Joyce came aboard the campaign, several key ward organizations were lining up against Rostenkowski. Joyce and Daley's camp won them back.

Joyce engineered the endorsements of the Fraternal Order of Police and the Firefighters Union for Rostenkowski. When polling showed that Rostenkowski had a gender gap, Joyce lined up endorsements from women officeholders and produced fliers that showcased Rostenkowski's strong record on women's issues.

In putting together a campaign that targeted every major ethnic group and community in the district, Joyce reduced Rostenkowski's negative rating by more than 20 percentage points. With the aid of Ald. Richard F. Mell (33rd) and former state Sen. Timothy F. Degnan, Joyce turned out the vote for Rostenkowski with a precinct army of more than 800 workers.

When John Cullerton sent 5th District residents a flier that billed himself as a champion of gun control, Joyce countered with the endorsements of anti-gun activists Jim and Sarah Brady.

By reaching out to the Southwest Side's top political organizer, Rostenkowski saved his congressional seat.

Edmund L. Kelly
Chicago Sun-Times, 6/20/97

He was Chicago's most successful playground coach.

It has been 49 years since former Chicago Park District Supt. Ed Kelly got his start as a coach at Welles Park on the Near Northwest Side. He taught more than a generation of kids how to drive for a lay-up, pass to the open man and play tight man-to-man defense.

Kelly, 72, who grew up in the Cabrini-Green area and won All City basketball honors at St. Phillip's High School in 1942, was an aerial gunner in a dive-bomber squadron with the Marines in the South Pacific during World War II. He later attended DePaul University and played professional basketball with the Oshkosh All-Stars of the National Basketball League. In sports and politics, Kelly always has played to win.

His earliest ambition was to become a coach in his hometown. After his start at Welles Park, Kelly later coached at River Park, Green Briar, Chase, Waveland, Pottawattomie and Lincoln parks. Tens of thousands of youngsters participated in Kelly's programs during his 38-year career with the Park District. Kelly coached city basketball and baseball champions and Catholic Youth Organization All-Star teams that were undefeated for four years.

"I still get letters from many of these kids," Kelly said Thursday. "They always remember their gym teacher. For me, it was a labor of love."

Texas A&M head basketball coach Tony Barone, who played for Kelly at Waveland Field, gained a scholarship to Duke University with Kelly's aid. Barone was co-captain of the 1968 Blue Devils and an Academic All-American. Barone, whose first head coaching job was at Mount Carmel High School, says that his association with Kelly was the turning point in his career.

Richards High School football coach Gary Korhonen, who won back-to-back state titles in 1988–89, was among Kelly's athletes at Chase Park. "He was a major influence on me and was part of a foundation that I've tried to give back to my players," said Korhonen.

Wes Pavalon, who played basketball for Kelly at Green Briar Park and went on to become the founding owner of the Milwaukee Bucks in the NBA, describes Kelly as "a priest, a rabbi, a psychiatrist, a physician, a coach, a friend—everything. He's spent his whole life in the Park District keeping kids out of jail, keeping kids away from narcotics, keeping families together. He fed me. He was a father to me."

Kelly coached many notable athletes, including John Jardine, who became football coach at the University of Wisconsin; Ron Rubenstein, a member of Louisville University's 1959 Final Four basketball team; Larry Coutre, a half-back on two Notre Dame championship teams; Northwestern's basketball All-American Frank Ehmann; and DePaul basketball stars Billy Haig and Howie Carl.

His playground alumni also include the film director William Friedkin, who won an Oscar for "The French Connection," CBS News national correspondent Bill Plante and NBC network executive Bobby Walsh. State's Attorney Richard A. Devine played basketball for Kelly at Chase Park. Ald. Bernard Hansen (44th) was a baseball standout at Waveland Field.

If Kelly hadn't gone into politics, he would have done well in college or professional sports. He was an assistant coach for the 1961–62 Loyola Ramblers basketball team, which won the NCAA championship in 1963. Kelly was on the board of directors for 10 years of the Milwaukee Bucks. He nearly left Chicago in 1968 to become the president of the Bucks. He was so close to the center Lew Alcindor that he made the arrangements in Chicago for Alcindor to change his name to Kareem Abdul-Jabbar. Kelly also engineered the trade for Hall of Famer Oscar Robertson, who teamed with Jabbar to win the 1971 NBA title.

The late Mayor Richard J. Daley talked Kelly out of moving to Milwaukee and recruited him into Democratic politics. Kelly, who has been the 47th Ward's Democratic committeeman for 29 years, said he has no regrets.

Richard F. Mell

Chicago Sun-Times, 7/25/93

Whatever happens in the 5th Congressional District, one thing is certain.

Ald. Richard F. Mell (33rd) will be in the middle of the fight.

Mell, 54, the Northwest Side's most influential Democratic ward committeeman, is promoting his son-in-law, freshman State Rep. Rod Blagojevich as a successor to U.S. Rep. Dan Rostenkowski, whose political future is less than certain.

Until recent developments in a federal probe of the House post office, Mell was tentatively committed to backing Rostenkowski in 1994 and lining up pledges of support for a 1996 Blagojevich congressional bid. But Mell's timetable may be changing.

Mell and Rostenkowski are longtime rivals. If former Mayor Jane M. Byrne had been re-elected in 1983, Mell was her candidate to oust the Northwest Side congressman. Rostenkowski once told me that the Byrne/Mell alliance was the reason he collected a $1 million political fund. Mell would have been a formidable challenger. But after Byrne narrowly lost the '83 primary to Harold Washington, Mell folded his candidacy against Rostenkowski.

In the last decade, Mell has gained recognition as among the few surviving powerhouses in local Democratic politics. He was the only committeeman who delivered every precinct for Byrne in the '83 mayoral primary. Last year, challengers supported by Mell crushed state legislators supported by Rostenkowski and 47th Ward Committeeman Edmund L. Kelly in the March primary. Blagojevich trounced former State Rep. Myron Kulas, a member of Rostenkowski's 32nd ward organization. Another Mell-backed candidate, community activist Nancy Kaszak, soundly defeated former State Rep. Alfred G. Ronan, Mell's former ally who defected to Kelly's organization.

How does Mell do it?

Mell loves the game of politics. A workaholic, he hardly sleeps in the closing weeks of a campaign; he lost 14 pounds in the final stretch of the '92 primary. The 33rd Ward Democratic committeeman has a political base of 500 patronage workers, which is the largest organization on the Northwest Side. Mell is also a prolific fund-raiser.

Mell, who owns two manufacturing companies that he founded and has a net worth of about $10 million, is among the city's wealthiest public officials. Partly because of his wealth, he doesn't hesitate to take chances. Mell's wife runs his businesses. He devotes most of his energies to politics.

Though Mell is among the town's more successful Democratic committeemen, he has been frustrated in attempts to win higher office. Following the death of Mayor Washington in 1987, Mell made a brief bid for acting mayor but then helped broker the election of Eugene Sawyer. Mell sought the chairmanship of the Cook County Democratic party in 1990, losing to 45th Ward Committeeman Thomas G. Lyons. Last year, Mell wanted to become the congressman from the new Hispanic-majority congressional district. But Mell, who is half Polish and half German, concluded that the district should be represented by a Hispanic. With Mell out of the running, Luis Gutierrez won the seat. Mell, who has the best organization in the district, could have won.

Mell, though, has no regrets about not going to Congress. He's passing the torch to his son-in-law. Whether it's in '94 or '96, Mell is committed to sending Blagojevich to Congress.

Edward R. Vrdolyak

Chicago Sun-Times, 2/24/97

Edward R. Vrdolyak is a tough infighter and shrewd political strategist.

Though it has been eight years since his last run for office, the former mayoral candidate and alderman from Chicago's Southeast Side hasn't given up the game. He is a player in Tuesday's bitterly fought GOP primary in Cicero.

A decade after he received 468,493 votes as a mayoral candidate against the late Harold Washington, Vrdolyak is mapping strategy for Cicero's Town President Betty Loren-Maltese, who is facing a stiff challenge from former allies in Tuesday's primary.

Vrdolyak, 59, describes Loren-Maltese as a friend. His loyalty to her isn't surprising given that he has received more than $1 million in legal fees from Loren-Maltese's administration.

"You help people, they help you," Vrdolyak once said of his political alliances. "Business or politics. It works that way."

The opposition slate to Loren-Maltese is attempting to make Vrdolyak an issue. Town Collector Alison E. Resnick alleged that Vrdolyak's only interest in Cicero is his fat legal fees. Resnick has also attacked him as an outsider. Town Supervisor Joseph A. DeChicio has accused Vrdolyak of bringing in political workers to intimidate Loren-Maltese's opposition.

Vrdolyak isn't falling for the bait. When Resnick and DeChicio held a news conference to attack him, Vrdolyak wouldn't respond on camera. He denied their allegations as "absolute nonsense" and "the desperate charges of a losing campaign."

His political advice to others is often good.

As the Cook County Democratic chairman in 1982, it was Vrdolyak who came up with the "Punch 10" campaign for straight-ticket voting that produced a massive Democratic vote. Though he later switched political parties, Vrdolyak's Punch 10 slogan was revived by Democrats last fall and helped elect Richard A. Devine as state's attorney.

In 1983, Vrdolyak helped Mayor Jane M. Byrne soften her confrontational image and make a surprisingly strong bid for re-election when early polls indicated she didn't have a chance. Byrne's commercials looked like an old Katharine Hepburn movie. She projected the image of an executive in charge and above the fray. Byrne surged into the lead but narrowly lost the Democratic primary to Washington. She finished ahead of Richard M. Daley.

Perhaps it's just a coincidence. But the Loren-Maltese '97 re-election message is similar to Byrne's in the campaign that Vrdolyak stage-managed. The Loren-Maltese campaign literature showcases her efforts to promote economic development and "more jobs for Cicero residents." Vrdolyak has sought to keep Loren-Maltese focused on her message, sources said.

When Loren-Maltese led police with drug-sniffing dogs into the town hall offices of two political rivals last week, a Republican source said that Loren-Maltese had hoped to embarrass one of these targets. If Vrdolyak's advice had been sought, he would have cautioned against a raid on just one office in the town hall.

But Vrdolyak also plays it tough. Ray Hanania, the campaign manager for the opposition slate, said he was fired last fall by Loren-Maltese as the town spokesman because of Vrdolyak's advice. Loren-Maltese responded that she had hired Hanania on Vrdolyak's recommendation but did not dispute Hanania's claim that Vrdolyak forced his ouster. "Vrdolyak said that I had to be fired if I wouldn't publicly defend Betty" in the face of a federal investigation, Hanania said.

Attacking Vrdolyak in Cicero could be politically risky. In 1988, as the Republican nominee for Circuit Court clerk, Vrdolyak got more votes in Cicero than George Bush. That's why Loren-Maltese is relying on his help.

Philip J. Rock

Chicago Sun-Times, 11/13/92

Philip J. Rock, who is ending a record tenure as president of the Illinois Senate, is going to be missed.

In typical fashion, he isn't making a big deal of his retirement. He knows who he is and doesn't need reminders about his political prominence and power. His official biography in the Illinois Blue Book is briefer than those of most freshman legislators. Rock is comfortable with himself.

He is among the few politicians I've ever covered who doesn't worry about the polls. More than any prominent Illinois political figure since the late Gov. Richard B. Ogilvie, he doesn't sweat the political consequences of doing the right thing. A former Golden Gloves fighter, Rock isn't afraid to lead with his chin. On no fewer than four occasions, he has taken the lead in promoting an increase in the state's income tax, which is among the lowest in the nation.

Throughout his political career, Rock has strived to make government more responsive. He has always sought to speak for the voiceless, for the poor, for working people and for children. He is the author of more than 450 Illinois laws, including important reforms in special education, child adoption and foster care, domestic violence and child support.

Rock, who grew up on the Northwest Side, is the son of Joe Rock, a native of Luxembourg, and Kathryn, a first-generation Irish-American. His political mentor is former Attorney General William Clark.

His personal and political philosophies aren't complicated. He says that he was born a Catholic, a Democrat and a Cubs fan in roughly that order. His loyalties haven't changed. He nearly became a priest. When Wrigley Field is almost empty, Rock is still there, a diehard fan. A loyal Democrat, he has ignored court rulings that banned political hiring and firing.

As for his public philosophy, he has noted: "Government exists to improve and enhance the quality of life. I should not impede free enterprise, but on the other hand there should be a recognition that government does have a role in attempting to be of assistance to those who can't assist themselves."

Tonight, a legion of Rock's friends, including Rep. Dan Rostenkowski and Ald. Edward M. Burke (14th) are gathering for a farewell tribute. Rock is being honored with Maryville Academy's fourth "Standing Tall" award.

For more than 20 years, Rock has served on Maryville's board. The Rev. John Smyth, Maryville's director and a former basketball All-American at Notre Dame, has been Rock's friend for 40 years. Rock was a playmaking guard for Quigley seminary. "Phil was a terrific competitor," recalls Father Smyth. "He was a fairly good shot and a good passer. But, most of all, he was a leader. He has a quiet confidence that inspires respect."

"Phil never asks anything for himself, which is unusual in politics. But he's always trying to help others," Smyth notes. "He gets a thrill out of making the process work for others."

Rock has shunned many opportunities to seek other top offices. Just last winter, he passed up almost certain election to the Supreme Court. He would have probably been a fine governor or U.S. senator.

But he is leaving a richer legacy than all but a handful of the state's chief executives. Rock will be remembered as among the more notable legislators in Illinois history.

Michael J. Madigan
Chicago Sun-Times, 5/24/98

House Speaker Michael J. Madigan is bringing a new discipline to the State Democratic Central Committee in his first month as party chairman.

Because of his dual role as legislative leader, he has the ability to unite the diverse factions that make up the Democratic Party. For the first time in the '90s, the party might be getting its act together.

Madigan, 56, has a track record of winning elections. Despite a Republican-drawn legislative map after the 1991 reapportionment, Madigan twice has won Democratic House majorities in the last three elections.

In taking over the party chairmanship, Madigan's goal is to create a winning environment for the statewide Democratic ticket, including gubernatorial nominee Glenn Poshard and Sen. Carol Moseley-Braun, and to retain control of the House.

Madigan, who is a master of coalition politics, is facing no small challenge.

The Democrats have lost six consecutive elections for governor, the last four elections for secretary of state and, in 1994, failed to win a single statewide executive office for the first time in 38 years. Madigan also lost his House majority in the '94 GOP sweep. He took on the chairmanship to make certain that doesn't happen again.

In his first fund-raising event as party chairman, Madigan netted about $100,000 during a reception at Springfield's private Sangamo Club. The event demonstrated that Madigan would take full advantage of his legislative leadership position to boost the Democratic Party's fortunes. Although GOP spokesmen publicly claimed to be shocked that the House Speaker was using his clout to help other Democrats, Madigan showed Republican officeholders that he meant business.

Madigan is convening twice-a-month strategy meetings with the state Democratic ticket at his Southwest Side political office, which shares space with the Balzekas Museum of Lithuanian Culture. Other members of the State Democratic Central Committee, the state AFL-CIO, state Senate and House Democratic campaign committees and Cook County Board President John H. Stroger's re-election campaign have been invited to participate in the strategy sessions.

During a recent interview in his office at the state Capitol, Madigan talked about his game plan for the '98 Democratic ticket.

"Keeping them together as much as possible is our goal," Madigan said. "These are political people, and some of them will want to pursue their individual agendas, but their chances for success are better if everyone is working together."

Madigan is scheduling his coordinated campaign meetings at 9 on Sunday mornings at his headquarters "as a test of resolve." Moseley-Braun recently attended one of the sessions. "We've had 40 to 45 people at each meeting," Madigan said. "I have the meetings on Sunday mornings because it's a day when almost everyone is available."

He runs the meetings with clockwork efficiency. When there is a disagreement between candidates or party officials, Madigan allows each side to be heard. But he won't be distracted. "I'll say, 'Let's end this discussion and move to discuss things that will bring us together,'" Madigan said.

Madigan has asked members of the statewide Democratic ticket and other party groups to pool their resources to pay for tracking polls and focus groups. "Some people want to know how much money there is to spend. My response is, 'What are you going to put in?' Some people seem to think that I'm going to be the major domo fundraiser, and I may wind up doing that. But everyone has got to do their share.

"I'm not going to be heavy-handed," Madigan said. "But I've told them that this [the tracking polls] will not go forward until I get an individual check from each of the campaigns."

Who's going to turn him down?

Warhorses

Thomas P. Keane

Chicago Sun-Times, 9/29/95

He is known as the Professor.

Former Ald. Thomas P. Keane (31st), who is celebrating his 90th birthday today, was the most influential member of the Chicago City Council in the second half of the 20th century.

Keane was Mayor Richard J. Daley's floor leader from 1955 until 1974 and served a record 16 years as chairman of the Council's Finance Committee.

It was 50 years ago this month that Keane gave up his seat in the Illinois Senate to succeed his late father Thomas P. Keane as alderman of the Near Northwest Side 31st Ward. "I enjoyed the Senate and didn't want to leave," he recalled.

As he lunched with former associates in a Loop restaurant across from City Hall, Keane recalled that he got his political start when he was about 9 years old working in his father's first race for Democratic ward committeeman. "We used to put up campaign cards on the counters of drugstores and saloons," he said.

During his four decades on the Council, Keane was a forceful debater and the Council's master parliamentarian. He wrote the rules of the Council and shaped the boundaries of the city's 50 wards. Keane also is the author of the 1955 executive budget law that gave the mayor instead of the Council the responsibility for shaping the budget. Under Keane's law, a professional budget division was established.

Keane also played a major role in the creation of O'Hare International Airport. He devised the plan for the annexation of the land on which the airport was built. Keane and Daley persuaded nine major airlines to pay landing fees, terminal costs and interest on a special reserve fund that enabled the city to build O'Hare.

He was and is respected for his political skills.

"I never met a man more able than Tom Keane in the affairs of city government," Daley said in 1974.

"Listening to Tom Keane is an education," said former Mayor Jane M. Byrne. "He knew the rules better than any alderman because he wrote them and if there wasn't a rule, he would make a new one."

"Tom Keane was a genius in running the Council," Mayor Harold Washington told William Braden of the *Chicago Sun-Times* in 1986. It is part of the Keane legend that he once moved 286 bills in 10 minutes.

Ald. Edward M. Burke (14th), who was part of a 1972 rebellion that protested Keane's iron rule, recalled Thursday that Keane never lost a vote in his years as Daley's floor leader. "Tom Keane's career in Chicago politics has never been fully appreciated," Burke said. "Without his incomparable knowledge of municipal finance, O'Hare couldn't have been built."

Keane's career was cut short in 1974 when he was convicted in federal court on charges of mail fraud linked to use of inside information on tax-delinquent properties. He still denies the allegations. More than a decade later, the U.S. Supreme Court restricted the government's use of the mail-fraud statute under which Keane was convicted.

Keane won partial vindication when the Illinois Supreme Court reinstated his license to practice law in 1984. But Keane failed to get his conviction overturned. Though a federal judge acknowledged in 1988 that Keane's appeal had some merit, the court concluded that the case was moot. Keane had done his time and gotten back his license.

Keane should be judged on his full record, which includes major achievements.

In looking back on his career, Keane once told writer Eugene Kennedy that he admired Daley and former President Truman "because they both knew government so thoroughly and they were both so decisive."

So is Keane.

Vito Marzullo

Chicago Sun-Times, 4/26/89

Former Ald. Vito Marzullo (25th) outdid himself this time.

Long renowned as one of the more accomplished scene-stealers since Lionel Barrymore, the 91-year-old Marzullo managed to upstage Richard M. Daley on the day of his inauguration as mayor.

Marzullo, who emigrated from Italy and settled on Chicago's West Side in the 1920s, rose to power and prominence as one of Richard J. Daley's key political lieutenants. A fourth-grade dropout, he has lectured on politics at Harvard University, been featured on TV's "60 Minutes" and profiled in the *New York Times*.

But this week, the plain-spoken Marzullo made his biggest splash. On the day that President Bush, Vice President Danny Quayle, and most of the nation's newspaper publishers were in town for a convention, Marzullo stole the show just by breathing.

"I've seen them come and go in public life from presidents on down, and thank God, I'm still here," Marzullo once observed. "The Lord has been so nice to me—good family, good health, and friendship in the city, the county, and the state."

In Sunday's editions of the *Chicago Tribune*, a front-page headline solemnly proclaimed that the legendary Marzullo had bought the farm. An article on the front page of the newspaper's Chicagoland section disclosed that Marzullo had been found dead shortly after 11 P.M. Saturday night in his home on South Oakley Boulevard.

Several of Marzullo's longtime friends, including Cook County Democratic chairman George W. Dunne and Ald. Edward M. Burke (14th), were awakened for quotes about Vito's untimely passing. The same article included a quote from a James Daley, identified as a brother of the city's new mayor although there is no Daley brother by that name.

As it turned out, the headlines about Marzullo's death were somewhat exaggerated. Like Mark Twain and former White House press secretary Jim Brady, Marzullo was inducted into the elite corps of prominent Americans who lived to read their own obituaries, despite news reports to the contrary. If Dan Rather had heard about Marzullo, it's probable that political buff Rather would have paused for a moment of silence in the "CBS Evening News" as he did for Brady.

"He couldn't care less about it," Letzia Marzullo, the former alderman's wife of 67 years said Tuesday of the premature obituary. "He's alive and well. He's doing just fine."

Marzullo, whose political career spans more than seven decades, has vivid memories of the *Trib*'s 1948 "Dewey Defeats Truman" election-night headline when the same newspaper that declared him dead picked the wrong winner in the presidential election. Some of Marzullo's former colleagues are pulling for him to make a triumphant return to the City Council's chambers, striking a Trumanesque pose by holding the headline announcing his demise.

When it comes to matters of life and death, Marzullo is not alone in being done in by the *Trib*. Under the headline "Jailhouse Rock," a back-page gossip column incorrectly reported that Jesse L. Jackson "might face the death penalty if prosecutors have their way on his murder indictment." Like Marzullo, Jackson got a next-day apology.

Always the philosopher, Marzullo once said, "Sometimes I feel just like Abraham Lincoln. He's the one who said you can only fool some of the people some of the time. But my people got confidence in Vito Marzullo all of the time." And, on the whole, he'd rather be in the 25th Ward.

Abraham L. Marovitz
Chicago Sun-Times, 8/9/95

The federal courtroom was packed.

Senior Judge Abraham Lincoln Marovitz asked the multi-ethnic group of men and women, young and old, to stand and take the oath of U.S. citizenship.

Standing behind the bench in the courtroom that bears his name, Marovitz asks the new citizens to renounce in unison their allegiances or loyalty "to any foreign prince, potentate, state or sovereignty," and to defend the Constitution of the United States.

He is a man for all people. Marovitz performs this ceremony twice a month, as he has for more than 30 years. For Marovitz, who celebrates his 90th birthday Thursday, the induction ceremony has a special significance. He is a believer in the American dream because he has lived it. His father, a Lithuanian immigrant, took the same oath of citizenship in 1894.

"Every time I perform the induction ceremony I think of my father," says Marovitz, who is wearing cuff links with portraits of his parents. He talks with love and pride of the legacy of Joseph and Rachel Marovitz. The U.S. Immigration Department has given Marovitz an award for administering the citizenship oath to more naturalized Americans than any other member of the federal bench.

Nearly everywhere Marovitz goes, he is approached by a man or woman who took the citizenship oath in his courtroom. His door is always open to the people whose lives he has touched.

Marovitz talks with nostalgia about the immigrant world in which he grew up. He is a West Sider from the old Maxwell Street neighborhood. His father had a tailor shop, and his mother ran a candy store in front of the family's three-room apartment. "It was a large Jewish community and we learned the importance of hard work, loyalty and fairness," said Marovitz.

His path to prominence wasn't easy. Marovitz still remembers the hurt, anger and humiliation he felt as a teenager when he was fired from his job in a Michigan Avenue clothing store after his employer learned that he was Jewish. "My father told me that anti-Semitism is an old story, but that one day I would do something about it," Marovitz recalled. The elder Marovitz lived to see his son become the youngest assistant state's attorney in Cook County history, and the first Jewish Illinois state senator.

A Marine veteran of World War II, Marovitz has served on the bench for half of his life. In the mid-1950s, he nearly became the Democratic nominee for governor of Illinois. But Marovitz recalled Tuesday that his mother told him not to quit the court because no office is more important than judge. Marovitz took her advice. He has no regrets.

Marshall Korshak

Chicago Sun-Times, 2/5/90

During a recent banquet in a Loop hotel, Marshall Korshak was holding court at one of the front tables when a waiter approached him with the message that Korshak had a telephone call.

"You're late," responded Korshak, biting off the end of a thick cigar of such richness that it could have heated a basketball arena. The white-haired Korshak, looking dapper in a dark suit, then rose and left the room. There was, of course, no phone call. In a political career that spans six decades, Korshak learned the art of making a graceful exit.

Korshak, who is among the last of the Democratic Party's great warhorses, will be 80 tomorrow. Few people in the city's history have held more top political offices than Korshak, whose titles included Democratic committeeman of the 5th Ward, state senator, Illinois revenue director, city revenue director, city treasurer, city collector and trustee of the agency now called the Metropolitan Water Reclamation District. But there was much more to Korshak's public career than winning a lot of elections.

From his youth in Lawndale on the old West Side, Korshak has been renowned for helping others. After he moved to Hyde Park and the 5th Ward, Korshak became one of the city's best 1930s precinct captains. "I knew my people. I knew the wives, and the children, and the relatives. I got to know them like I was a member of their family, and they a member of my family," Korshak once told his friend Milton Rakove. The voters of the 5th Ward knew that their problems were also Korshak's.

In his response to a *Chicago Sun-Times* candidate questionnaire, Korshak wrote in 1950 that he was running for the Illinois Senate "because I have the ability to serve my constituents and the people of the State of Illinois in an efficient and honest manner and because I have the experience and political know-how which qualify me to be an effective state senator."

Korshak lived up to his campaign promises. In his first term, he was among Gov. Adlai E. Stevenson's chief allies in the Illinois General Assembly. During his four terms in the Senate, Korshak wrote laws creating a Fair Employment Practices Commission, increasing state aid to education and establishing a four-year branch of the University of Illinois in Chicago.

During Richard J. Daley's long reign as Democratic Party boss, Korshak was among Daley's chief political lieutenants. At Democratic rallies, Korshak seldom failed to rouse audiences by raising his voice and sharing some of his political wisdom. For 20 years, he was the Democratic committeeman of the 5th Ward. Korshak was among the few regulars on friendly terms with independents. When Korshak sensed it was time for change, he eased out his old friend, U.S. Rep. Barrett O'Hara and slated Abner Mikva to replace him.

In his long political career, Korshak met just one defeat, for county treasurer. That loss was by a narrow margin in the 1966 Republican sweep. Sen. Paul H. Douglas, who was defeated in the same election, wired Korshak: "Crushed by your defeat but not by mine."

In victory and defeat, Korshak remains among the best politicians this city has ever produced.

George W. Dunne

Chicago Sun-Times, 9/27/89

When Cook County Democratic chairman George W. Dunne was informed about an impending vacancy on the Illinois Supreme Court, he promptly made a recommendation.

The silver-haired Dunne urged the appointment of a black lawyer as the next justice of the Illinois Supreme Court. It has been nearly a quarter of a century since Lyndon B. Johnson named Thurgood Marshall to the U.S. Supreme Court, ending a tradition of nearly two centuries as a whites-only club. And Dunne believes that it's long overdue for the Illinois Supreme Court to do the same.

Over the last dozen years, Dunne has arguably done more for black political empowerment than any major Democratic political figure.

In other states, blacks are traditionally slated by Democrats and Republicans for statewide and countywide offices in which chances of victory are remote. Dunne, though, is a strong advocate of black political empowerment. When he proposes a black for a major political office, it isn't tokenism. Dunne has always managed to get his candidates elected.

Dunne was largely responsible in 1978 for the Democratic party's slating of Loop banker Roland Burris for state comptroller. Burris became the first black to win statewide constitutional office in Illinois. Dunne has encouraged Burris to run for attorney general next year.

When Harold Washington stunned the local establishment in 1983 by winning the Democratic mayoral primary, Dunne was among the handful of prominent Democratic regulars to support Washington's candidacy. His support was a major factor in Washington's narrow election over Republican Bernie Epton.

Dunne actively supported Washington's re-election in 1987 when other prominent Democratic regulars were backing third-party alternatives. Later that year, Washington took the lead in reinstating Dunne as the boss of the local Democratic party.

Following Washington's death, Dunne thwarted City Council regulars who had the votes to elect a white ethnic as acting mayor. Dunne provided the swing vote that made Eugene Sawyer the city's second black mayor. Without Dunne's intervention, Ald. Terry Gabinski (32nd) or another member of the old Vrdolyak 29 bloc would have been elected as Washington's successor. But Dunne wouldn't let it happen.

To the displeasure of ambitious politicians, Dunne pushed through the appointment last spring of Cecil A. Partee as the first black Cook County state's attorney.

In addition to Partee, Dunne played a major role in the election of blacks Wilson Frost to the County Board of (Tax) Appeals and Carol Moseley-Braun as Recorder of Deeds; and of Board of Appeals Commissioner Joe Berrios as the first Hispanic elected to countywide office. State Rep. Jesse C. White, sponsored by Dunne, is the first black legislator elected in Illinois from a district with a white majority.

One of the reasons that Dunne is likely to win renomination in next winter's Democratic primary for County Board president is that his record on black empowerment hasn't been forgotten by black voters. He is being challenged in the primary by a suburban lawyer who until recently was a member of a country club that bars blacks and women.

Stanley T. Kusper

Chicago Sun-Times, 3/28/90

Landslide Stanley was in a foul mood.

County Clerk Stanley T. Kusper Jr., who began the 1990 Democratic race for the Cook County Board presidency as the early favorite, had watched himself finish dead last and in single-digits. He didn't win a single ward or township.

Kusper, who had been among the county's leading vote-getters for 16 years, failed to even be nominated for the County Board. Though 10 people were nominated, Landslide Stanley finished 14th in the field of 37.

From his election-night headquarters in the penthouse of the Executive House, Landslide Stanley showed grace and poise in declaring that the voters of Cook County "have decided that it is time for Stanley Kusper to retire from office."

But when the TV lights went off, Landslide Stanley made little effort to disguise his bitterness. Kusper told a TV reporter that he would like to kick his teeth down his throat.

Landslide Stanley blamed everyone but himself. Cook County Democratic Chairman George W. Dunne, who chose not to slate Kusper for the board presidency, will have to "drink his bitter vial of vengeance," Kusper declared. Then he took a few swigs himself.

State Sen. Ted Lechowicz, who received more than twice Kusper's countywide vote for the board presidency, and who nearly doubled Kusper's vote for county commissioner, reached out to Landslide Stanley on the morning after the primary. A conciliatory Lechowicz complimented Kusper on a good fight and said that they should resume their friendship. Landslide Stanley responded that Lechowicz had been the spoiler and berated him for not dropping out of the race. In the campaign's final week, Democratic committeemen had urged Kusper to pull the plug on his faltering candidacy.

With the wit and charm for which he is renowned, Landslide Stanley later telephoned a TV reporter to "congratulate" her for sinking his candidacy with a critical news report about his operation of the clerk's office. Landslide Stanley then referred to the reporter with an epithet that rhymes with rich.

Landslide Stanley suggested to another reporter that the media had been out to sabotage his quest for the County Board presidency. Kusper subscribed to the theory that news organizations told each other about what dates their pollsters would be gathering data so that articles about his shortcomings could be timed for maximum impact. "He's the Polish Dick Nixon," chortled a Kusper crony.

Until last week's primary, Kusper had never faced a real political contest because he had always been backed by the organization. His slogan "Kusper Cares" began to lack credibility when it was disclosed that he had an annual income of more than $600,000 while claiming to be a full-time clerk; that residents had lost homes because of Kusper's inattention to details; and that $6.8 million of public funds had been left in a non-interest bearing account. Landslide Stanley blamed a staffer.

If Nixon, Winston Churchill and former Mayor Mike Bilandic could make comebacks, Landslide Stanley figured that he, too, would return. "Stanley Kusper will be in the public arena," he vowed. "I think I have something to offer."

Cecil A. Partee

Chicago Sun-Times, 6/24/94

He is renowned for making history.

Cecil A. Partee has broken more barriers and achieved more historic firsts than anyone in Illinois. Partee, 72, is the only African American to serve as president of the Illinois State Senate, the first African American nominated for statewide executive office (attorney general in 1976), and the only African American to serve as acting governor of Illinois. He was elected to three terms as Chicago's city treasurer and ended his public career in 1990 as Cook County state's attorney. He has left footprints with each step of his career.

The historymaker was celebrated the other night at the Chicago Historical Society, where Partee was honored by Montay College. It was a moving tribute to a man with an invincible spirit, who is fighting serious illness.

The African-American historian Alex Haley, who knew and admired Partee, noted that the achievements of black leaders of Partee's generation "deserve to be multiplied or magnified at least 10 times in comparison with what similar young men would be faced with today."

Born and reared in rural Arkansas, Partee was an honor student. But he was denied admission to the all-white University of Arkansas Law School. State officials offered to pay his expenses to a northern law school. He chose Northwestern University. When Partee was admitted to the Illinois bar in 1947 in Springfield, he couldn't attend the dinner for new lawyers at the Abraham Lincoln Hotel because blacks weren't allowed in the hotel.

With his remarkable energy and drive, Partee became one of the top precinct captains on Chicago's South Side. From Harry Truman to Bill Clinton, he has played a role in the election of Democratic presidents. He helped Truman win Illinois by converting an all-black GOP precinct to Truman in '48. As Democratic leader of the 20th Ward, he helped deliver Illinois for John F. Kennedy in 1960. In '64, Partee delivered the 20th Ward for Lyndon B. Johnson by a 37,000-to-1,000 margin over Barry Goldwater. In 1992, Partee was among Bill Clinton's earliest Illinois allies.

Serving in the Illinois General Assembly from 1957 to 1977, Partee was among the more accomplished legislators of his era. Partee sponsored fair employment, open housing and consumer rights legislation. With his rich and resonant voice and precise articulation, Partee was among the few law-makers whose comments in legislative debate could persuade colleagues to shift votes.

Partee is proud of his role as a mentor to African-American leaders from the late Mayor Harold Washington, whose career he rescued, to

John Rogers, president of the Chicago Park District's board of commissioners.

He cares about people. As state's attorney, Partee once intervened in a street fight. Partee stopped his car when he noticed two women attacking each other. One had a knife and was stabbing the other. The victim credited Partee with saving her life. The parents of the attacker also thanked Partee for preventing their daughter from taking a life. Partee has always practiced what he preached. His strength and compassion will be long remembered.

On the Edge

James D. Heiple

Chicago Sun-Times, 4/16/97

Illinois Supreme Court Chief Justice James D. Heiple is guilty of bad judgment.

But is that reason to throw him out of office?

The Illinois House is setting a dangerous precedent in voting to create a panel to determine whether there is just cause to impeach Heiple.

Heiple is under attack because he was the author of the unpopular Baby Richard decision that awarded custody of the infant to his biological parents, which angered the baby's adoptive family and public opinion.

Even though legislators have cited other reasons for the impeachment probe, it all comes back to Baby Richard. If Heiple hadn't written the decision, he wouldn't be paying this price. Heiple was rude in seeking to use his clout to avoid traffic tickets. He also was sneaky in naming his pal Justice Moses W. Harrison II as chief of the Illinois Courts Commission. But if it weren't for the Baby Richard case, Heiple wouldn't be under siege.

It is unfair when judges are punished for controversial rulings. California voters recalled Chief Justice Rose Bird in 1986 after she voted to overturn convictions in death-penalty cases. Tennessee Supreme Court Justice Penny White was ousted last year after she also overturned the death penalty in a high-profile case. "Those who want judges to rule based on majority public opinion have never been in the minority," White said.

Last year, U.S. District Judge Harold Baer Jr. of the Southern district of New York came under fire for suppressing evidence that had been seized by cops in a drug case. More than 200 members of Congress called for his ouster, as did presidential candidate Bob Dole. President Clinton demanded a reversal.

Judge Jon O. Newman, chief of the U.S. Court of Appeals for the Second Circuit, warned that these attacks on Baer could weaken an independent judiciary. "The recent attacks on a trial judge of our circuit have gone too far. They threaten to weaken the constitutional structure of this nation, which has well served our citizens for more than 200 years," Newman said in a statement issued with his two predecessors as chief judge.

"These attacks do a grave disservice to the principle of an independent judiciary, and more significantly, mislead the public as to the role of judges in a constitutional democracy," he asserted.

"Judges are called upon to make hundreds of decisions each year. These decisions are made after consideration of opposing contentions, both of which are often based on reasonable interpretations of the laws of the United States and the Constitution. Most rulings are subject to appeal, as is the one that has occasioned these attacks.

"When a judge is threatened with a call for resignation or impeachment because of disagreement with a ruling, the entire process of orderly resolution of legal disputes is undermined.

"We have no quarrel with criticism of any decision rendered by any judge. Informed comment and disagreement from lawyers, academics and public officials have been hallmarks of the American legal tradition.

"But there is an important line between legitimate criticism of a decision and illegitimate attack upon a judge. Criticism of a decision can illuminate issues and sometimes point the way toward better decisions. Attacks on a judge risk inhibition of all judges as they conscientiously endeavor to discharge their constitutional responsibilities."

Heiple shouldn't be punished because you or I don't agree with him. He isn't guilty of high crimes and misdemeanors. This judicial lynching is absurd.

Jack O'Malley

Chicago Sun-Times, 9/30/96

He bills himself as a tough prosecutor.

But in six years as Cook County State's Attorney, Jack O'Malley has never tried a case. When confronted with a high-profile case, he looks for TV cameras. O'Malley, who wants to run for governor, has a flair for the dramatic.

"There is a killer on the loose," he declared in 1993 at a news conference after seven people were murdered at Brown's Chicken and Pasta restaurant in Palatine. He warned area residents to keep their doors locked.

Eight months later, with the killer still at large, O'Malley rationalized the unsolved mystery. "Murder cases, generally, if they're not solved within a day or a couple of days, the likelihood of them being solved diminishes," he said on WMAQ-AM radio.

O'Malley, 45, a former vice president of the National District Attorneys Association, claims his office is "a national model of efficiency." But last winter he obtained a 1,238-count indictment of Gerald Hill in a child abuse case, and O'Malley's spokesman gloated: "It's the biggest indictment anyone has ever seen around here." But all charges were dropped in March. So much for being "a national model of efficiency."

The state's attorney's office has a high conviction rate (93.2 percent of felonies), which has improved slightly during O'Malley's tenure. But O'Malley hasn't done well in high-profile cases. He was embarrassed last year when a jury acquitted Helmut C. Hofer in the 1993 bludgeoning death of North Shore socialite Suzanne Olds.

Another setback for O'Malley was the 1992 trial of former Teamsters Union leader Daniel Ligurotis, who shot and killed his son Daniel Jr., also a union official. Police said the men had argued over the son's drug use. Both men had guns. The father said he shot in self-defense. O'Malley charged him with murder. He was found not guilty.

O'Malley, a former Chicago police officer who recently was endorsed for re-election by the Fraternal Order of Police, has been criticized for his handling of police brutality cases. O'Malley declined to prosecute three Chicago police officers whose actions led to the death of Jorge Guillen, whose family called police because he was acting strangely. Although a police report cited the officers for using "excessive force," O'Malley said there was no basis for criminal charges. O'Malley nearly gave a pass to Chicago policeman Gregory Becker, who last summer shot and killed Joseph Gould, a homeless man. After a public outcry, O'Malley finally obtained an indictment of Becker on charges of armed violence and involuntary manslaughter.

His political career got a boost last year with the conviction of Rep. Mel Reynolds (D-Dolton), who was charged with having a sexual relationship with a 16-year-old girl. Reynolds was guilty of misconduct, but O'Malley doesn't show the same zeal to prosecute less-prominent citizens for identical offenses. O'Malley may have been guilty of over-kill. Reynolds' accuser, who recanted her charges, was jailed until she agreed to testify.

O'Malley has done a good job of recruiting assistant state's attorneys. He hired Andrea Zopp, a former assistant U.S. attorney, as first assistant state's attorney. He has promoted more women and minorities than his predecessors.

There are morale problems in O'Malley's office, however. He filed a lawsuit in 1994 and thwarted a move by prosecutors to form a union. O'Malley has lost talented prosecutors, including Thomas Epach, a criminal courts supervisor, Dean Morask, former chief of criminal prosecutions, and Tony Calabrese, former chief deputy of the criminal division.

O'Malley would like to follow in the footsteps of his mentor, James R. Thompson, who used the U.S. attorney's office as a springboard to become governor of Illinois. But there's an important difference. Thompson prosecuted cases and was a tiger in the courtroom. O'Malley is a publicity hound.

John J. Flood
Chicago Sun-Times, 3/2/90

John J. Flood, the president of the Combined Counties Police Association, a Wheeling-based union that represents suburban policemen, knows how to promote himself.

Flood, 50, a Northbrook resident, is a Democratic candidate for Cook County sheriff. In preparing for the March primary, Flood has modestly portrayed himself in CCPA journals as one of the genuine legends of Illinois law enforcement.

"When he enters a room, he rarely, if ever, goes unnoticed," begins a profile in Flood's journal. "Heads turn and those that are not sure who he is, ask. . . . Meeting Flood can be an intimidating experience. One soon realizes, however, that beneath his exterior of toughness beats a compassionate heart and a mind that is entrepreneurial."

Another Flood profile in a CCPA journal is headlined, "Flood's Career Grew From Militant to Labor Statesman." Flood's official biography omitted his four arrests for driving under the influence of alcohol and his refusal to take blood-alcohol tests. Flood was found guilty on each occasion, and his driver's license was twice suspended.

Flood contends that the arrests were linked to his controversial union activities in attempting to organize suburban police departments.

By taking advantage of his union's nonprofit organization postal rate, Flood has sought to boost his political fortunes. A recent issue of his magazine featured 11 pictures of himself, including a candid shot with the Emerald Society's Pipe and Drum Corps, and photographs with Mayor Daley and former Mayor Washington.

Flood, who has accused Republican Sheriff James E. O'Grady of being too political, has frequently made political endorsements as CCPA president. He was among O'Grady's more prominent supporters in 1986.

When Flood decided to challenge his former ally, O'Grady was suddenly portrayed as a villain in CCPA publications.

When Flood appeared as a witness recently in federal court, he issued a press release headlined, "Sheriff's Candidate Flood to Testify in Reputed Mob Hitman's Sentencing." It is considered highly unusual for a witness to publicize a court appearance. But Flood has always prided himself on being a nonconformist.

Flood, who would be in charge of an annual budget of more than $100 million as sheriff, isn't renowned for his administrative skills. The CCPA credit union was put into federal receivership in 1987 by the National Credit Union Association and the Illinois Department of Financial Institutions.

Though Flood has attacked opponent Ald. Michael F. Sheehan (19th) as a tool of the regular Democratic organization, Flood often forgets to tell audiences that he unsuccessfully sought party slating. Flood doesn't always seem to mind the company of politicians. His CCPA publications have often featured pictures of Flood chatting it up with Democratic ward committeemen.

"No one who seeks him out for help is turned away, and his energy and brilliant mind spring forth to endeavor on their behalf," according to Flood's own magazine.

Burton F. Natarus

Chicago Sun-Times, 2/10/95

Ald. Burton F. Natarus (42nd) said he was only doing a favor.

But it was more than that.

He was acting on behalf of Pat Marcy, "an actual made member" of organized crime. In 1989, Natarus sought to help Marcy obtain the city's approval for a 4 A.M. liquor license for Eddie Rockets on West Division. Marcy was then the secretary of the 1st Ward's Democratic Organization.

In testifying about his role, Natarus asked for and was granted immunity by federal prosecutors. While awaiting trial on corruption charges, Marcy died in 1993. But for Natarus, the controversy lingers on.

Natarus, a 24-year member of the City Council, is running for re-election from a new 42nd Ward that includes the Near North Side. Also running are Kevin Flood and Dennis O'Neill, who is distributing court records of Natarus' conversations.

Natarus is on the defensive about his past. By listening to a couple of secretly taped telephone conversations between Natarus and Marcy, federal prosecutors learned about his role. "If he [the city inspector] goes out on the square, you're not gonna get it," Natarus told Marcy about the license.

Because the bar is in a residential area, Natarus noted that residents would normally have to be polled to determine if they favored the 4 A.M. license. But Natarus gave more priority to Marcy than to his constituents. Natarus told Marcy that he would "push" Sidney Jones, who was then the city's liquor commissioner.

Natarus later testified before a federal grand jury: "The support of the 1st Ward [organization] was so important to me that I used my influence to try to obtain the license without regard to whether Eddie Rockets was, in fact, entitled to receive the license."

He also told the grand jury: "This support is vital because the 1st Ward organization is responsible for a number of city services, such as Streets and Sanitation Services, that I need to be able to provide to my constituents promptly upon request."

In his 1983 testimony before the Senate Permanent Subcommittee on Investigations, former FBI agent William F. Roemer Jr. provided another view of the politics of the 1st Ward. He noted that Marcy was "an actual made member" of organized crime and was "actually the conduit through which the orders from the mob passed to . . . public officials."

Roemer also said: "The umbrella which protects the Chicago mob, and the linchpin which holds it together, is its alliance between crime and politics. Nowhere can organized crime be effective without the connivance of politics."

In his phone conversation with Marcy, Natarus was deferential and ingratiating. Natarus addressed Marcy as "sir." He also told Marcy that liquor commissioner Sidney Jones "is not a good guy." Marcy responded: "I know that."

Natarus told former Ald. Fred Roti (1st), Marcy's sidekick, that the building inspector was "a phony" for holding up the late-night license. The inspector was trying to comply with regulations. If the residents had been polled, Natarus knew they probably would have opposed the license.

Natarus testified that he told a city official that the license should be approved "at all costs." He told the grand jury: "Whether the applicant was entitled to the license or not, I wanted it issued, and so I told [city inspector Patrick] Gamboney to do whatever was required to get the license issued."

"I told Gamboney I wanted the license issued and that I wanted it at all costs," Natarus told the grand jury. "By my words I intended to communicate to Gamboney that he should do whatever was necessary to make certain that the license was issued."

In his second phone conversation with Marcy, Natarus blamed Jones for the delay in the license. Marcy told Natarus that Jones "should cover it" when Natarus asked for the license.

Natarus told Marcy that an official blocking the license was a resident of Ald. William J. P. Banks' 36th Ward. "I know but that don't mean nothin'," Marcy told Natarus. "I know how he got there. It wasn't through Banks or anybody."

During his testimony at Roti's trial, Natarus said: "I wasn't asking anybody to break the law. I was getting a little frustrated because I wasn't getting the results that I wanted, so I told them to do it at all costs."

Though he took immunity, Natarus said that he did nothing wrong. When asked under oath why he took immunity, Natarus answered: "I was fearful that during the course of some transactions somebody might lie about me, and as a result of that false testimony I might be indicted."

Robert Shaw

Chicago Sun-Times, 2/6/98

There's no business like Shaw business.

Ald. Robert Shaw (9th), a Democratic candidate for the Cook County Board of Review, is an old-style politician without apologies.

When Mayor Daley proposed a tougher ethics code for aldermen, Shaw's response was a classic. "Members of the City Council aren't the only crooks in Chicago," Shaw quipped.

Shaw, who also is a Democratic ward committeeman, began his political career on the West Side as a member of the late Arthur X. Elrod's 24th Ward Regular Democratic organization. He gained power and prominence in the early 1980s as mayor Jane M. Byrne's chief ally in the African-American community. Shaw took heat from black independents when he voted to support Byrne's City Council map, which a federal court later ruled was unfair to African Americans and Latinos.

During the Byrne administration, Shaw and Ald. Edward R. Vrdolyak (10th) were co-sponsors of legislation that would have gutted the city's personnel code by increasing the number of political employees. Byrne vetoed Shaw's legislation.

In a move that stunned the African-American community, Shaw called for the removal of blacks from the City Council's galleries when they showed up to protest Byrne's ouster of blacks from the School Board and the Chicago Housing Authority Board. He stood firmly with Byrne and CHA Chairman Charles Swibel.

"I will not be silenced and will continue speaking out against the injustices and wrongs against my people," Shaw later declared, though he supported Byrne over Harold Washington in the 1983 Democratic mayoral primary. Washington garnered 80 percent of the vote in the 9th Ward. Shaw's support of Byrne cost him re-election that year.

But Shaw reinvented himself as a Washington supporter in 1987 and recaptured his Council seat. Since then he has been most passionate in his support for aldermanic pay raises. Washington dismissed Shaw as a "two-bit hustler." The Rev. Jesse L. Jackson, with whom Shaw has clashed on several occasions, described him as "a hack."

Shaw, though, is among the more durable and resourceful players on the local political stage. When Washington died in November, 1987, Shaw joined forces with Ald. Edward M. Burke (14th), who had been the late mayor's arch foe, in thwarting the bid of Ald. Timothy C. Evans (4th), a Washington ally, as acting mayor. Shaw was the driving force in the selection of Eugene Sawyer as Washington's successor. If Shaw hadn't joined forces with Burke, it is probable that Evans would have been Washington's heir.

In 1990, Shaw crossed party lines to support Republican Jim Edgar over Democrat Neil F. Hartigan for governor. Before his death, Washington had indicated that Hartigan was his preference for governor. Maybe that's why Shaw worked against him.

Shaw, who has long been ambitious for higher political office, grabbed his opportunity after getting a tip that 12-year incumbent Wilson Frost planned to step down from the Cook County Board of Tax Appeals. Two years ago, the GOP-controlled General Assembly voted to replace the two-member Board of Appeals (which was elected countywide) with a new three-member Board of Review, to be elected from single districts.

As Democratic committeemen met in November to choose a 1998 ticket, Frost caught most of them by surprise with his announcement that he would not be seeking re-election. Shaw moved quickly to take advantage of Frost's retirement. He took charge of slatemaking for Frost's 3rd District, called a meeting without notice and had himself slated as the party's candidate.

Among Shaw's problems is that he doesn't know much about the office he is seeking. He has suggested that the Board of Review has the authority to grant a four-year tax reduction when it is limited by law to making a one-year reduction. Shaw also seemed remarkably uninformed about the office in his response to a questionnaire from the Independent Voters of Illinois. In describing his political history for them, Shaw listed his involvement in eight political campaigns, though not Byrne's 1983 re-election bid. Maybe he forgot.

Alfred G. Ronan

Chicago Sun-Times, 4/14/95

Money talks.

That's the political philosophy of former state Rep. Alfred G. Ronan (D-Chicago). "I never met a special interest I didn't like," he once declared on the floor of the Illinois House.

Ronan, 47, who served in the General Assembly from 1979 until 1993, has parlayed his political connections into a lucrative career as a lobbyist.

As a state legislator, he set up his own lobbying firm. Though it's not unusual for ex-legislators to lobby former colleagues, Ronan had the audacity to openly shill for special interests while holding public office. As a full-time lobbyist, he has summoned legislators off the House floor and handed them checks of $50 to $100 as campaign donations from his clients.

"An important component of government relations is political contributions to elective members," Ronan noted in a written description of his lobbying services. "Elective office requires financial assistance, and we provide the assistance through our clients' political actions committees. Alfred G. Ronan Ltd. provides assistance to clients throughout the process, including: analysis and recommendations for fund-raising for political action committees; recommendations for specific contributions; and assistance with setting long-range goals for successful PACs. Financial contributions are a necessity in the current political environment. It is important to contribute wisely."

While in office, Ronan was a good investment for special interests. He collected more than $1.4 million in campaign funds from special interests between 1982 and 1991. Ronan also pocketed another $500,000 in lobbying fees. He took $24,000 from insurance companies and was among a handful of Democrats to vote against universal health care. He took $12,000 from the tobacco interests and was absent for House votes to ban smoking in public places and to put restrictions on the sale of tobacco products to children.

His constituents eventually got angry about Ronan's dual role. He was defeated for renomination in the 1992 Democratic primary, in which his wheeling and dealing were the major issues.

Since his loss, Ronan has become even more successful at trading on his political connections. He has snagged dozens of new clients and now represents 45 firms or organizations. Among his blue-chip clients are investment bankers Smith Barney, 3M, Unisys Corp. and Philip Morris tobacco. Ronan also represents the Joliet-based Empress River Casino, the Illinois State Medical Society, the Independent Insurance Agents of Illinois and the Illinois Road Builders Association. He also has worked for Quaker Oats and for the Chicago Bears.

Ronan, who said that his firm "operates in a bipartisan fashion when working with government officials," claims to have special clout with Gov. Edgar. "Once legislation is passed by both chambers, Alfred G. Ronan Ltd. meets with the governor's office to explain the merits of the legislation and to ensure that the legislation is signed into law," Ronan said in his pitch to prospective clients.

What a smooth-talking guy.

Mel Reynolds

Chicago Sun-Times, 8/23/94

U.S. Rep. Mel Reynolds (D-Ill.) knows something about the politics of sexual misconduct. His public career was made—and may be broken—by sex scandals.

On Monday, Reynolds was booked on charges of child pornography, sexual assault and obstruction of justice. Ironically, it was his predecessor's alleged sexual misconduct that set the stage for Reynolds' rise to power.

Five years ago, Reynolds took advantage of sexual-harassment allegations against then-Rep. Gus Savage (D-Ill.). In August, 1989, the House Ethics Committee began an inquiry into charges that Savage had made improper sexual advances to a young woman during a congressional visit to Africa. Reynolds showed no mercy in exploiting Savage's personal troubles.

Reynolds, who was about to launch his second campaign against Savage, was gleeful about Savage's plight. In the 1988 Democratic primary, Savage won renomination with 52.4 percent of the vote. Reynolds, who garnered 13.6 percent, finished a distant third in a five-way primary. But in the wake of the sexual misconduct charges against Savage, Reynolds became a contender as the alternative to Savage.

The charges against Savage were serious. The woman alleged that Savage grabbed her, kissed her, asked her to spend the night with him, and that he attempted to force her to have sex. The House Ethics Committee's six-month investigation concluded that Savage had violated congressional "standards of conduct." The committee reported that Savage "did, in fact, make sexual advances to the Peace Corps volunteer." The report said that the Ethics Committee "clearly disapproves of Rep. Savage's conduct."

During his '92 campaign against Savage, Reynolds kept Savage on the defensive by commissioning two polls that, among other things, asked 2nd District voters about their perception of the sex scandal. A September, 1989, poll by Market Shares Corp. reported that 79 percent of likely Democratic primary voters were aware of the allegations against Savage and that only 27 percent believed that Savage was innocent. Reynolds generated publicity for himself by leaking the poll. He later hired another firm to conduct a survey about Savage's troubles. Reynolds got even more favorable press coverage. Reynolds ridiculed Savage as "a national embarrassment."

There are haunting similarities in how Reynolds and Savage responded to charges of sexual misconduct. Both Reynolds and Savage blamed the news media for hyping their respective scandals. Both claimed that investigations of their alleged misconduct were racially motivated. Reynolds used another Savage tactic in appealing to anti-gay prejudice in the African-American community. Savage viciously criticized Rep. Barney Frank (D-Mass.), who is openly gay. Frank was among three congressmen who requested the House Ethics probe of Savage. Reynolds is seeking to discredit his accuser, a teenage woman, by making negative comments about her alleged homosexuality.

Weakened by the charges of sexual misconduct, Savage barely survived the 1990 primary. There was even more rage against Savage in the 1992 primary, which followed the Clarence Thomas–Anita Hill hearings. Reynolds, in that race, vilified Savage's conduct and won the seat.

What goes around comes around.

Perks

Lee A. Daniels

Chicago Sun-Times, 6/11/97

If you've got the money, he's got the time.

House Minority Leader Lee A. Daniels (R-Elmhurst) is asking special interests to sponsor his 8th annual golf outing and pig roast.

For the pleasure of his company, Daniels is charging $10,000. Golf outings are among the great perks of Illinois politicians. Daniels sees no reason why he can't charge top dollar.

As the nation's top golfers head for Washington, D.C., this week to play in the U.S. Open, Daniels is planning his own invitational in August with nine levels of sponsorship. He has a lot of green to work with—and fairways, too.

The Medinah Country Club, the site of the last three locally held U.S. Open championships, which has among the nation's best golf courses, is where Daniels is hosting his fund-raiser. Applicants have to wait up to seven years to gain membership in the posh country club. Daniels is offering lobbyists the chance to walk in the footsteps of Arnold Palmer, Jack Nicklaus and Gene Sarazen.

Daniels is offering special inducements to the big hitters. For $10,000, a "Main Event Host" has ready access to Daniels, a sign displaying his or her corporate logo at the check-in, an ad in the Daniels ad book, and a foursome on Medinah's finest course—No. 3.

Though some traditionalists have grumbled about the tacky commercialism, a Republican fund-raiser explained Tuesday that without all the logos, Daniels couldn't charge as much.

The Illinois Campaign Finance Project, a bipartisan task force headed by former Sen. Paul Simon and former Gov. William G. Stratton, last winter recommended a $2,000 limit on contributions from groups, corporations, associations and individuals. This panel also sought to limit transfers of funds from committees controlled by legislative leaders such as Daniels to individual legislative campaigns. Unfortunately, their proposals went nowhere.

Under federal election law, corporations are banned from making contributions to candidates for national office. There also is a $5,000 limit from political action committees to federal candidates. But Illinois permits unlimited contributions from special interests to candidates for state office.

In four neighboring states—Iowa, Wisconsin, Michigan and Kentucky—corporations are prohibited from making political contributions. In Indiana, there is a limit on the amount that corporations may donate to political candidates. Daniels is taking full advantage of Illinois election law.

Daniels also is selling "hole sponsorships" on Medinah's three golf courses. For $3,500, a "Three-Hole Sponsor" gets to golf on the No. 3 course, a twosome on Medinah's course No. 1 or a foursome on the less-prestigious No. 2 course. For $3,000, a "Two-Hole Sponsor" may golf on the No. 1 course or have a twosome on No. 2. For $2,000, a "One-Hole Sponsor" may golf on course No. 2.

For golfers with large checkbooks, Daniels has other propositions. A $5,000 "Dinner Sponsor" gets a "prominent sign displayed at dinner," a foursome on the lower-rent No. 2 course, and an ad in the Daniels yearbook. A $3,000 "lunch sponsor" buys an "exclusive sign displayed at lunch" and an ad in the book. A $2,500 "Caddie Sponsor" doesn't get to put his or her logo on the caddy's back but does get to display an "exclusive sign" at check-in and an ad in the Daniels book. A $1,000 "Halfway House Sponsor" purchases an "exclusive sign" at the halfway house and an ad in the book.

Daniels hasn't put a price on the caddyshack or ball-washers. He is willing to have his picture taken with his high-rolling guests. Daniels may even sign their golf caps.

George H. Ryan

Chicago Sun-Times, 7/15/94

Illinois Secretary of State George H. Ryan has a $1.2 million security detail.

With seven bodyguards, Ryan has more protection than any of the other 49 secretaries of state. Most of them have none. Of the 40 states that provide bodyguards for their governors, Illinois is the only state that offers such protection to a half-dozen statewide officeholders.

"This is Illinois, not Iowa," Ryan said in a telephone interview. "I think anyone who has statewide office should have security. State officials are constantly in the spotlight. The world is full of crazy people."

Not all statewide officials talk about the state's 11.6 million residents as a health hazard. Lt. Gov. Bob Kustra and State Treasurer Pat Quinn declined to take bodyguards. On taking office, Gov. Edgar downsized his security detail.

Even though Ryan's taxpayer-funded security is emerging as an issue in his bid for re-election, he insists that he's entitled to such protection. If re-elected in November, Ryan said, he will retain his bodyguards in a second term.

Ryan's security detail is made up of five Illinois state troopers and two investigators from the Secretary of State's police force. Since Ryan took office in 1991, nine policemen have been paid about $1.25 million for guarding him, including $106,417.93 in overtime. The bodyguards also are Ryan's chauffeurs and advance men.

As Illinois secretary of state, Ryan is the state's librarian, chief administrator of motor vehicles, and the official keeper of the "great seal of the state of Illinois." In defending his decision to have bodyguards, Ryan said: "I suspend guys' driver's licenses. We take away privileges and repossess their cars. We're not dealing with characters from Disneyland. We deal with a lot of folks who are bad people. When they get mad and upset, they don't look for the cop. They look for the guy at the top of the list."

Ryan also noted that he made himself vulnerable by speaking out against a Ku Klux Klan rally in Springfield and by calling for a ban on assault weapons. But Ryan's out-of-state travels with bodyguards are even more controversial.

As lieutenant governor, George the Jet was the state's goodwill ambassador. With his bodyguards as his baggage handlers, Ryan swept across Denmark, Sweden, Germany, Belgium, Scotland and England. During Ryan's golfing vacation in Scotland, a bodyguard moved more than 20 pieces of his luggage. His bodyguards also accompanied Ryan to Hawaii and Australia.

As secretary of state, Ryan has taken bodyguards to such hardship posts as the Indian River Resort in Stuart, Fla., to the Orange Tree Resort in Scottsdale, Ariz., and the Hyatt Regency in Waikoloa, Hawaii. If there was a clear and present danger at these resorts, then what was Ryan doing there? Why did the working people of Illinois have to pay for his security?

Ryan said that he doesn't determine how many bodyguards accompany him to public events. With a rising murder rate, why are Illinois cops serving as valets for politicians?

Phil Crane

Chicago Sun-Times, 2/27/94

He's got a ticket to ride.

Rep. Phil Crane (R-Ill.), the second-ranking Republican on the Ways and Means committee, has it all figured out. In his quarter-century congressional career, he has perfected the art of the working vacation.

Because of his seniority on the tax-writing committee, Crane has become a most popular fellow with the special interests. He listens to their concerns. And the special interests pay for his working vacations. The Illinois Republican lives for the sun. He has become a stranger in much of his northwest suburban 8th congressional district. But he's no stranger in paradise.

Crane has made a career out of taking trips to faraway places on other people's money. The Illinois Republican has taken full advantage of a loophole that allows legislators to be reimbursed for expenses that were incurred on speaking engagements, fact-finding trips, and seminars.

If Crane has few legislative accomplishments in his House career, he has gained national recognition for his travels. Special interests have paid for Crane's working vacations in Hawaii, Puerto Rico, Florida and Sun Valley. The sunshine congressman took his wife on a seven-day Caribbean cruise that was paid for by Norwegian Caribbean Lines. He also took a cruise courtesy of Royal Caribbean Cruises.

Instead of sending out a congressional newsletter, Crane ought to be sending his constituents "Wish You Were Here" postcards of sandy beaches, where he has left more footprints than on Capitol Hill.

Crane makes no apologies for spending so much time on the sunshine trail. Last spring, he had a starring role in an ABC News undercover report of a congressional junket to a resort on Florida's Captiva Island. The trip was sponsored by lobbyists for the electronics industry. The report was aired on "Primetime Live." Crane told ABC's Chris Wallace that there was absolutely no conflict in accepting the free trip to the luxury resort because the sponsors got something in return: his participation in the conference.

A national television audience watched Crane sunbathing by the pool, yawning as he left a seminar, golfing with a lobbyist, and drinking imported beer. He appeared to be having a pretty good time. "It's a working event," Crane told Wallace. "I don't consider it a vacation."

Though Crane claimed that he didn't take all that many junkets, an ABC News graphic showed that he had taken 67 such trips in four years, more than one a month, to some of the more exotic places in the world. "I don't see any problem with that because there's no compromising of my position and it's all a matter of record," Crane said in the ABC interview.

When asked if he planned to continue accepting such trips, Crane replied: "Certainly. It's a way of maintaining that contact with your constituents." But Crane is facing a tough race for renomination in the March 15 primary because some of his constituents aren't certain that the district needs a sunshine congressman.

Uncommon Valor

The Fighting Sullivans

Chicago Sun-Times, 5/31/93

Thomas Sullivan, who worked 40 years as a conductor for the Illinois Central, was the patriarch of a remarkable family.

The United States has been involved in 10 major wars in less than 10 generations, and all of our veterans are honored on Memorial Day. In the history of the United States, no family has sacrificed more than the Sullivans.

Sullivan, the son of Irish immigrants, and his wife, Aletta, lived in Waterloo, Iowa. Their marriage produced five sons and a daughter: George, Francis, Joseph, Madison, Albert and Genevieve. Sullivan didn't expect his sons to grow into heroes. They were normal kids with a zest for life.

As youngsters, the five Irish-American brothers listened for the lonesome whistle of the Illinois Central and made it a daily ritual to climb the water tower above the tracks and greet their father. The Sullivans were separated just once, when George and Francis joined the navy in 1937 and served in the Pacific. Bill Ball, who had dated Genevieve for nearly six years and was almost a member of the family, enlisted in the Navy a few months after the two Sullivans. Following the discharge of George and Francis in the spring of 1941, the five brothers and their sister worked in a packing house.

Then it happened. When Japan attacked Pearl Harbor on Dec. 7, 1941, Bill Ball, then serving on the Arizona, was among the casualties. "You never know how people will react to war," Ernest Hemingway wrote. But for the Sullivans, it wasn't a tough call. They vowed to avenge their friend's death and the four oldest brothers enlisted in the Navy. Albert, the youngest brother and the only one with a family, was expected to stay home. But his wife, Katherine Mary, told him: "You belong with them. It's always been the five of you."

And it always had been. As the Sullivans signed up for naval service, they asked the recruiting officer to bend regulations so that they might serve together. "It's always been the five of us. We stick together," George declared. Though rejected, the brothers made a successful appeal to the War Department. They were assigned to the cruiser Juneau. "If the worst comes to worst," George wrote his mother, "then we'll all have gone down together."

When the brothers embarked for war, the Sullivans displayed a service flag with five blue stars in their front window. "Worrying does no good. Neither for the children nor their parents," Hemingway wrote. "A good soldier does not worry. He knows that nothing happens until it actually happens and you live your life up until then. Danger only exists at the moment of danger."

In November of 1942, the Sullivans took part in the naval battle of Guadalcanal, the most fierce naval battle of World War II. It went on for three days. Nine ships were destroyed, six American and three Japanese, and there were thousands of casualties. The Juneau, struck by a Japanese torpedo, was sunk in 42 seconds. More than 700 men went down with the ship. All five Sullivan brothers died.

The American people shared in the Sullivans' grief. Eleanor Roosevelt wrote Mrs. Sullivan: "You and your husband have given a lesson of great courage to the whole country and in thinking of the war and what it means to all mothers of the country. I shall keep the memory of your fortitude always in my mind. It is heartening to feel that parents who have suffered the loss you have can always find solace in your faith and your abiding love for our country."

Fifty years ago, a U.S. destroyer was named for the Sullivans, the only family to gain such recognition. A plaque on the mast quoted George: "We stick together." They never had a homecoming. But America will never forget them.

Jim and Sarah Brady

Chicago Sun-Times, 8/26/96

Their courage has inspired America.

Jim and Sarah Brady, lifelong Republicans and gun-control advocates, will be at the podium tonight at the Democratic National Convention. She will address delegates. It will be among the convention's special moments.

They're not abandoning their party. Their party abandoned them.

Former White House press secretary Jim Brady, who turns 56 this week, was shot and partially paralyzed during John Hinckley's 1981 assassination attempt of President Ronald Reagan.

For more than a decade, the Bradys have fought to keep handguns out of the wrong hands. They introduced a gun-control measure called the Brady Bill that requires a seven-day waiting period for handgun purchases to give law-enforcement organizations a chance to run background checks on gun buyers. Their goal is to prevent criminals and unstable people from buying guns.

To most Americans, the Brady Bill was common sense. But the gun lobby is a powerful special interest. It took seven years and three presidential administrations for the Bradys to prevail.

Though Brady took a bullet meant for Reagan, two Republican administrations failed to push the Brady Bill. Every police organization supported it. Reagan endorsed the bill only after leaving office. Former President George Bush gave it lukewarm support.

The Bradys are grateful to President Clinton for signing the Brady Bill into law in 1993. Unhappily enough, many of their Republican friends were too cowardly to take on the National Rifle Association. But Clinton refused to be intimidated by the powerful special-interest group.

"This is a very important day for me and for Sarah and for all of those who have worked so hard to see the Brady Bill become law. But it is an even more important day for America and America's children," Jim said when Clinton signed the Brady Bill.

Since then, the NRA and right-wing extremists have sought to overturn it. They have also sought to repeal the assault-weapons ban. The Bradys have been vilified in the NRA's direct-mail campaigns. "The only political groups doing well in America right now are those preaching hate," the NRA claimed in a mailing. "And the No. 1 group on the list that is selling hate to raise funds is Handgun Control Inc." Sarah Brady is chairman of that group.

The Bradys have the gun lobby on the run because they're talking straight. The NRA lobbyists are the slicksters. Sarah has been particularly effective in exposing the NRA's distortion of the Second Amendment of the Constitution—that it guarantees the right to bear arms. It doesn't.

I've known the Bradys for a long time. Before meeting them, I was a friend of Sarah Brady's father, the late Stan Kemp, a former FBI agent who was the administrative assistant to a Republican congressman. I got to know Jim and traveled with him when he was former Texas Gov. John B. Connally's press secretary in the 1980 GOP presidential primaries. Sarah was a former staffer for the Republican National Committee.

What I liked immediately about Jim was his irreverent wit and his love of the game. After Connally withdrew from the race, Brady was hired by Reagan. For those of us who covered Reagan's 1980 campaign, Brady made it more fun. I'll never forget Jim's excitement when he told me that Reagan had selected him as White House press secretary.

In March, 1981, I was in the lobby of the Washington Hilton when Jim was shot just outside. As the presidential motorcade pulled away, I saw Jim lying on the ground with blood running from his head. Almost no one thought he had a chance. It was a miracle that he lived.

The Bradys' crusade has made America safer. They have turned tragedy into triumph.

Thomas J. Stack

Chicago Sun-Times, 4/20/94

He was among the more decorated soldiers of the Vietnam War.

But Thomas J. Stack seldom talked about his combat record.

On his return from Vietnam, Stack had a reunion in his basement with some of his pals from the Southwest Side. He wanted to know how they were doing. Stack never talked about himself much. But he helped a generation recover its lost pride.

Stack, 50, who died on Saturday after a 17-year bout with cancer, was a sergeant in the 9th Infantry Division in Vietnam who earned two Silver Stars, three Bronze Stars for valor and the Air Medal for taking part in more than 25 aerial missions over hostile territory.

"He was a hell of a man," said retired Gen. William C. Westmoreland, who commanded U.S. forces in Vietnam from 1964 to 1968. "Tom showed great bravery and valor on the battlefield. He put his life on the line to protect his men," Westmoreland said Tuesday. He recalled that Stack was among the more selfless men that he had known.

In Stack's final hours, his spirits brightened when he received a phone call from Westmoreland at St. Francis Hospital in Blue Island. Stack smiled when he got the call from his wartime commander. "I just told him how much he meant to all of us and that we were pulling for him," said Westmoreland, 80, who frequently corresponded with Stack. "He's going to be missed."

When he was under fire in Vietnam, Stack responded with toughness and courage. In the face of enemy fire, he dove into a stream, saved an American soldier from drowning and also captured a Viet Cong officer. While serving as a platoon leader, Sgt. Stack was under fire with his men behind a rice-paddy dike. Stack led a charge that wiped out five bunkers, rescued wounded American soldiers, and took heavy Vietnamese casualties. On another occasion when his platoon was under heavy fire, Stack led an assault that knocked out enemy snipers. Stack was a soldier's soldier.

On coming home from the Vietnam War, Stack and other veterans were greeted by protesters who called them names. It bothered him that Vietnam veterans weren't treated fairly. Stack was in Washington, D.C., in 1982 for the dedication of the Vietnam Veterans Memorial. He was deeply moved by the Wall and visited it often.

As part of the healing process from the Vietnam era, Stack organized the 1986 Vietnam Veterans Welcome Home Parade that brought more than 250,000 Vietnam veterans to Chicago. It was an extraordinary event. Westmoreland said Tuesday that Stack played an important role in the process of national reconciliation. "That cracked the ice. Vietnam was an unpopular war, and that rubbed off on the veterans," said Westmoreland. "But the Chicago parade cracked the ice on the country's attitude toward the Vietnam veteran and the veteran's attitude about himself. Other cities began honoring their veterans. Tom Stack started it all."

Stack received thousands of letters from parents and children of soldiers who had died in Vietnam, from veterans and from families of surviving veterans that thanked him for honoring the courage and sacrifice of American soldiers.

He was among the more heroic figures of his generation.

William F. Roemer

Chicago Sun-Times, 6/19/96

He never pulled his punches.

With his broad shoulders and powerful build, William F. Roemer Jr. was a born fighter. For more than 30 years, he battled the Chicago crime syndicate. The veteran FBI agent, who died last week at 69, never lost his zest for combat with the underworld. He fought crime with the swagger of John Wayne in the role of Big Jim McClain.

He installed the first electronic surveillance of a mob headquarters. Roemer also was among the first FBI agents to develop an informant within the crime syndicate. He was the cartographer for the Illinois attorney general's organized crime chart.

One of the reasons that the Chicago mob has lost influence is that Roemer was so good at doing his job.

Nothing intimidated him. Roemer was the first four-time heavyweight boxing champion at Notre Dame and a Marine boxing champion during World War II. In his middle 40s, Roemer tried unsuccessfully to persuade his hero Muhammad Ali to spar with him. Roemer said once that his biggest regret was that he didn't get to trade punches with John Dillinger.

He claimed to have had more face-to-face showdowns with mobsters than any Chicago G-man since Eliot Ness. His image as a tough guy was enhanced by his confrontation with mob boss Sam Giancana at O'Hare Airport in the early 1960s. Giancana had walked off an American Airlines plane. FBI agent Roemer presented his credentials and asked Giancana about an illegal wiretap that the mobster may have arranged. But the don was non-responsive. "I've got nothin' to say to you guys," he snarled.

When Roemer kept pressing for answers, Giancana got surly. He cut Roemer short with obscenities and boasted that he could have him killed. Roemer accused the mobster of threatening federal officers.

Giancana accused Roemer of violating his rights. Roemer mocked Giancana for carrying his girlfriend's purse and questioned his manhood. Giancana vowed to get him.

As a crowd gathered, Roemer berated the mobster as "garbage" and a "piece of slime." Harold Sell, Roemer's FBI supervisor, pulled Roemer back and told him that he had gone too far.

But Roemer made his point. Giancana told Roemer that he would get even if it was the last thing he did. Roemer said that Giancana once put out a $100,000 contract on him. But Roemer outlived his old adversary by 21 years.

After his retirement from the FBI in 1980, Roemer opened a private investigative firm that specialized in organized crime. Though he moved to Arizona, he became a consultant for the Chicago Crime

Commission and returned here often. When the Senate Rackets Committee held hearings in Chicago in 1983, Roemer was the star witness.

"The umbrella which protects the Chicago mob, and the linchpin which holds it together, is its alliance between crime and politics. Nowhere can organized crime be effective without the connivance of public officials. This would include law enforcement officers, legislators, judges and key officials," said Roemer.

He wasn't talking about the distant past. Roemer referred to specific Democratic ward organizations that had mob ties and named elected officials who did business with the mob.

In 1989, Roemer wrote his autobiography, *Man Against the Mob*, which provided a detailed and colorful account of his FBI career. Roemer added to his own myth. He told about his face-to-face meeting with mob boss Anthony Accardo. He wrote that Accardo did him a favor by calling off a contract on a government witness against a New York mobster.

Roemer's closest friend in politics was Illinois Gov. Richard B. Ogilvie. They struck up a friendship in the late 1950s when Ogilvie was chief of the attorney general's Midwest office on organized crime. Roemer helped Ogilvie in his prosecution of Accardo. Though Ogilvie won a conviction against Accardo for tax fraud, it was overturned on appeal. When Ogilvie was later elected sheriff, county board president and governor, he tried each time to recruit Roemer from the FBI. But Roemer liked what he was doing.

Until his book was published, Roemer wasn't well known outside of Chicago. But he gained more prominence after his book became a best seller and was made into a movie for television.

Roemer wasn't above embellishing his achievements. When a crime reporter once referred to him as "the most decorated agent in the history of the FBI," Roemer asked for his source. It was the reporter's opinion. "That is not official. The Bureau has never said that I am—though they haven't said the guy is wrong," Roemer wrote in a 1989 letter to a friend. "So I may be and I may not be."

Though the FBI never made any such designation, it became part of his official biography. As the old editor noted in John Ford's "The Man Who Shot Liberty Valance," "When the legend becomes a fact, print the legend." Roemer became one.

Ringmasters

Ben Bentley

Chicago Sun-Times, 1/25/99

He has been boxing's voice in Chicago for a half century.

Ben Bentley, 79, is among the last of the Damon Runyon characters.

Former Illinois Senate President Philip J. Rock, who was once an amateur fighter, has nominated Bentley for the Chicagoland Sports Hall of Fame.

There's no doubt that Bentley deserves induction. As a ring announcer, he was the best there ever was. A former amateur boxer and song-and-dance man from the West Side, Bentley was born to grab the microphone when it came down from the ceiling. He worked more than 50 world championship fights in the 1950s.

"Benny is Chicago, if you know what I mean," the late Jack Brickhouse told the *Chicago Sun-Times* in 1994. "I don't think there's a street in this town he doesn't know, a street that he hasn't walked down."

With his low-pitched voice, he has worked with ring legends from Jack Dempsey to Muhammad Ali. He was among the few boxing experts to predict Ali's stunning 1964 upset over Sonny Liston.

For Bentley, the music has never stopped. He still sings the jingle for the Wednesday night fights. "What'll you have? Pabst Blue Ribbon. What'll you have?" The late ringside announcer Don Dunphy, who often worked with him, said that Bentley was "superb" as boxing's voice.

Bentley is enjoying a second life as his main events are being aired again on ESPN's "Classic Sports." Looking dapper in his tuxedo, Bentley is shown in grainy black-and-white announcing that Sugar Ray Robinson has won a split decision over Carmen Basilio for the middleweight championship. On the same channel, he is also featured in the Rocky Marciano–Jersey Joe Walcott rematch.

In the golden age of boxing, Bentley was a reliable source for sports-writers like Jimmy Cannon and Red Smith. About 10 years ago, Bentley found himself sitting next to Saul Bellow at Eli's. When Bentley asked Bellow what he did for a living, Bellow responded that he was a writer. "Who do you write for?" Bentley asked.

"I write novels," Bellow responded.

"Have you ever written anything about Chicago?" Bentley asked.

Bellow noted that he had written *The Adventures of Augie March*.

"Who's Augie March?" Bentley asked, as if March might have been a contender for the middleweight championship.

When Mike Royko was writing for the *Chicago Daily News*, this is how he described Bentley: "Most people, when they think of a fight promoter, envision a burly man, wearing sunglasses, a diamond ring, houndstooth slacks, a wine-colored shirt, a white tie, a blue blazer and a cigar between his teeth. In the stereotype, the promoter talks like he was born near Humboldt Park and can snap your spine like a wishbone. As a matter of fact, that's the way Benny Bentley looks. I'm told he looked that way when he was 9 years old."

Bentley likes to tell the story about when he took heavyweight champion Sonny Liston to meet Vice President Lyndon B. Johnson. Liston got bored after LBJ gave them a few trinkets. "Let's blow this bum off," Liston whispered to Bentley.

When boxing declined here, Bentley was hired as the public relations director and first stadium announcer for the Chicago Bulls. He worked for the NBA team from 1966 until 1973. General manager Pat Williams named the team's mascot "Benny the Bull" after Bentley.

Only Bentley could make a basketball game sound like a title fight. Utah Jazz coach Jerry Sloan, who played for the Bulls, recalled in the team's oral history: "I'll never forget the first night we played in the Amphitheater, and Benny announced us coming out on the floor. That was the greatest thing I ever heard in the world. I thought we were coming out for round one of a boxing match."

Bentley, who knew a few hoods in the fight game, once got stopped on Michigan Avenue by a couple of detectives, one of whom thought he was mobster Tony Accardo. "That's not Accardo," said one of the cops. "He's just a small-time burglar from Omaha."

He wasn't upset at being confused with Accardo. "The thing that really made me mad was that they accused me of being from Omaha," Bentley says with a laugh. That's why they call him Benny the Burglar.

Jack Brickhouse

Chicago Sun-Times, 5/18/94

It was a night to remember.

In celebration of Wrigley Field's 80th birthday, Jack Brickhouse was back in the broadcast booth for seven innings on Monday night. Brickhouse, 78, is a living legend of baseball broadcasting. Brickhouse, who began covering the Cubs on radio in 1940 and broadcast the Cubs on TV from 1948 to 1981 and the White Sox from 1948 to 1967, has telecast more games than any other sportscaster. His love of the game is still captivating.

On Monday night, Brickhouse achieved another milestone by telecasting a Major League game in six different decades. He described the action in one of the season's more exciting contests, a 4–2 Cubs victory over the San Diego Padres, while also conducting a history seminar for fans. "Give me a shot of the upper deck," said Brickhouse, who recalled that the upper deck's construction in 1927 drew record crowds.

With two outs in the sixth inning and Sammy Sosa at the plate, Brickhouse was talking about Sosa's crowd-pleasing style as the Cubs outfielder connected for a triple. And when third baseman Steve Buechele blasted a home run into left field, Brickhouse said it: "Hey-Hey! In the basket."

"If you're from the Midwest, given the words 'Hey-Hey,' who comes to mind in an instant? Unless you have spent the last 35 years plus under an Arctic snowdrift, the answer is elementary—Jack Brickhouse," according to a Cubs program of the early 1980s. "His exclaiming the famous 'Hey-Hey' following a Cubs home run has become synonymous with Brickhouse not only in Chicago but throughout the baseball world."

And on Monday night, he was back, reunited with Hall of Famer Lou Boudreau and Vince Lloyd, for a night of memories. When a color photograph of Brickhouse from the 1960s was aired, his colleagues pressed him to identify the other man in the picture. "It's not Abner Doubleday," chortled Brickhouse. It was former Twins manager Sam Mele.

In his book, *Voices of the Games*, Curt Smith wrote that Brickhouse gave the finest speech in the first half century of the Baseball Hall of Fame when he was inducted at Cooperstown in 1983.

"I stand this day on what I consider the hollowed baseball ground of Cooperstown," he began. "I feel at his moment like a man who is 60 feet 6 inches tall. On a clear day in this quaint New York village, you can hear and see and feel the echoes of baseball's storied past. The atmosphere to me is breathless and humbling.

"It has been my privilege to broadcast the exploits of the Chicago Cubs and the White Sox for 40 years or more. There is Wrigley Field and Comiskey Park. I have experienced the joy and the heartbreak—probably more of the latter than the former—but Chicago and its beautifully loyal fans have a resiliency which has kindled a perpetual flame of hope.

"The trains, the planes, the cabs, the buses—they have carried me millions of miles through the years to get me where I most wanted to be—the ballgame. A reporter once told me that even if I didn't make Cooperstown, my suitcase probably would. Fortunately for me, we arrived together. . . . Here on this memorable afternoon, my heart tells me I have traveled the 90 feet from third to home and scored standing up." He scored again Monday night.

Harry Caray
Chicago Sun-Times, 10/4/89

When the lights go on at Wrigley Field tonight for the National League playoffs, Hall of Fame baseball announcer Harry Caray will be working off-camera.

In a baseball career that spans nearly a half century, former semi-professional second-baseman Caray lamented that the voices of baseball's championship teams are pre-empted by the networks for post-season play.

It is one of the quirks of major league baseball that its best local announcers are inevitably the victims of their team's championship flags.

And Caray made little effort to hide his disappointment at getting bumped off the air.

While NBC is televising the Cubs playoff game tonight, Caray's WGN will be airing the second installment of "Lace," a mini-series about a porn star.

Instead of watching the white-haired man shouting "holy cow" from his perch at Wrigley Field, Channel 9 viewers will be treated to a soft-core drama starring a couple of bimbos. With the possible exception of former Angels pitcher Bo Belinksy, who once dated the legendary Mamie Van Doren, baseball aficionados will miss Caray's presence on the little screen.

Caray, though, is likely to be responsible for an autumn revival of home-entertainment centers.

A hefty percentage of Cubs fans are planning to watch NBC's video presentation of the National League playoff series without the sound.

At the same time, they will be tuning in to the inimitable Caray on the Cubs radio network.

These folks have nothing against NBC's much-respected commentator Vin Scully, except that he isn't Harry.

Since making it to the majors as an announcer in 1944 with the St. Louis Cardinals, Caray has witnessed some of the game's more memorable innings while following the Cards, Athletics, White Sox, and Cubs.

One of the reasons that he has worked for multiple franchises is that Caray, a former radio newsman, stubbornly refused to go along with the tradition in some major league towns that sports announcers are mouth-pieces for the team's owners and players. Long before it was fashionable for the talking hairdos of the networks to "tell it like it is," Caray had gained the respect of the fans for his independent judgments.

On several levels, this season has been Caray's most fulfilling. For starters, Caray was inducted in July into the Baseball Hall of Fame with two other superstars, Johnny Bench of the Cincinnati Reds and Carl Yastremski of the Boston Red Sox.

In his speech, Caray graciously paid tribute to another Chicago broadcasting legend and fellow Hall-of-Famer, Jack Brickhouse.

Caray's engaging and highly readable autobiography, *Holy Cow!* was published earlier this year by Villard Books. Not only did the book enjoy brisk sales but it also was critically well-received.

His steakhouse, Harry Caray's, has become among the town's better and more popular restaurants.

As much as anyone, Caray has been astonished by the success of the National League East champion Cubs. And the national TV audience will be missing considerably more than the town's worst singing voice in tonight's game.

Dick Biondi

Chicago Sun-Times, 2/7/97

What's that sound?

In the winter of 1963, Chicago's Dick Biondi was the first American disc jockey to play a new record by four lads from Liverpool. They were then touring in England as a supporting act for Roy Orbison.

Biondi, who was with WLS radio, was among the nation's more influential disc jockeys with an audience that reached 40 states and Canada on the 50,000-watt, clear-channel station. He was voted in 1961 and 1962 as the nation's most popular Top 40 disc jockey.

The new group he introduced was the Beatles. Their single "Please Please Me" was released in February, 1963, by Chicago's Vee-Jay Records. "It was just a fresh, original sound that nobody else was doing," Biondi recalled Thursday. "I played it and played it."

Not everyone shared Biondi's enthusiasm. Capitol Records, which had the first option on their music, turned them down. On Dick Clark's television program "American Bandstand," the kids didn't like the Beatles. Biondi, though, sensed that they were special.

"Dick had a great ear and he was always ahead of the curve," said Howard Bedno, a rock promoter and former Vee-Jay Records marketing representative. "I don't think that anyone in rock 'n' roll had more impact in a short period of time than Dick Biondi. He was Mr. Rock 'n' Roll."

"He introduced rock 'n' roll to a huge segment of America," added Bruce DuMont, founder and president of the Museum of Broadcast Communications. "Dick was an important voice in bringing new music to a new generation in the early '60s" DuMont noted that President Clinton and Vice President Al Gore were among Biondi's early fans.

Biondi, 64, who plays classic rock weeknights on Chicago's oldies station, WJMK-FM (104.3), still is going strong after nearly a half century in rock music. Though he seldom talks about himself, he talks with wit and knowledge about the music that changed America.

"The first reaction to the Beatles wasn't fantastic," he said. Even though Biondi had a 56 percent share of Chicago's rock audience, he couldn't get the Beatles on the charts with their first record. Biondi was fired at WLS in May of '63 because he thought the station was airing too many commercials and not enough music.

Biondi then went to KRLA in Los Angeles and attempted to promote the Beatles. "The phones would ring with kids calling me to take that crap off the air and put on the Beach Boys," he said. "They were so used to the surfing music that they didn't know what to make of this new sound."

Later, when the mass hysteria of Beatlemania swept across America, the Fab Four remembered Biondi's early support. He introduced them in concerts at the Hollywood Bowl and Dodger Stadium. "They're all nice guys. But I liked George [Harrison] the most because he was quiet but could be very funny. He was also skinny like me," said Biondi.

Biondi, who has known most of rock's legendary performers, also was among Elvis Presley's first champions. He was fired in Buffalo in the late 1950s for ignoring an edict that he couldn't play Presley's records. At a '56 Presley concert in Cleveland, Biondi got Elvis to sign his shirt and then jumped into the crowd. Biondi went to the hospital after a horde of Presley's fans tried to tear off his shirt. "Elvis couldn't quit laughing," he said.

In the middle 1950s, Biondi was a disc jockey in Youngstown, Ohio, when he brought in Jerry Lee Lewis on his first Northern tour. "The Killer had never been up North before," said Biondi. "We also brought in Michael Landon, the actor, for a record hop. Landon was so good-looking the girls went crazy. Jerry Lee took it on as a challenge and did 14 songs straight. He came off, looked at me, and said, 'Now let's see if that pretty kid can top that.' Nobody could top Jerry Lee."

Biondi, who grew up in Endicott, N.Y., has worked for 23 radio stations in a career that spans more than 50 years. He is passionate about rock 'n' roll because it united the music of black and white performers. His short list of rock 'n' roll greats includes Chuck Berry, Little Richard, Presley and the Beatles. The Great Biondi should be next to them in the Rock and Roll Hall of Fame.

Champions

Red Grange

Chicago Sun-Times, 1/30/91

Football legend Red Grange, who died Monday at the age of 87, is still a larger-than-life presence in his hometown of Wheaton.

In the main corridor of the DuPage Center in Wheaton stands a heroic mural of Grange. The Galloping Ghost is wearing a leather helmet and clutching a football. Though the building is the center of DuPage County government, it is also a shrine to a man who never held political office.

There are still a few people around who saw Grange play for Wheaton High before he gained national prominence as the first football superstar. Even more remember him as the delivery man for a local ice company in the pre-refrigeration era. Grange recalled that he toted chunks of ice that weighed from 50 to 100 pounds and would cut pieces of ice "to the weight desired, give or take a few pounds." He once took a break from his ice route to win six first places in a high school track meet, then returned to the ice wagon.

Grange, a native of Pennsylvania, moved to Wheaton when he was 6 years old. His father is remembered in Wheaton as a tough, plain-spoken policeman who eventually became the local police chief. Red's mother had died before the family moved to Illinois. In downtown Wheaton, the Granges lived in a small flat above a store.

In his youth, Grange cut classes to attend White Sox games. Though Grange came up with alibis, he said that his teachers weren't fooled and asked him how the Sox were doing. Grange said that his father at first discouraged him from playing football but later became his chief booster.

At Wheaton High, Grange earned 16 varsity letters, won individual state track championships each year and scored 75 touchdowns in football. Some of Grange's sports memorabilia is on display in the DuPage

Center. Grange kept little for himself. The lion's share of his collection is at the Pro Football hall of Fame in Canton, Ohio.

Grange, who never played on Astroturf, recalled that he often got bruised in his high school football career. In Wheaton, his team's home field was the surface of an old gravel pit. Until Grange brought professional football into major-league stadiums, NFL games were played on harvest fields and village squares.

Football wasn't everything, Grange often noted. He recalled the time that former Sen. William B. McKinley (R-Ill.) took Grange and his pal George Halas to meet President Coolidge at the White House. "This is Mr. Grange and Mr. Halas," the senator told Coolidge. "They're with the Chicago Bears." Silent Cal replied, "Glad to meet you fellows. I always did like animal acts."

Though Coolidge wasn't familiar with Grange, everybody else was. Red even starred as himself in two movies, "One Minute to Play" and "The Galloping Ghost," produced by Joseph P. Kennedy, a former Harvard football player. Grange's Hollywood career was brief, but he kept in touch with Kennedy, who told him of his family's enthusiasm for football. "He was especially proud of young Jack," Grange recalled. "I kept the family in mind and thought perhaps someday George Halas could sign young Jack for the Bears. Things didn't work out that way."

Sid Luckman
Chicago Sun-Times, 12/15/96

It was fought in the cold.

On Dec. 15, 1946, in New York's windswept Polo Grounds, the Chicago Bears met the New York Giants for the NFL championship.

The drama began even before the kickoff. It was revealed that a New York halfback had been offered a bribe to throw the game. Though the player didn't take the money, he didn't report the attempted bribe to league officials. The NFL commissioner suspended the player. A second player who knew of the offer was allowed to play in the game.

A half-century later, Bears quarterback Sid Luckman has vivid memories of his last championship game. It was the fifth time in seven years that Luckman had led the Bears to the NFL title game. In a 12-year career, he guided the Bears to four championships and six second-place finishes. He is a legend of the fall as the greatest player on the greatest NFL team of his era. Luckman was renowned for his ball handling, passing and leadership.

During most of 1944 and for part of the 1945 season, Luckman had served in the U.S. Merchant Marine. Bears coach George S. Halas, who had been in the Navy for four years, was back for the '46 season.

"I remember it all as if it were yesterday," said Luckman, who recently turned 80. He is still trim and wears tinted glasses. "That '46 championship game with the Giants was the most vicious football game I ever played in. The Giants wanted to win. But they also had something to prove. They hit harder than any team I ever played against."

The largest crowd up to that time in pro football history (61,000) had gathered for this game. It also was televised on the old DuMont Network. Even though the Giants had defeated the Bears earlier in the regular season, Chicago was narrowly favored in the rematch.

For Luckman, it was a homecoming. He grew up in Brooklyn, where he led Erasmus Hall High School to the city championship. He was later an All-American at Columbia University. "Coming back to New York was a tremendous thrill for me," he said.

His fans weren't disappointed.

Luckman opened the scoring with a 21-yard touchdown pass. With the score tied 14–14 late in the fourth quarter, Luckman led a drive deep into Giant territory. In the game's turning point, Luckman faked to halfback George McAfee, who drew most of the Giant defenders. Luckman tucked the ball in his right arm and sprinted 19 yards for the winning touchdown.

"Coach Halas would never let me run," said Luckman. "But I called a timeout and walked over to the sidelines. We had a play called 'Bingo keep it,' where I kept the ball. I asked Halas, 'Now?' and he knew what I meant. We had been watching their defense keying on McAfee."

Giants quarterback Frank Filchock, who had passed for two touchdowns, led a comeback. But Luckman made an interception that killed the Giant threat.

The Bears won 24–14.

Of Luckman's four championships, the '46 title was the hardest-earned.

His most famous game was the 73–0 triumph over the Washington Redskins in the 1940 championship. His performance in that game as a pioneer of the T-formation revolutionized the game at all levels.

During 1941–42, the Bears won 18 straight games, including two playoff victories. They were upset in the '42 title game.

In the '43 season, he set a record that has stood for more than a half-century by throwing seven touchdown passes against the Giants. In the championship game that year, he threw five touchdowns against the Redskins. He also intercepted two passes. He was the NFL's MVP.

A half-century ago, Luckman was avidly courted by three teams in the new All-America Football Conference. The Chicago Rockets deposited $125,000 in the bank and offered it to Luckman. But he declined the offer. "The Bears and Coach Halas meant too much to me," said Luckman. "How could I quit a club that had done so much for me?"

Kenny Washington

Chicago Sun-Times, 6/24/96

It was a hard road.

But Kenny Washington blazed the trail.

Washington, who died 25 years ago today, played an important role in the social revolution that changed America. It has been 50 years since he broke the color barrier in the National Football League.

When Washington was signed by the Los Angeles Rams in March, 1946, it had dramatic impact. He was the first black to sign with a major league sports team in the modern era. Washington opened the way for other African-American athletes in professional sports, though it would take another 17 years for blacks to be listed on all NFL teams. A year after he joined the Rams, college teammate Jackie Robinson broke baseball's color barrier with the Brooklyn Dodgers.

Washington was an inspiration and role model to many who knew the pain of racial exclusion. "I grew up with the legacy of Kenny Washington. He was a great football player. But he had to be as much of a champion off the field as on the field because of the social conditions," said the Rev. Jesse L. Jackson, who played football in high school and college.

"Kenny Washington was the greatest football player I have ever seen. He had everything needed for greatness—size, speed and tremendous strength," Robinson said after Washington's death in 1971. "Kenny was probably the greatest long passer ever. He could throw 60 yards on the fly consistently."

In the early years of professional football, blacks had been allowed to participate, and African Americans Paul Robeson, Fritz Pollard and Duke Slater were among the league's stars. But in 1934, the league's owners made an agreement to keep blacks out of the NFL.

Soon afterward, Washington became UCLA's first superstar. He excelled in football, baseball, track and boxing for the Bruins. Washington batted .454 for the UCLA baseball team, 200 percentage points higher than Robinson. But it was in football that Washington gained national acclaim. He had breakaway speed as a runner and six times threw complete passes of more than 60 yards. Washington led the nation's collegiate teams in total offense with 1,370 yards his senior year.

Washington was such a spectacular talent that George Halas of the Chicago Bears made an effort to persuade other owners to end the league's policy against black players. After the 1940 College All-Star Game at Soldier Field, Halas asked Washington to stay in Chicago.

"I waited about a week, and then I was told that he couldn't use me," Washington recalled.

When Halas struck out with NFL owners, former Chicago Cardinals Coach Paul Schissler signed Washington with the Hollywood Bears of the Pacific Coast Football League. Washington became the dominant player in the PCFL.

Other NFL owners objected when Dan Reeves, owner of the Rams, signed Washington. The Rams were negotiating to use the publicly owned Los Angeles Coliseum. "Reeves had the league over a barrel," Washington later recalled. "The Coliseum people warned the Rams that if they practiced discrimination, they couldn't use the stadium. When those NFL people began thinking about all those seats and the money they could make filling 'em, they decided my kind wasn't so bad after all."

Washington played only three years in the NFL. He often played hurt and had to endure more than his share of cheap shots from racist opponents. "When he first began to play, they'd tee off on him," recalled former coach Bob Snyder. "They'd drop knees on him." But Washington always came back. His 92-yard run against the Cardinals is still a Rams record. He led the NFL with a 7.4-yard-per-carry average in 1947.

It's an injustice that Washington isn't in the Pro Football Hall of Fame.

George Connor
Chicago Sun-Times, 9/7/93

In the golden age of professional football, George Connor of the Chicago Bears was the toughest of the 60-minute men.

No one tackled harder than Connor, who was called the Moose.

A linebacker and tackle, Connor was an all-pro for the Bears at three positions during his 1948–1956 professional career. He played the equivalent of six modern football positions.

His lethal tackle against the Green Bay Packers in a 1955 game at Wrigley Field is part of the NFL's folklore. On a kickoff, Connor broke through the Packer line and slammed running-back Verl Switzer with such speed and force that he fumbled the ball and Switzer's helmet was knocked into the air. Linebacker Bill George scooped up the ball and took it into the end zone for a Bears touchdown. Connor's hit was unforgettable.

So, too, was his performance against the Baltimore Colts, which changed NFL history. George Shaw, the Colts quarterback and NFL Rookie of the Year, was going back for a pass against the Bears when Connor smashed through the line and dropped him with a shoulder tackle that broke Shaw's face mask, broke his nose, and knocked out several teeth. By knocking Shaw out of the game, Connor forced the Colts to give an opportunity to Johnny Unitas, a backup quarterback who became the NFL's greatest star of the 1950s and '60s.

Nobody was better than Connor at diagnosing enemy plays. Connor, now 68, recalls the time that he was playing right linebacker against the Lions at Tiger Stadium and he outfoxed Lions quarterback Bobby Layne and intercepted a pass on the left side. "You're not supposed to be over there, you big ape," Layne told Connor.

"I'll remember that next time, Bobby," Connor shot back.

It was an era of powerful running backs, including Ollie Matson, Joe Perry, Steve Van Buren, Hugh McElhenny and Marion Motley. Connor says that Cardinals halfback Elmer Angsman was the toughest to stop. But Connor chortles as he recalls the time he dropped Angsman for a loss when the Cardinals had a fourth and goal on the Bears half-yard line.

Connor, who played at 6 feet 3 inches and 240 pounds, was the first of the big, fast linebackers of the modern era. The other day, at Schaller's Pump in Bridgeport, he hosted an 80th birthday luncheon for his De La Salle Institute coach Joe Gleason. Connor, an all-star tackle for De La Salle, recalled how he became a linebacker. He said that a knee injury limited his mobility. The coach moved Connor to middle linebacker, and he dominated both sides of the line.

In the 1940s, Connor gained All-American honors at Holy Cross and Notre Dame, where he captained two of Frank Leahy's four national championship teams. *Sports Illustrated* named Connor as one of 11 members of the All-Century college football team. He is also a member of the Pro Football Hall of Fame.

In recognition of Connor's achievements, a fund has been established in his name at De La Salle to benefit needy student athletes.

A kickoff for the fund will be held Sept. 15 at the Gold Cup Room at Hawthorne Race Track. Legions of his friends will be there.

It's a fitting tribute to a remarkable man.

John Lattner

Chicago Sun-Times, 12/27/93

He was known as the bread-and-butter ball carrier.

In the history of Notre Dame football, John Lattner is a player for all time. Playing on both offense and defense, he averaged more than 50 minutes a game. Lattner was an outstanding runner, passer, receiver, kicker, punter and tackle, and was the first to win back-to-back Maxwell trophies as the nation's premier football player. John F. Kennedy and Ronald Reagan were among his fans. Lattner was featured on the cover of *Time* magazine.

It was 40 years ago this month that he won the Heisman Trophy as the best college football player. At the awards ceremony in New York, Knute Rockne's legendary Four Horsemen were reunited for the first time in 18 years.

Lattner showed a special grace in accepting the Heisman. The Notre Dame All-American said that football wasn't the most important thing in life. He paid tribute to his mother, his late father, his coaches, and his teammates.

"Without a good team behind him, there is no such thing as a so-called star," Lattner said in accepting the trophy. "It's not false modesty but common sense. I wouldn't have been able to do what I did this year without those teammates and the coaches who made it possible."

Since winning the Heisman, Lattner has devoted much of his time to doing good. He has worked tirelessly for Maryville Academy and other worthy causes. It's doubtful whether anyone in the Chicago area has done more for charity than Lattner. He still lives in Oak Park, where he starred in basketball and football for Fenwick High School. Lattner is a former commissioner of Oak Park's park district.

Lattner made a strong but losing race for an at-large suburban slot on the Cook County Board in 1986. If Lattner had run as a Republican, he would have won. But for Lattner, who grew up as a Democrat, switching parties to gain political office was unthinkable. During appearances at charitable events, Lattner was urged by Democratic strategists to make a pitch for his candidacy, but he said self-promotion would be inappropriate at such events. He knows there are more important things than winning an election.

If Lattner had won his Heisman a generation later, he would have become an instant multimillionaire. He was drafted in the first round by the Pittsburgh Steelers, made the all-pro team, and was acclaimed the top rookie in the NFL. An injury cut short his NFL career. Lattner, now a vice president of a business-supply firm, has no regrets.

For all of Lattner's football achievements, there are members of eight Chicago families who remember Lattner even more fondly. Thirty years ago, Lattner and his wife, Margaret, ran into a burning West Side apartment building in the wee hours of the morning and helped rescue 35 tenants, including eight people who had been overcome by smoke.

Frank Leahy, Lattner's coach at Notre Dame, once said of Lattner: "He's more than an All-American off the field than on." He still is.

Tony Zale

Chicago Sun-Times, 3/23/97

He might have been the toughest fighter who ever lived.

Tony Zale, boxing's "Man of Steel," ruled the middleweight division in the 1940s with courage, ferocity and a quiet dignity.

He twice knocked out Rocky Graziano in three bloodbaths in the most celebrated series in middleweight history.

"They weren't fights. They were wars without survivors," said boxing historian Bert Randolph Sugar.

Zale, who grew up in Gary, where he was a steelworker, and then lived in Chicago for a half century, died Thursday at 83. If they start counting 10 over Zale, there are fighters who wouldn't be surprised if he got up.

He always found a way to win. Graziano, who was eight years younger than Zale, was the favorite in their first fight at Yankee Stadium in 1946. Zale broke his hand below the right thumb in the second round. Graziano hurt Zale with a barrage of punches in that round, and Zale was saved by the bell. But he came back.

"This guy is tougher and he is quicker than anybody I ever fought," Graziano said. Zale, who was losing on points, stunned Graziano in the sixth round with a right to the midsection. Then came the left hook. Graziano recalled: "I saw it coming. I couldn't stop it. It hit me. The jolt shot from my head down to my feet. The feeling went out of my feet and I went whang on the canvas like I didn't have any feet at all."

In July, 1947, at the Chicago Stadium, they fought again. Zale nearly stopped Graziano in the third and fourth rounds. He closed Graziano's left eye, and the blood from another cut impaired Graziano's vision in his right eye. A determined Graziano fought back and trapped Zale on the ropes in the sixth round. Zale was knocked down. But he got back up. As Graziano pounded Zale on the ropes, the referee stopped the fight.

In June, 1948, Graziano was a 12–5 favorite in the rubber match, which was held at an outdoor stadium in Newark, N.J. Zale dropped Graziano in the first round with two crushing left hooks. Graziano landed with fierce combinations in the second, and Zale's legs buckled. But in the third round, Zale hit him with a right to the body and a smashing left hook to the jaw. Graziano's short reign had ended.

Zale, who first won the title in 1940 with a 13th-round knockout over middleweight champion Al Hostak, fought seven world champions. Former middleweight champion Billy Soose said that when Zale hit him it was like getting a hot poker stuck in your ribs.

When the United States entered World War II, Zale joined the Navy and served as a fight instructor. He was offered a fortune to defend his title, but declined on grounds that he shouldn't fight for profit in wartime. President George Bush, another Navy veteran, fought back tears in 1990 when he awarded Zale the Presidential Medal of Freedom and recalled Zale's wartime service and dedication.

Zale regretted passing up a college boxing scholarship in favor of a pro career. He took great pride in serving as a mentor to young men. For a generation, he was a boxing coach for the Catholic Youth Organization and the Chicago Park District.

Former Chicago Park District Supt. Edmund L. Kelly, who hired Zale, said, "He was very disciplined and soft-spoken. Nobody worked better with kids than Tony."

Illinois Attorney General Jim Ryan, who was among the young fighters coached by Zale in the early 1960s, won the middleweight title in the Chicago Golden Gloves. Zale was his role model.

John F. Sandner, chairman of the Chicago Mercantile Exchange, who grew up on the South Side, said Zale changed his life. Sandner, who won CYO and Golden Gloves titles, dropped out of high school to pursue a fight career. Zale motivated Sandner to resume his studies and go on to Notre Dame. "He was the greatest influence in thousands of lives," Sandner said. "He was the model of virtue, hard work and integrity."

Zale wasn't just tough. He was also one class act.

Jersey Joe Walcott
The Philadelphia Inquirer, 2/3/74

Before Muhammad Ali, 32, and Joe Frazier, 30, take too seriously the allegations that they are over the hill, they might consider the case of the oldest fighter to win the heavyweight championship of the world.

Jersey Joe Walcott was 37 when he finally won the title.

It is somehow reassuring that Walcott, with his broad shoulders and muscular arms, looks about as strong and physically fit today as he did in 1951 when he knocked out Ezzard Charles in the seventh round to win the heavyweight crown. Walcott celebrated his 60th birthday last week. His face is fuller, and at 211, he's about 15 pounds over his fighting weight. But Jersey Joe has aged gracefully.

Other things about Joe Walcott haven't changed much either. He still lives in Camden, the town where he grew up as Arnold Cream. His four sisters live there. His wife is principal of the high school. And he's the sheriff of Camden County.

Walcott is the heavyweight champion who never forgot where he came from. Ali, Frazier, Floyd Patterson, and Sonny Liston moved into suburban mansions after winning the title. Jersey Joe's life style is unique among modern heavyweight champions.

No one could blame Joe Walcott if he gave up on this fading industrial city and moved to one of those fashionable gated communities in the suburbs. Camden's gray old rowhouses, blighted waterfront, and crumbling business district are not a pretty sight.

But Joe Walcott insists that will never happen. He remembers the day when 200,000 of his neighbors crowded Admiral Wilson Boulevard to celebrate his championship. "I couldn't be happy if I left Camden to live on some country hillside," he says. "I probably wouldn't know anyone. The name Joe Walcott wouldn't mean anything there.

"I'd be letting myself down knowing that I had walked out on what is most dear to me. I'd be a real ingrate. I've received so much that I like to give something back."

He's still the local hero in Camden. If he wanted to run for mayor, there's little doubt that he'd win. Four years ago, he ran for sheriff on the Democratic ticket and won in a landslide. A wonderful honor, he says, but politics isn't for him.

"I'm not running for another term," he says. "I seriously doubt if I'll run for office again. We've done everything possible at the jail, but it just makes you realize how much more should be done. I'm more interested now in keeping people out of jail, getting back on the streets, and working with young people."

Clearly, Walcott doesn't want to be associated with politicians in this age of Watergate. The credibility of public officials has declined even further in Camden where the incumbent mayor was recently indicted for allegedly accepting payoffs. "That's a touchy subject," he says. "It's really not in my makeup to talk about these things."

Walcott wants to go back into youth work, which is what he's been doing nearly full-time since he quit fighting. There are countless stories in this community about Joe Walcott visiting sick children at Cooper Hospital, working with church youth groups, and walking the streets to keep things cool during potential riot situations.

His wife, the former Riletta Twayne, shares his interest in young people. But Mrs. Cream says she had doubts about taking the principal's job at Camden High two years ago. She was contented with her role as principal of an elementary school, and the manifold problems of Camden High seemed intimidating. "My husband was instrumental in my decision," she says. "I was so apprehensive that if he had been negative or expressed any reservation, I wouldn't have taken the job. But he was enthusiastic about it and urged me to accept."

While there may be few visible signs that Camden is destined to become anything other than South Jersey's only lighted graveyard, Joe Walcott is a hard man to convince.

Walcott is, if anything, a man of persistence. He says that he'd probably still be boxing if he hadn't captured the title. "It was my life's dream," he says. "I vowed to win the championship when I was nine years old. It took me 21 years after turning professional. Then, at the age of 37 and a half, my life's dreams were fulfilled. I guess if things hadn't turned out right, I'd still be trying for the championship even at this late date because my life wouldn't have been complete."

But Jersey Joe Walcott reached his goal—and then some. He was, for example, recently elected to Boxing's Hall of Fame. And, just last month, a *Sports Illustrated* poll rated him, along with such ring immortals as Joe Louis, Jack Dempsey, Muhammad Ali, Jack Johnson, and Rocky Marciano as one of the ten greatest heavyweights. "All of this makes me feel real proud," Walcott says. "I've never considered myself one of the greatest, although I guess I probably was one of the most determined fighters to win the championship."

The modest Walcott doesn't particularly enjoy reminiscing about his career. And, much to the disappointment of his friends, he won't show his fight films. "I'm too self-conscious," he says. "The fact is, if I'd show my films, I might as well be walking around with a sign saying 'Here I am.' I've loaned out my prints of the Louis, Marciano, and Charles fights to different people and don't even know where they are."

Walcott's career is one of boxing's more remarkable tales: a gallant struggle against almost impossible odds, with a storybook ending. Jersey Joe, who was the son of immigrants from Barbados and one of 12 children, adopted the ring name of Joe Walcott after a legendary fighter from his native island. He was only 16 when he fought his first professional fight at Vineland, N.J., knocking out Cowboy Wallace in the first round. His purse? A big $7.50.

In 1936, Walcott was hired as a sparring partner for Joe Louis, the undefeated number one heavyweight contender. Walcott caught Louis with a hard straight right and floored him during a sparring session. "They said I couldn't go another round," Walcott recalls. "They paid me $25 and chased me out of camp."

A year later, Louis won the championship, and, being a prudent man, ignored Walcott. Meanwhile, times were hard for Joe Walcott. He couldn't get fights against leading contenders. He worked on a road gang, did odd jobs, worked on an ice truck, and on a garbage truck. When he broke his arm, Walcott was forced to go on relief. He lived in a house with broken window panes covered by burlap bags. But things improved during World War II when he got a job in the Camden shipyards.

Walcott, after retiring from boxing no less than six times, made a strong comeback in 1945 under the direction of a new manager and sponsorship of a promoter who provided him with the means to go into full-time training. In the summer of 1945, Walcott won a surprising but well-earned decision over Joe Baski, who was then rated as the number two heavyweight contender. In the winter of 1946, Walcott was matched against top contender Jimmy Bivins in his hometown of Cleveland. Louis had predicted that Bivins would be the next heavyweight champion. Walcott knocked him down and gave him a lopsided beating. Walcott says these two fights may have been his best performances.

At any rate, Louis finally agreed to meet him at Madison Square Garden on Dec. 5, 1947. Nobody gave Walcott a chance. He was a 10-to-1 underdog. Walcott dropped Louis in the first minute of the fight, knocked him down again in the fourth round, and punched and jabbed the unbeaten champion at will. Louis graciously congratulated him at the end of the fight. Walcott appeared to have won boxing's greatest upset.

But something happened.

Louis, who had started to leave the ring, was awarded a controversial split decision. The sportswriter Grantland Rice spoke for most who witnessed the fight when he observed: "Walcott won by as far as a guy can shoot."

Walcott says there was no bitterness. "I'd proven that I could beat anybody."

There was a rematch. Once again, Walcott took charge. He knocked Louis down, closed his eye, and going into the 11th round, seemed to be headed for the title. But Louis trapped him in a corner, nailed him with a hurricane of punches, and it was all over.

When Louis quit boxing in 1949, he invited Walcott and Ezzard Charles to fight for his vacant title. Charles outpointed Walcott in Chicago and decisioned him again in Detroit in March of 1951. It seemed unlikely that he would get another chance. But four months later, when Walcott got his fifth title shot, the old man from Camden hit Charles with a left hook to the chin that sent him down for the count. Walcott retained the title with a close decision over Charles in their rematch.

Walcott defended his title against Rocky Marciano at Philadelphia's Municipal Stadium on Sept. 23, 1952. Marciano, nearly a decade younger than Walcott, was the heavy favorite. But it would be an epic struggle, one of the most exciting and closest battles in the history of the heavyweight division. Walcott's left hook dropped Marciano in the first round. It was the first time that Rocky had been knocked down. "He hit me so hard I thought the roof had caved in," Marciano recalled.

"I hit him in the temple. If that punch had been lower, he'd have never gotten up. But Rocky was a tough game fighter," Walcott says. The Marciano fight may have been Walcott's best. He staggered the Rock again in the 11th round, he had piled up an insurmountable lead. That's when Marciano connected with the hard right to the jaw which ended Walcott's reign.

Unfortunately, there was a rematch. This time, Walcott didn't survive the first round. "I'd have to say this was my biggest disappointment," he says. "Not so much failing to come back. It was just so frustrating to lose my last fight by a knockout. I realized then that it was the end of the road, that I could no longer produce or give what was expected of me.

"It's hard for most fighters to hang the gloves up. You always think you can come back. And, of course, there's the glamour and excitement that you hate to give up. But it's regrettable to see a great champion, Ezzard Charles, lose his last fights to men who couldn't have carried his water pail in earlier years. But you have to understand how good fighters love this profession."

When asked about today's heavyweights, Walcott says the champion George Foreman and Frazier "would have done well at any given time." But Ali is something special. "Ali could have been champion at any time," Walcott says. "He's one of the greatest fighters I've ever seen. He's clever. He's fast. He knows what he's doing at all times. He may be the greatest of all heavyweights."

Well, then, how would Walcott expect Ali to do against Foreman? "I wouldn't try to guess," he says. "After I predicted that Joe Walcott would knock out Marciano, I realized that Joe Walcott wasn't much of a handicapper."

Muhammad Ali

Chicago Sun-Times, 8/8/93

Muhammad Ali is the heavyweight champion who transcended boxing.

He still does. At the age of 51, he remains a player on the world stage.

Ali is currently mediating a prisoner of war exchange between the governments of Iraq and Iran, who waged a long, bloody, fruitless war in the 1980s. He has reached a tentative agreement with both governments for an exchange of 25,000 prisoners. Because of Ali's status as one of the world's more prominent Muslims, he was asked to intervene in the negotiations by the governments of the two predominantly Islamic nations. "They are aware of my personal commitment to the fundamental principles of Islam," said Ali. "The basis for the agreement of the leadership of Iran and Iraq to cooperate is also based upon Muslim tenets."

President Clinton would do well to consider using Ali in a diplomatic role as U.S. ambassador to the world. In 1990 Ali negotiated for the release of 14 Americans who were held hostage by Iraq's Saddam Hussein. After the Iranian takeover of the U.S. embassy in Tehran, Ali offered himself to Iran's government as a political prisoner in exchange for the Americans held hostage. Ali was turned down. Former President Jimmy Carter, who used Ali on several diplomatic assignments, said that he chose him as "the most famous person in our country."

More than any sports figure of the 20th century, Ali has touched our lives. It has been 29 years since he stunned the world by upsetting Sonny Liston for the heavyweight title, then changed his name and announced that he was a Black Muslim.

Ali showed extraordinary courage when he publicly criticized Lyndon B. Johnson's escalation of the Vietnam war. The power elite struck back. He was unfairly stripped of his heavyweight title after he refused induction into the Army because of his Islamic beliefs. He was convicted of draft evasion by LBJ's Justice Department and sentenced to five years in prison. Ali gave up his title and millions of dollars in income because of his principles and humanity.

As he did so often in the boxing ring, Ali won a unanimous decision in 1970 when the U.S. Supreme Court heard his appeal. He never went to jail. The courts ruled that the suspension of his license had been "arbitrary and unreasonable."

When he returned to the ring, the best was yet to come. His epic battles with Joe Frazier, Ken Norton and George Foreman established Ali as arguably history's all-time heavyweight champion. With style and grace, Ali saved a sport that had been dying.

Contrast Ali's humanity with the lighted firecracker that New York Met fielder Vince Coleman recently tossed out of the window of a car in a parking lot at Dodger Stadium. Some fans were hoping to get Coleman's autograph. Coleman's response was to throw a firecracker. Three people, including a one-year-old girl and an 11-year-old boy were injured by Coleman's firecracker.

"I feel like I should be doing more with what I've got to help people," Ali said. "My main goal now is helping people."

Steve Prefontaine
Chicago Sun-Times, 2/2/97

He was born to run.

With the style and flair of a rock star, Steve Prefontaine was the most exciting track-and-field performer of the early '70s. Like Muhammad Ali, Prefontaine took on the establishment. He made us all participants in his drama.

He demanded fairness for American athletes. It bothered him that the old men of the American Athletic Union dictated where U.S. athletes could train and compete.

Prefontaine, killed in a 1975 automobile accident, is remembered as the James Dean of track and field because he was an extraordinary talent who died before his time.

In no small part because of Prefontaine, running for fitness became a cultural phenomenon in the '70s. The Nike running shoe was invented for Prefontaine.

"To many, he was the greatest U.S. middle-distance runner ever, but to me he was more than that," said Nike founder Phil Knight. "Pre was a rebel from a working-class background, a guy full of cockiness and pride and guts. Pre's spirit is the cornerstone of this company's soul."

He is the subject of a new movie, "Prefontaine," written and produced by the team that collaborated on "Hoop Dreams." The film, starring Jared Leto as Prefontaine, effectively captures what Prefontaine was all about.

Prefontaine held 14 American records, including the record for every distance from 2,000 to 10,000 meters.

I had a front-row seat for Prefontaine's run to fame. As a student at the University of Oregon, I worked part time in the sports information office of the athletic department, where I met Prefontaine. He was friendly and personable. Prefontaine already had a following. While still in high school he had set a national record in the 2-mile run. When kids wrote him fan letters at Oregon, Pre always found the time to write back. He worked with disadvantaged youth and liked to give running clinics for area high school students. He even started a running program for inmates in the state prison.

When Pre ran it was always a happening. Even though the University of Oregon is a track-and-field powerhouse, which has produced many world-class runners, it had never seen anyone like him. He became the first runner to win four NCAA titles in the same event (the 5,000 meters). He also won the Pacific Eight Conference 3-mile championship four times and in his sophomore year also won the conference championship in the mile. Prefontaine dazzled the crowd with his enthusiasm and showmanship. He invented the victory lap.

Until Prefontaine, the mile was the most prestigious distance event. His ambition was to be the world's greatest miler. He ran the mile nine times in under four minutes. But Oregon Coach Bill Bowerman told Prefontaine to run longer distances, where his toughness and stamina would give him the edge.

Prefontaine always ran to win. In the 5,000 meters at the 1972 Munich Olympics, he sprinted into the lead in the final lap but burned himself out going for the gold. If he had run a more pragmatic race, he would have brought home the silver or bronze medal. But Prefontaine never cared about consolation prizes. By going for the gold, he was so spent at the finish that he was overtaken for third place in the final second.

He couldn't wait for a rematch with Finland's Olympic champion Lasse Viren.

Prefontaine was so eager to run against Viren that he defied the U.S. track-and-field establishment. He took on the American Athletic

Union, which sought to force him to compete against runners from the Soviet Union. Prefontaine wanted another chance to beat Viren.

At the risk of suspension, Prefontaine declined to run against the Soviet Union, Poland and Czechoslovakia. He didn't want to be a pawn in U.S.-Soviet politics. His argument was that the toughest competition in distance running was in Scandinavia. He resented the AAU's political agenda. "I wish they'd leave me alone to do what I want to do—run against the best," he said.

His conflict with the AAU is among the themes of the movie. Prefontaine, who was voted the most popular track star in the world by Track & Field News in 1975, had turned down what was then the largest contract that had been offered a track star—$200,000. He wanted to retain his amateur status for the 1976 Olympic games.

On his own, Prefontaine invited a group of Finnish athletes to compete in several track meets. The AAU threatened to punish him. But Prefontaine got them to blink. On the day he was killed in the car wreck, Prefontaine won a 5,000-meter race against the Finnish runners.

"Pre had incredible determination and passion," recalls his friend Geoff Hollister. "A message for kids today that can be taken from Steve's story is that there are no short cuts to success."

Men in Black

Monsignor Ignatius D. McDermott

Chicago Sun-Times, 8/28/92

On the streets of the Near West Side, the big, husky man in the dark suit has been a presence for nearly a half century.

The Rev. Monsignor Ignatius D. McDermott, 82, known in Chicago as "Father Mac," has devoted his life to the poor and dispossessed. He has had remarkable impact on thousands of lives. "I'm the luckiest guy alive," he says. "If I'd accepted a pastorship, I'd have been retired years ago."

He walks with more vigor than persons half his age. Since the 1940s, he has walked nightly through the Near West Side, providing comfort and shelter to the downtrodden. At the old Desplaines Street police station, which had a holding area for alcoholics and a court known as "the Drunk Court," Father Mac was troubled by the daily ritual of sentencing intoxicated persons to 30 days in jail. He became their advocate, the Skid Row priest, the apostle of the alcoholics. His creed is from St. Vincent DePaul: "When you no longer burn with love, others will die of the cold."

Through his persistence and the force of his personality, McDermott promoted legislation that recognized alcoholism as a treatable disease and provided for treatment. "My philosophy of life is that God never gives up on anybody until the undertaker picks up the body," Monsignor McDermott says.

In his fine biography of McDermott, *The Liquid Cross of Skid Row,* former *Sun-Times* columnist Bill Gleason wrote that Father Mac walked streets that most Chicagoans are afraid to walk. Father Mac talks to the people of the street in their language. "He doesn't ask whether they are Catholic, Protestant or Jewish," Gleason wrote. "He asks if he may help them. He tries to help them even when they say no. He cooperated in setting up a soup line for them. He prays for them. He writes to their anguished or indifferent families. He arranges for them to be hospitalized to take the cure or for the treatment of diseases that ravage the row."

Monsignor McDermott has won international acclaim for his efforts. It has been nearly 30 years since he founded the McDermott Center to serve troubled families, and he also established the Central States Institute of Addiction to provide training for treatment of addictions, including alcoholism. In 1988, he opened a three-building center for the homeless, the disadvantaged and substance abusers at 932 W. Washington Blvd. The center includes a 24-hour residential program, an overnight shelter, single occupancy rooms for the homeless, a rehabilitation center, cafeteria and chapel.

It's been a remarkable run. And he's still at it. Monsignor McDermott delivered the invocation to the Illinois House of Representatives last spring, then lobbied legislators against cuts in aid to the disadvantaged. He has just returned from Switzerland, where he sits on the World Council of Alcoholism.

The Chicago City Council recently renamed Washington Boulevard between Morgan and Halsted in Monsignor McDermott's honor. Today, a group of Father Mac's friends, including Judge Abraham Lincoln Marovitz and Illinois Secretary of State George H. Ryan, will dedicate McDermott Boulevard. It's a fitting tribute to Chicago's churchman of the century.

Joseph Cardinal Bernardin

Chicago Sun-Times, 11/15/96

He cared.

Joseph Cardinal Bernardin, who died early Thursday, leaves a legacy of compassion.

In his 30 years as a bishop, he became one of the more influential religious leaders of his time. But he is deeply mourned because he was a good and decent man. Bernardin gave all of us hope.

He showed vision and leadership in 1983 as the author of a pastoral letter against nuclear war, issued by the National Conference of Catholic Bishops. Bernardin called for an "immediate bilateral, verifiable agreement to curb the testing, production and development of new nuclear weapons." His words had impact. President Ronald Reagan, who talked tough against the Soviet Union, became an advocate for arms control.

During his long and courageous fight with cancer, Bernardin wrote a pastoral letter reflecting on his illness and outlining his social philosophy.

"I have experienced in a very personal way the chaos that serious illness brings into one's life. I have had to let go of many things that had brought me a sense of security and satisfaction in order to find the healing that only faith in the Lord can bring," he wrote on Nov. 6, 1995.

Bernardin voiced strong views on health care in a March, 1994, address before the National Press Club in Washington, D.C. "Health care is an essential safeguard of human life and dignity, and there is an obligation for society to ensure that every person be able to realize this right.

"The only way this obligation can be effectively met by society is for our nation to make universal health care coverage a reality. Universal access in not enough," he said.

In the pastoral letter, he rebuked the forces that thwarted President Clinton's 1993 initiative for national health care. He also worried about the social consequences of welfare reform.

Bernardin criticized the influence of the "special interests" that had defeated Clinton's health-care initiative. "I was deeply disappointed by our inability as a nation to move forward with systemic reform of our nation's delivery of health care," he wrote. "While now is not the time to attribute blame, I am troubled that our constitutional process for decision-making seems increasingly incapable of addressing fundamental issues."

Bernardin rejected the new harshness of American politics. He warned against an "ethic of punishment" as a replacement for social responsibility.

"I sense a meanspiritedness that, under the guise of encouraging responsible living, is, in fact, judging the poor and the marginalized as a class or social group who are responsible for their own situation. The logical conclusion of this judgment is that society need do nothing. And because we are now in the realm of so-called 'personal failure,' some have concluded that the not-for-profit- sector of society, and in particular religious institutions, and not the government, should care for the needs of such people."

Bernardin ardently defended government's role in providing such care. "Over the last half-century, we have come to recognize certain human and social needs, which, as a nation, we could not ignore. In effect, we concluded that in these areas the demands of the common good required action. Attempts to eliminate inefficiency and ineffectiveness must be carefully evaluated to ensure that . . . they do not result in our walking away from these communal and social responsibilities."

He believed in America as a family. Maybe that's why so many of us are mourning a loss in ours.

Father Andrew M. Greeley

Chicago Sun-Times, 8/28/89

The forests of North America have been getting smaller since the Rev. Andrew M. Greeley started writing books in 1959. He has been accused of never having an unpublished thought.

Over the last 30 years, Father Greeley has written 109 books that have collectively sold more than 15 million copies. He has written much-acclaimed and provocative studies of the American Irish, the Catholic Church, and Democratic ethnic politics. But he is more widely known for his best-selling fiction written in the last decade.

Indeed, Father Greeley has become one of the more popular novelists of his generation. The majority of his 17 novels have been national best sellers. His latest, *St. Valentine's Night*, which is just off the presses at Warner Books, is selling briskly at bookstores.

With his deep-set piercing blue eyes, a Jimmy Cagney presence, and light, thinning hair, Father Greeley is among the city's more distinctive personalities. Although he also owns houses in Grand Beach, Michigan, and in Arizona, he is a lifelong Chicagoan who has remained close to his roots.

Father Greeley has given away some of the millions that he has earned from his books, including a substantial grant to Chicago's inner-city schools. When the University of Chicago foolishly denied him tenure, Father Greeley later responded by giving more than $1 million to the university to endow a chair for Roman Catholic study. He is still affiliated with the National Opinion Research Center at the university.

In the tradition of James T. Farrell, who chronicled the lives of Studs Lonigan and Danny O'Neill in his classic novels about the Irish neighborhoods of the city's South Side, Father Greeley writes with passion and narrative force about the parishes where he grew up and has spent much of his life.

"To those who object that my novels are always about the neighborhood Chicago Irish, I am constrained to reply that I really don't know anyone else well enough to write about them," Greeley responds to those who have suggested that his works are too narrowly parochial and autobiographical.

St. Valentine's Night is set against the backdrop of former Mayor Washington's death. Former Mayor Eugene Sawyer, Ald. Edward M. Burke (14th), Ald. Timothy C. Evans (4th), political gadfly Walter "Slim" Coleman, *Chicago Sun-Times* columnist Vernon Jarrett, and Mayor Richard M. Daley are among the local personalities to gain mention in Father Greeley's new book. But the book's dominant characters are the Rev. Monsignor Blackie Ryan and his lifelong friend, Neal Connor, a network television correspondent.

Without giving away the book's plot, Greeley aficionados may be assured that *St. Valentine's Night* is both readable and compelling. His next book, *Andrew Greeley's Chicago*, scheduled for publication this fall, will give special attention to the neighborhood communities including Saint Angela ("Saint Ursula") and Christ the King ("St. Praxides") settings for his fiction.

About the only creative field into which Father Greeley hasn't ventured is the movies. He was offered the role of a priest in *The Mission*, a movie with Robert DeNiro. But he turned it down, saying he didn't have the time.

Storytellers

Dashiell Hammett

Chicago Sun-Times, 5/29/94

In the final scene of *The Maltese Falcon*, Brigid O'Shaughnessy is taken into custody after confessing to a murder. She was turned over to the cops by private investigator Sam Spade, whose partner was the victim.

One of the cops is intrigued by a black sculpture of a falcon and asks, "What's that?"

Humphrey Bogart, in the role of Spade, replies, "The stuff that dreams are made of." So, too, is the writing of Dashiell Hammett, the creator of *The Maltese Falcon, The Thin Man, The Glass Key, The Continental Op, The Big Knockover,* and other American classics.

On the 100th anniversary of his birth, Dashiell Hammett is remembered as one of the more influential writers in American literature. He was the dean of tough-guy writers, the founding father of detective stories. He elevated crime stories from pulp magazines to some of our more enduring literature. "His prose was clean and entirely unique," the *New York Times* noted when he died in 1961. "His characters were as sharply and economically defined as any in American fiction. His stories were as consistent as mathematics and as intricate as psychology. His gift of invention never tempted him beyond the limits of credibility."

"Hammett gave murder back to the kind of people that commit it for reasons, not just to provide a corpse; and with the means at hand, not with hand-wrought duelling pistols, curare, and tropical fish," Raymond Chandler wrote of Hammett's achievement. "He put these people down on paper as they are, and he made them talk and think in the language they customarily used for these purposes. He had style, but his audience didn't know it, because it was in a language not supposed to be capable of such refinements. They thought they were getting a good meaty melodrama written in the kind of lingo they imagined they spoke themselves. It was, in a sense, but it was much more."

Hammett, who was born May 27, 1894, quit school at 14, then worked as a freight clerk, stevedore and railroad employee. His life was as colorful as the characters he wrote about. At 20, he became an operative for the Pinkerton Detective Agency. In the 1920s he began setting a new standard for crime fiction with his stories for the magazine *Black Mask*.

As a detective, Hammett knew a man who stole a Ferris wheel. How did Hammett find it? "You don't steal something that big for your backyard," he said. "I knew it had to be at another carnival." He recalled that he once had to give directions to a subject he was shadowing because the man had gotten lost. Hammett recalled the chief of police in a Southern town who "once gave me a description of a man, complete even to a mole on his neck, but neglected to mention that he had only one arm."

Hammett, a veteran of two World Wars, became involved in left-wing politics in the 1930s. In 1951 he was convicted on contempt of court for refusing to testify about his role as a trustee of the bail fund for the Civil Rights Congress. He served six months in prison. "If it were more than jail, if it were my life, I would give it for what I think democracy is," said Hammett. "I don't let cops or judges tell me what I think democracy is."

He was later harassed by Sen. Joseph R. McCarthy's witch-hunting committee. McCarthy had his novels removed from government libraries abroad. President Dwight D. Eisenhower, who denounced the book burners, challenged this policy. Hammett is buried in Arlington National Cemetery. His work endures.

Ernest Hemingway

Chicago Sun-Times, 6/2/97

The legend under his picture in the 1917 Oak Park and River Forest High School yearbook captured him perfectly:

"None are to be found more clever than Ernie."

It was 80 years ago this month that Ernest Hemingway ended his formal education with his graduation from high school. Hemingway read the class prophecy, which he wrote, at the graduation ceremony.

Hemingway shunned opportunities to attend college and took a job out of high school as a reporter for the *Kansas City Star*. In 1918, he went to Europe and drove an ambulance in World War I for the Red Cross. He was wounded by mortar fire and returned to talk about his wartime experiences at his high school.

Though Hemingway went on to achieve international fame and became one of the more influential writers of the 20th century as the author of *The Sun Also Rises, A Farewell to Arms,* and *For Whom the Bell Tolls,* his writing was treated with scorn by residents of his hometown.

Hemingway responded that Oak Park was a village of "broad lawns and narrow minds." But he resisted the impulse to get even with his critics in print. "I had a wonderful novel to write about Oak Park," he wrote a biographer, "and would never do it because I did not want to hurt living people. . . . Nobody in Oak Park likes me, I should suppose. The people who were my good friends are dead or gone. I gave Oak Park a miss and never used it as a target. You wouldn't like to bomb your hometown, would you?"

The village that never honored the Nobel laureate during his lifetime now recognizes the importance of being Hemingway. His birthplace at 339 N. Oak Park Avenue has been restored and is open to the public. The Hemingway Museum at 200 N. Oak Park Ave. has exhibits on his life and writing. A book, *Ernest Hemingway: The Oak Park Legacy,* edited by James Nagel, was published last winter by the University of Alabama Press. A book of his earliest writings, *Hemingway at Oak Park High,* published by the high school in 1993, shows that Hemingway was exploring themes that would become central to his later fiction.

In a short story for the high school literary magazine, "Judgment of Manitou," Hemingway wrote about a dispute between two trappers in a remote Canadian territory that leads to violence and death. "As he took a step forward Pierre felt the clanking grip of the toother bear trap, that Dick had come to tend, close on his feet." As the story ends, Pierre reaches for his rifle to kill himself.

Hemingway, who boxed in his youth, wrote a short story about a con man attempting to fix a prize-fight. It begins: "What, you never heard the story about Joe Gans's first fight" said old Bob Armstrong, as he tugged at one of his gloves. "Well, son, that kid I was just giving the lesson to reminds me of the Big Swede that gummed the best frame-up we ever almost pulled off."

Susan Lowrey, a classmate, recalled years later: "His themes were almost always read aloud in class as examples of what we should all strive for."

Hemingway didn't want his Oak Park writing to be published. In the early 1950s, he blocked an attempt to include his early work in an anthology. He wrote a biographer that "writing that I do not wish to publish, you have no right to publish. I would no more do a thing like that to you than I would cheat a man at cards or rifle through his desk or wastebasket for read his personal letters. . . . You know the worst thing you can do to a writer is to dig out his worthless and childish stuff which he deliberately never allows to be collected or republished. It is like publishing the contents of a wastebasket."

But it's also an invaluable portrait of the artist as a young man.

Saul Bellow
Chicago Tribune Magazine, 9/16/79

"I am an American, Chicago born—Chicago, that somber city—and go at things as I have taught myself, free-style, and will make the record in my own way."

—from "The Adventures of Augie March"

It is a bright summer afternoon at the University of Chicago, and the leaded glass windows sparkle in the Gothic towers along the Midway.

In his fifth-floor office, Saul Bellow is wearing slacks and a blue golf shirt. He is a slightly built man with expressive, heavy-lidded eyes, well-chiseled features, and white hair, and he projects the aura of a literary person. The small room is dominated by tall metal bookcases with foreign language editions of his works, a set of leatherbound Coleridge, a multi-volume history of Jewish literature, and a miscellany of other books.

He is an intensely private man who shuns the talk-show circuit and the trappings of celebrity.

At age 64, Bellow is recognized as America's master storyteller, a superb craftsman, one of the most gifted novelists of his generation. He has been honored—the first American writer since Steinbeck to receive the Nobel Prize. At the same time, he is a commercial property whose books are best-sellers and book-club selections.

In novel after novel he has returned to the slums and ethnic neighborhoods of Chicago, and he is now writing a nonfiction book on the city that has been home for most of his life. "I thought it was time, after so many years in Chicago, to put down my ideas and feelings about it," says Bellow, "partly my own recollections of the '20s, '30s, and part of the '40s, and the book will contain some comparisons between the old Chicago and the new."

From "Dangling Man," his first novel, through, "To Jerusalem and Back," his most recent book, Chicago has been the setting for some of Bellow's most memorable prose. A native of Canada, Bellow moved to Chicago when he was 9 years old. "I grew up there and consider myself a Chicagoan, out and out," he once said.

As a youngster he lived in the vibrant multi-ethnic neighborhood of Humboldt Park, and he has drawn heavily from those formative years. His Chicago book began as an affectionate tribute to the old Chicago, but it soon evolved into a more ambitious project.

"When I set about this task," he says, "I was confident I knew the city. I soon learned how little I knew of contemporary Chicago. So much of what I thought was my knowledge of the city turned out to be inapplicable to present conditions. You have to look very closely to find the Chicago of the '20s and '30s."

He laments the passing of ethnic Chicago, the throbbing, immigrant neighborhoods that gave the city a special vitality. "Chicago was a collection of small towns German, Irish, Polish, Italian, Jewish, Czech," he says. "Where these small communities survive, they survive on a reduced scale. The suburbs have drained so much of the old Chicago. And there have been generational changes. The descendants of immigrants have given up the old trades and occupations. They have experienced what people like to call upward mobility. In the old neighborhoods, there were cabinet makers, cobblers, pastry cooks, tinsmiths, locksmiths, and blacksmiths. I doubt that many people now follow these occupations in the Old Country. Technology has put them out of business everywhere. Those locksmiths, pastry bakers, and printers of the old days have vanished."

Bellow's present neighborhood is Rogers Park, where he lives with his fourth wife, Alexandra, a Northwestern mathematics professor, in a fashionable apartment on Sheridan Road. "It's nothing like a Chicago neighborhood of the old days," he says. "What you have on the North Side is a fringe of high-rises and people in a state of semi-siege, especially the elderly, for whom shopping or simply getting about presents difficulties. Last winter during the blizzards I saw very old people trying to make their way from Sheridan Road to the shops on Broadway. Some used aluminum frame walkers while trying to manage their bundles. Many of them were quite frightened at having to venture out. They walked in mid-street."

Born in Lachine, Quebec, in 1915, Bellow was the youngest of four children. Until he was 9 years old, he lived in an old and impoverished Jewish neighborhood of Montreal.

As a youngster he learned four languages—English, Hebrew, Yiddish, and French—and, when he came to Chicago, quickly discovered the city's libraries and the works of Mark Twain, Poe, Dreiser, and Sherwood Anderson.

From boyhood his ambition was to make his mark as a famous writer. To school chums he confided titles of books he one day planned to write. At the Mission House in Humboldt Park, he read his work aloud to kids from the neighborhood. At the same time, Bellow was a determined athlete—a runner on the track team, swimmer, and tennis player.

"I used to go often to the Humboldt Park branch of the Chicago Public Library," he says. "It was located in a storefront of North Avenue and, later, in a storefront on California Avenue facing the park. I would combine my library visits with activities in the Association House on North Avenue, where kids of my neighborhood played basketball. So I would carry my Sherwood Anderson to the Association House, put it in my locker, then read it as I walked home.

"I was a determined athlete, but not outstanding. I was not in a class with Julius Echeles, now a criminal lawyer, who was the school's (Tuley High) basketball star. 'Lucky' was his nickname. I'd been a sickly child and was determined in adolescence not to be a convalescent adolescent. And I drove myself hard. Characteristically, I read a great deal about body building. I studied physical development books like 'How to Get Strong and How to Stay So.' From the great Walter Camp I learned to carry scuttles filled with coal, holding them out at arm's length."

Bellow graduated from Tuley in 1933 and entered the University of Chicago, where he found himself restless and confined in what he termed "the dense atmosphere of learning, of cultural effort." In 1935, he transferred to Northwestern University, studying anthropology and sociology, and graduating with honors two years later. He wanted to become a graduate student in English literature but the dean of Northwestern's English department told him that it would be unwise because anti-Semitism might thwart his career.

Instead, Bellow went to the University of Wisconsin and studied anthropology but found it less than compelling. "Every time I worked on my thesis, it turned out to be a story," he said. "I disappeared for the Christmas holidays, and I never came back."

For a time he worked for the New Deal's WPA Writers Project, writing short biographies of Midwestern novelists. It was one of the most unusual cultural aid programs ever launched by a government, a massive project that gave jobs to hundreds of writers, poets, playwrights, masters and hacks, radicals and right-wingers. Among the WPA writers were John Cheever, Nelson Algren, Loren Eiseley, Richard Wright, and Ralph Ellison, and they produced hundreds of books and pamphlets including the celebrated state guide series. "We adored the project, all of us," Bellow wrote in a 1969 letter. "This was in the days before gratitude became obsolete. We had never expected anyone to have any use whatsoever for us. With no grand illusions about Roosevelt and Harry Hopkins, I believe they behaved decently and imaginatively for men without culture—which is what politicians necessarily are."

As a struggling young writer, Bellow had looked forward to making friendships with such published novelists as Nelson Algren and Jack Conroy. It didn't happen. "I rather looked up to them," said Bellow, "and they rather looked down on me."

In Depression Chicago, Bellow did his writing on yellow sheets from the five and dime. "I became attached to this coarse, yellow paper which caught the tip of your pen and absorbed too much ink," he said later. "It was used by the young men and women in Chicago who carried rolls of manuscripts in their pockets and read aloud to one another in hall bedrooms or at Thompson's or Pixley's cafeterias."

Bellow taught for several years at Pestalozzi-Froebel Teachers college and then worked on the *Encyclopaedia Britannica*'s "Great Books" project.

In the early 1940s Bellow sensed that he was on the threshold of a writing career. He went to New York and mixed with such gifted young artists as poet Delmore Schwartz and critic Alfred Kazin. Bellow struck Kazin as witty, cultivated, supremely confident, a writer with a sense of destiny. "Bellow was the first writer of my generation," said Kazin, "who talked of Lawrence and Joyce, Hemingway and Fitzgerald, not as books in the library but as fellow operators in the same business."

Bellow served in the Merchant Marine during World War II and wrote what would become his first published novel, "Dangling Man."

It was a remarkable book, a journal of a young Chicago man who quits his job, expecting to be drafted, but is left dangling for nearly a year. It was a powerful document, often moving, and it captured the tensions and anxieties of wartime America.

"Dangling Man" served notice that Bellow was a somebody, a talent to be reckoned with, a young artist of extraordinary promise. Edmund Wilson, *The New Yorker*'s renowned critic, called it a wonderful book, "one of the most honest pieces of testimony on the psychology of a whole generation who have grown up during the Depression and the war."

Soon afterward, Bellow joined *Time* magazine as a film critic. "I was young, inexperienced, and tired of knocking about," he recalled. It was a short-lived career. On Bellow's second day, *Time* senior editor Whittaker Chambers, who would win notoriety as Alger Hiss' accuser, asked what Bellow thought of Wordsworth. "What does that have to do with film reviewing?" asked Bellow. When Chambers demanded an answer, Bellow said that Wordsworth was a romantic poet. Chambers said, "There's no place for you in this organization." So Bellow went back to writing books.

Bellow's second novel, "The Victim," came in 1947 and was also well received, but he was uncomfortable with the form. "I labored and tried to make it letter perfect," he said in a Paris Review interview. "In writing 'The Victim' I accepted a Flaubertian standard. Not a bad standard, to be sure, but one which, in the end, I found repressive—repressive because of the circumstances of my life and because of my upbringing in Chicago as the son on immigrants. . . . A writer should be able to express himself easily, naturally, copiously in a form which frees his mind, his energies."

In his next book, Bellow chose to write directly of his own experience, of the old neighborhood, and the result was nothing less than a classic, "The Adventures of Augie March," a long, crowded, picaresque novel that captured Jewish Chicago with a richness reminiscent of James Farrell's portrait of Irish Chicago. "The great pleasure of the book was that it came easily," said Bellow. "All I had to do was to be there with buckets to catch it."

Bellow started the novel in Paris and Rome while on a Guggenheim fellowship. Augie, Bellow's protagonist, the salesman, thief, union organizer, merchant seaman, and genuine character, was based on a kid from Humboldt Park. "When I was in Paris in the '40s, I vividly remembered a boy who had been my playmate," says Bellow. "He came of just such a family as I described. I hadn't seen him in 25 years, so the novel was a speculative biography."

His snapshots of Chicago were fresh and descriptive. "It is a city with the bloody-rinded Saturday gloom of wind-borne ash, and blackened forms of five-story buildings rising up to a blind Northern dimness from the Christmas blaze of shops." He wrote with verve of poolrooms and clipjoints and City Hall.

"Years ago, I found it was much better to write a book about Chicago while living in Paris," Bellow says. "From abroad, the hometown seemed a very exotic place."

"Augie March" earned Bellow the first of three National Book Awards, and it made his reputation as a literary heavyweight.

Few major American writers have managed to cope with such charmed success. When an early book is widely acclaimed, some writers find it impossible to live up to the standard. Scott Fitzgerald and Thomas Wolfe lost their grip, cracked up, and died years before their time. Ernest Hemingway became so consumed by his macho image that he committed suicide. Others, like Sinclair Lewis and Norman Mailer, turned to producing potboilers, cashing in on their names.

By contrast, Bellow's success has grown with each novel. He has the longest hitting streak in American letters, an unbroken string of first-rate books.

A 1965 *Book Week* poll of novelists and critics found Bellow to have written the "most distinguished fiction of the 1945–1965 period." In the same poll, three of Bellow's books were voted among the six "best" novels of the post-war years.

When the *Philadelphia Inquirer* recently polled readers on the American author whose works would be read into the next century, Bellow was an overwhelming winner.

Bellow's work has staying power, for he is recognized as a serious artist with a great deal to say and, at the same time, an engaging and exciting writer. He has given us painfully moving tragedy in "The Victim" and "Seize the Day," where the West Side of New York is the setting for the fall of Tommy Wilhelm, one of Bellow's most memorable losers. He has also written very funny comedy in "Henderson the Rain King," "Herzog," and "Humboldt's Gift," and these books are his special favorites.

In his view comedy is the bright hope of American fiction, for he contends that it is difficult for American writers to grasp the nuances and subtleties of tragedy.

"I think people in America have been spared the worst of the 20th Century," he says. "They didn't know wars as other countries knew them. They were spared the experience of totalitarianism. Even the least fortunate Americans can scarcely be compared with the Latin American or Asian poor. So either the gods have spared us or they have shown their contempt for us.

"We have not seen the worst of extremism, and this has made us less aware of what reality can be—in the way of cruelty, sadism, forced labor, mass murder. We American writers can hardly expect to compete with those who have known the worst of war in their own cities, or who have been condemned to slave labor camps.

"I think we are intimidated by those who have seen human life at its worst. But perhaps we can do in the realm of comedy what we are unable to do in the realm of terror. Totalitarianism, extremism, turn us away from the middle range of human experience and make us intolerant of life as most people know and always have known it."

In his novels, Bellow draws heavily on experiences, including some very personal ones. Herzog, for example, was twice divorced and suffered in relationships with women. Bellow went through three divorces, including a long, nasty court fight over alimony with his third wife, Susan. He is the father of three sons by his first three marriages and remains close to them.

Bellow is a city man. He plays handball at a downtown club. He is a devoted fan of the Chicago Art Institute. He is a keen observer of the local political scene. He is not, however, much of a sports fan. A friend says that Bellow enjoys watching a game for a few minutes to pick up color but gets bored.

In the summer he prefers more rustic surroundings, a place of learned retreat where he can work without distraction. This summer he and Alexandra stayed at a country home in Vermont.

Bellow's best writing is marked by its attachment to the urban environment, particularly Chicago. He came of age during Chicago's literary renaissance, when such writers as Dreiser, Sherwood Anderson, and Carl Sandburg brought the city special distinction. "When the '20s ended, so did the era of Dreiser, Anderson, Masters, Hecht, and all the rest," says Bellow. "The East drew most of them away from Chicago, and Hollywood took the rest. Chicago did not export as much poetry as it did pork."

That Bellow not only writes about Chicago but continues to live here has long baffled the New York literati. "I seem to have had an intuition long ago that it wouldn't do much good to bounce about looking for the best place for a writer," he says. "I think that so many American writers have a need, even a hunger, for the good great place where they don't have to explain themselves to the neighbors, where they are surrounded by cultural riches and enjoy the fellowship of other writers and artists.

"For American writers, there are no such conditions—never have been. Most of our writers are solitaries. I don't mean that they are absolutely deprived of companionship or understanding. But, as writers or painters, they have to make it on their own.

"Some went to Paris in the '20s and some headed for San Francisco in the '50s and '60s. But I always thought that there was no answer to the problem of place. The only answer was to accept it for what it was. Karl Shapiro has pointed out that nine-tenths of American poetry in the 20th Century complains about the unpoetic character of life in the United States. The theme is not a rich one."

In Bellow's most recent novel, "Humboldt's Gift," the hero, writer Charlie Citrine, discloses, "I came back to settle in Chicago with the secret motive of writing a significant work."

"The main thing about Chicago," Bellow once said, "is that it's not New York. There are no writers to talk to in New York, only celebrities on exhibit. In Chicago, you have a city in which the most dressed-up people are artistic, in which restaurants and shops and wines and cheeses and parties and sexual delinquencies are all the art life the city boasts."

Which suits Bellow very nicely. He writes for several hours each morning in his apartment. "Sometimes the subject leaps at you and you can write a story in a few days or a novel in several months," he says. "But a novel generally takes years."

Bellow sets high standards for himself. When his first novel was accepted for publication, he had second thoughts and destroyed the manuscript. He is a meticulous craftsman who writes and rewrites.

One of Bellow's listeners and a favorite critic is Richard Stern, a novelist and faculty colleague at the University of Chicago. "Humboldt's Gift" was more than eight years in the making, and Bellow signed Stern's book, "For Richard, who endured 10,000 versions of it."

"The idea that a novel should be formally perfect is a recent one. Novels had always been loosely written, even slovenly. Until the period of Flaubert and his heirs, no one paid much attention to the well-

187

made novel. Dickens, Dostoyevski, and Victor Hugo did not write well-made novels. Those are a 20th-Century specialty. The well-made novel comes to us by way of Flaubert and Henry James.

"I have sometimes written novels the form of which had to be discovered," says Bellow. "The novel couldn't be completed until I had succeeded in discovering its form.

"Since young writers are and should be imitative, in my first book ('Dangling Man'), I imitated Rilke's 'Journal of My Other Self.' After all, composers would be considerably handicapped if each had to invent the form of the sonatas for himself. No one is or should be entirely original. Each writer has his ancestors, and he knows perfectly well who they are. Without Merimee (19th-Century French writer and dramatist), who wrote 'Carmen,' without Stephen Crane, there would have been no Hemingway. I know perfectly well to whom I owe."

Though he is the most honored American novelist of his age and is already part of literary history, Bellow is not content to rest on his laurels. As long as the story juices are still flowing, he will keep writing. As Bellow looks at his career, he concludes that he has fallen short of his talents, that there are new mountains to climb.

"Some people mature very slowly," he says. "I think I had an extraordinarily long adolescence. For some reasons I held back, I sat on my own intelligence. I discovered how timid I had been about subjects I should have treated more boldly. Sometimes it seems I've been quite stingy with my talent, saving myself for what was to come. There's no little egotism in such a view of the future. I seem to have felt that I would live to do better."

Bellow's literary parents

"The bedrock writers, those I have read repeatedly, fall into two categories: the 19th-Century writers—Dickens, Balzac, Thomas Hardy, Melville, Hawthorne, the great Russians such as Dostoyevski, Tolstoy, and Chekhov—and the 20th-Century writers, whom I read over and over. Somehow I don't think of Mark Twain as a 19th-Century writer. He seems so contemporary.

"Among modern writers, those whose influence was greatest are Dreiser, Sherwood Anderson, Hemingway, Fitzgerald, Faulkner. Among the Europeans, Joseph Conrad, Joyce, and Proust.

"Each generation finds fault with its predecessors. There would be no progress made if that weren't true. So I naturally have an ambivalent attitude toward my literary parents. I love them, but I'm also quite critical of them. I love them because they were great artists, passionately moving writers. I quarrel with them sometimes because I feel them to have been simple-minded about life in the United States.

"Reading Dreiser was a revelation in the sense you saw what could be done with people like those you knew, people completely familiar—neighbors, relatives, working people, shopkeepers—and you saw them, with astonishment, as characters. In Dreiser it struck you with the force of revelation that they could provide material for novels and stories. That was what one felt immediately for Dreiser and Anderson, who had this wonderful power to make art out of the commonest American experience.

"In some respects Dreiser was Horatio Alger inside-out. He took exactly the reverse view of success. He could prove that to thrive in America could be to fail humanly. But some of his ideas were primitive. His notions about nature or his chemical and physiological explanations of motives—his theories were fairly elementary—were not what you'd expect to read in the pages of a great novel.

"Fitzgerald at times displayed a kind of naive snobbery, a passion for social climbing that a man of genius would have been better without.

"I think Ernest Hemingway one of our greatest writers. I don't hold much with the villainous acts of certain of his women, and his macho attitudes sometimes seemed unworthy of such a great writer. But no one can be perfectly 'worthy.' A preposterous idea."

John Updike

Philadelphia Inquirer, 6/9/74

Ipswich, Mass.—John Updike, the Pennsylvania author who now lives in Massachusetts, has spent most of his career writing stylish fables about the plain-spoken, unmuddled people and rolling landscape of Southeastern Pennsylvania.

The books, like "Rabbit, Run" and "The Centaur," have made Updike, at the ripe old age of 42, one of the most important figures in American letters. Literary critic Alfred Kazin calls Updike, "the most amazing prodigy and performer we have in our fiction, the Mozart of our technological culture."

Now Updike has served notice that his newest book, "Buchanan Dying," a historical play about James Buchanan, Pennsylvania's only President, "is my final volume of homage to my native state."

If Updike is serious, this signifies as radical a departure as Alexander Solzhenitsyn's deciding to quit writing novel set in Russia, or William Faulkner's vowing to desert the South.

He sounds serious. "I keep telling myself that I'm through with Southeastern Pennsylvania," Updike says, "but I find that going back, even a little bit, is inspiring."

"There is something tolerant and amiably confused about the Pennsylvania life style," says Updike, who was born in Shillington, Pa., in Berks County. "This (Pennsylvania) habit of tolerance and the ability to articulate may not encourage future Presidents, but these are good qualities for poets or novelists—people like Conrad Richter and Wallace Stevens. I would like to express my gratitude to Pennsylvania for this atmosphere."

Updike confesses that seemingly trivial happenings related to his home territory make him sentimental. "The other night I watched a detergent commercial," he says. "They were interviewing a number of women in a small Pennsylvania town. And it almost made me cry . . . just the way they said vowels."

Updike's regarding of Pennsylvania is, to be sure, done from afar these days, mainly from the neo-federalist house here that became his home some years ago after an unhappy period of living in New York.

And Updike has certain reservations about his native Berks County, including, in particular, the high pollen count. "I got asthma when I went back last Easter," he says. "Fortunately, they knew just what to do about it at Reading Hospital."

Updike finds other things disagreeable about his native region. In one of his books he ridiculed Pennsylvania Dutch restaurants for "trying to sell what in the old days couldn't be helped . . . making a tourist attraction out of fat-fried food and a diet of dough that would give a pig pimples."

Nonetheless, it was his unusual local patriotism for Pennsylvania that moved Updike to resurrect James Buchanan, perhaps our most un-heroic chief executive, in his latest work.

"I was always curious why Buchanan was never mentioned," he says. "There isn't even a Buchanan, Pennsylvania. There are no monuments, no Buchanan avenues."

As a schoolboy, Updike was disappointed at the absence of children's biographies with titles like "Jimmie Buchanan, Keystone Son in the White House," or "Old Buck, the Hair-Splitter who Preceded the Rail-Splitter."

Updike discovered, years later, that Buchanan was forgotten because he was a boring politician who never accomplished much. Indeed, historian Henry Steele Commager has called Buchanan "by universal consent the worst Presidency in the history of our country."

Not only was Updike unconvinced that his hero was a national disgrace, he was determined to set the record straight.

Updike intended initially to write a Buchanan novel. In it, Buchanan, like Harry (Rabbit) Angstrom, George Caldwell, and other Updike characters, would be a well-intentioned protagonist.

But after reading Penn State historian Philip S. Klein's Buchanan biography, he decided it would be more natural to do a play.

"Buchanan's life is something of a Greek tragedy," he says. "It was almost as if God pounced on him at the end of his life—just as he always feared. My idea was to have Buchanan dying in order to show a parallel between the two great crises of his life: not going to Philadelphia to save Anne Coleman (his fiancee) from her desperate suicide, and not saving the South from plunging into succession."

Instead of the contempt and scorn heaped upon him by historians, Buchanan deserves credit, Updike says, "for all the people who lived for more years after 1857. He could have forced war earlier by acting in a Jacksonian manner . . . but Buchanan was an intelligent, conscientious, immensely tender-minded man whose life was one long attempt to play it safe."

Updike, furthermore, says the time has come to "reopen the casebooks" on all Presidents, including Buchanan, and, for that matter, Lincoln.

Arthur Schlesinger Jr., a Buchanan detractor, says that while Updike makes Buchanan seem like a drawing room dandy out of an Oscar Wilde comedy, "few historians . . . will be convinced by Mr. Updike's glittering case for the Old Public Functionary.

"But," Schlesinger adds, "it (Updike's play) is an abundant, even opulent creative act," that is "infinitely more interesting than most of the trash that finds its way to New York these days."

Updike, though, has no illusions about "Buchanan Dying" becoming a Broadway hit. "It probably won't ever have a commercial presentation," he says. "I didn't want to get my head scrambled by trying to make it a New York play. I sent it to Roger Stevens, director of the Kennedy Center in Washington, who tells me that it is too long. My guess is that it might be produced, in part, on a college campus, or in Lancaster."

Updike would enjoy watching his play produced in Buchanan's home town. For, though he refuses nearly all speaking and interview requests, he likes having an excuse to visit Pennsylvania.

This spring, for example, while turning down other invitations, he accepted an honorary degree from Lafayette College and an award from Drexel. Public appearances are particularly taxing for Updike, who has a stuttering problem.

"I don't think I'm inordinately shy," he says. "I'll do what I must. What is useful about me is that which I do in private. It's not worth an hour of my time to bemuse or entertain 300 students. I would rather spend that hour writing one thing that might amuse one person in Saskatchewan."

There was a time when Updike wanted to entertain millions as a newspaper comic strip cartoonist. "My boyhood heroes were people like Al Capp and Chic Young, not Faulkner, Hemingway, or Fitzgerald," he says. "I had seen New York in the movies and I wanted a little piece of that. I wanted to be a media man." (Drawing, he says, is still his first love. He designed the dust jacket of the Buchanan book.)

Updike finally made it to the Big Apple after attending Harvard and Oxford, landing a coveted writing job on *The New Yorker*. Those who read his polished, sophisticated prose and poetry predicted great things for Updike.

But Updike, like Hemingway, found literary New York "a bottle of tapeworms trying to feed each other." "I wasn't in New York long before I got out," Updike says.

Nonetheless, from time to time he still hears from the New York literary world. Norman Podhoretz, editor of *Commentary*, once wrote that Updike is "a writer who has very little to say and whose authentic emotional range is so narrow and thin that it may without too much exaggeration be characterized as limited to a rather timid nostalgia for the confusions of youth."

The personal attack offended Updike. "It seemed to go beyond the call of reviewing a book," he says. "Podhoretz was trying to do the literary world a favor by bringing me down."

Podhoretz, of course, hasn't been Updike's only detractor. Many highbrow critics accused Updike of wasting his talents on "Couples," a novel about sex as a suburban community activity. Kazin called it "inferior." The *New York Review of Books* judged it "a poor novel irritatingly marred by good features."

He has sort of broken even on his last two books. "Bech: A Book," a satirical work about the problems of a Jewish writer, drew critical approval, while the comments on "Rabbit, Redux," his 1971 sequel to "Rabbit, Run," received comments that can be charitably described as mixed.

Updike claims to be largely unaffected by critics.

"You can't steer by critical decision. After all the hundreds of reviews I've read, I can't say that I'd make any changes. A book is a little like a person. It could be better. But if you change it, you're apt to lose its identity."

Updike feels he has preserved his own identity in Ipswich.

"I've lived my life as I've tried to produce a book a year and raise my children. This little town has been as nice for them as Southeastern Pennsylvania was for me."

"I feel only like a kind of guest here in New England," he says. "But I am a happy guest. I have no dreams of going back to Pennsylvania, but I would hate not to visit there often."

Updike says, "I was very much in love with the landscape in Pennsylvania. My family had a special closeness, possibly because we all knew I wouldn't live my years out there in Pennsylvania. The first 20 years were very precious. The region was kind and mild, sort of non-Puritanical, poor but not really impoverished. All in all, it was a nice setting for a child, except for the fact that I had hay fever and spent one out of every four days in bed."

Updike's parents were a profound influence. His father, the late Wesley Updike, "was a special kind of eccentric." The elder Updike, a high school math teacher, was affectionately portrayed as George Caldwell in "The Centaur," the book which won a National Book Award and still ranks as Updike's favorite.

"It was a child's view of my father," he says. "It has a nice beat, a funny amusing shape with the father and everyone representing a God. I like all of my books pretty well, but I like to forget them after reading the last proofs."

His mother, Linda Grace Hoyer Updike, 69, "was slightly shy and sensitive. She wanted to be a writer and always had longings for New York and Flaubert."

Mrs. Updike was the model for the strong, domineering Mrs. Robinson in "Of the Farm." She lives today on the 93-acre farm near Plowville that her family has owned, except for a brief interval, since 1834, and to which young John Updike moved with his parents at age 12.

Mrs. Updike was depicted in one Updike biography as being the driving force behind her son, urging him to leave the little industrial town of Shillington at all costs, nudging him toward a writing career.

But she resents being viewed as a Pennsylvania Dutch version of Rose Kennedy who pushed and pressured her son to Harvard and national fame.

Mrs. Updike says, "I didn't feel I was driving him. I'm not capable of driving an Updike. I saw he had a willingness to work that he inherited from his father. Updikes are very willing to work. And it wasn't hard to see that his intelligence was higher than usual in our community. He was willing to use this intelligence to please others—and what else does a writer write for."

"It was more encouragement than criticism," Updike agrees. "I was just made to feel that I could do things. If you get this feeling early and can hold it until you're 15, you tend never to lose it."

In recent years, Mrs. Updike has realized her own writing ambitions. Writing under her maiden name of Linda Grace Hoyer ("I never liked the name of Updike. Linda and Updike don't go together"), she has sold a number of articles to *The New Yorker*; published "Enchantment," a book of prose; and just finished writing a historical novel about her lifelong hero, Ponce de León, the seeker of the Fountain of Youth.

"Writing has helped me feel less frustrated, more like a person," she says.

Her favorite Updike novel is, not surprisingly, "Of the Farm." She says, "I'm trying very hard to be like Mrs. Robinson (the character in the book). I don't think I'm as witty and I'm certainly not as tough, but I'm trying very hard."

Meanwhile, Updike seems to be reconsidering his mysterious decision to abandon the Pennsylvania setting in his novels and short stories.

In 1960 he published "Rabbit, Run," the novel about a former high school basketball star who married too early, searches for meaning in life, and flees from his family and responsibility. A sequel, "Rabbit, Redux," appeared in 1971 with the hero still bored and restless.

Updike hopes to "make a man's life through four or five volumes—doing a book every ten years. I'll always be Harry's age. I have about six years to go before doing another book. It will be an idyllic book, half the length of 'Redux.'"

He jokes that the future titles might include "Rural Rabbit" and, in 1991, "Rabbit Is Rich."

"I'll have to wait and see what happens," he says. "But I'd love to continue with this project. It is always fun to be back in Pennsylvania—fictionally."

Barbara Tuchman

Chicago Sun-Times, 2/12/89

In an age when the nonfiction bestseller lists are crowded with as-told-to biographies by television personalities and books about how to be your own best friend, Barbara W. Tuchman was something special.

Mrs. Tuchman, who died last week at the age of 77, was born into a family of considerable accomplishment. Her uncle, Henry Morgenthau Jr., was FDR's close friend and Treasury secretary. Her father, Maurice Wertheim, was the publisher of the *Nation*. She earned more prominence than either of them, gaining a place on the short list along with Francis Parkman, Samuel Eliot Morison, Henry Steele Commager and Dumas Malone as among the more notable American historians.

More than anyone else in the last quarter-century, Mrs. Tuchman was responsible for the revival of narrative history in the United States. Her historical works, including *The Guns of August, The Proud Tower* and *Stilwell and the American Experience in China* are unsurpassed for their vivid descriptions of war and of the personalities who helped to shape the 20th century.

"I want the reader to turn the page and keep on turning to the end," Mrs. Tuchman once said. "This is accomplished only when the narrative moves steadily ahead, not when it comes to a weary standstill, overloaded with every item uncovered in the research."

Her books sold hundred of thousands of copies and won two Pulitzer Prizes because Mrs. Tuchman was a master of her craft. Her final book, *The First Salute*, a study of how the American Revolution was received beyond our shores, has been on national best-seller lists for 18 weeks.

It rankled some of the academic nitpickers that her popular and scholarly works have proven to be more readable and enduring than their eminently forgettable and boring tomes.

"My stuff is assigned in college courses," Mrs. Tuchman once told me. "They need us if they're going to make history interesting to students, or enrollments will drop and they'll be out of jobs.

"I've found that the more readable historians, Cecil Woodham-Smith, Veronica Wedgwood, Antonia Fraser and Catherine Drinker Bowen, are women. And all of us have been fortunate in escaping graduate education.

"Our present form of education should be turned upside down. It's terribly stifling. Instead of giving graduate students a sense of history, it ruins their imagination. For one thing, you must have a passion for your subject. You can't write a fascinating book about a junior senator from South Carolina in 1822 just because he happened to deposit his papers in the archives and no one has used them."

Although Mrs. Tuchman was a woman of strong political views, she was not a polemicist. She criticized the revisionist history movement of the early 1970s, saying, "It's always dangerous to use history as an ideological weapon. When I was writing *Stilwell* I would get into a point of rage reading Claire Chennault's memoirs. I had a strong desire to point out all of his lies. But I wouldn't let myself intrude."

Mrs. Tuchman, whose books were always compelling, had little patience with the new wave of biographers whose books seemed to be narratives of footnotes.

"Unhappily, biography has lately been overtaken by a school that has abandoned the selective in favor of the all-inclusive," she said. "I think this development is part of the anti-excellence spirit of our time that insists on the equality and is thus reduced to the theory that all facts are of equal value and that the biographer or historian should not presume to exercise judgment. To that I can only say, if he cannot exercise judgment, he should not be in the business. A portraitist does not achieve a likeness by giving sleeve buttons and shoelaces equal value to mouth and eyes."

Robert V. Remini

Chicago Sun-Times, 6/2/91

On Monday night, University of Illinois at Chicago scholar Robert V. Remini is giving a command performance.

Remini, 69, one of the nation's more prominent historians is playing the White House. At the invitation of President Bush, Remini is lecturing about Andrew Jackson. Earlier speakers in the series have been David Herbert Donald of Harvard about Abraham Lincoln and David McCullough about Teddy Roosevelt. Remini contends that Jackson's presidency was a historical turning point.

Though Remini is a New Deal Democrat, he promptly accepted Bush's invitation. Remini, who retires from UIC this month after 26 years, said that Bush is a scholar of presidential literature. Bush is also an avid Remini fan.

A 1943 graduate of Fordham University, Remini received his master's and doctorate from Columbia University, where he was a protege of Pulitzer Prize-winning historian Dumas Malone, Thomas Jefferson's multivolume biographer.

"He taught me how to write," said Remini.

Malone, who lived into his 90s, placed Remini among the nation's leading presidential scholars. Remini's Jackson biography is frequently compared with Malone's Jefferson as a model of well-written history. Remini is among Chicago's civic treasures.

Remini, the first chairman of UIC's history department in 1965, built his department from six to 45 professors. In 1982, Remini was named as the first director of the Institute for the Humanities. "Coming to UIC was the wisest and best thing I could have done in my academic life," Remini said. He is talking about writing a history of UIC.

As for Jackson, Remini says that Old Hickory was the indispensable player in America's expansion from the East Coast to the heartland. In his three-volume biography, Remini shows that Jackson drove the Spanish out of Florida and also fueled the movements against the English and Spanish in what would become the western United States.

"No American ever had so powerful an impact on the minds and spirits of his contemporaries as did Andrew Jackson," Remini wrote in his Jackson biography. "No other man ever dominated an age spanning so many decades. No one, not Washington, Jefferson, or Franklin ever held the American people in such near-total submission."

Remini traveled to Spain for his research and uncovered records from imperial officials saying that Jackson was the most dangerous man in America and the foremost threat to Spain's empire. He also contends that Jackson's victory over 10,000 British forces at New Orleans saved the United States from an invasion that might have undone the Louisiana Purchase and left the young nation vulnerable to Old World powers.

"The pure Jackson," says Remini, "was without subtlety, pretense or political fakery."

In presenting the National Book Award to Remini, Arthur M. Schlesinger Jr. said, "Professor Remini's biography brings a great American leader to full and vibrant life against the backdrop of tumultuous times. It is a splendid work, meticulous in its scholarship, masterful in its control of sprawling materials, sympathetic while intelligently critical in its assessment of its powerful, willful and irascible hero, arresting in its portrayal of a whole generation of commanding political figures, vivid in its sense of the era, written with spirit, passion and high drama. It places the life in a grand historical context, displaying Jackson's significance in the expansion of the nation, the growth of presidential power, and the transition from republicanism to democracy. It is superb history that makes the past alive and exciting."

Remini, whose Jackson biography is nothing less than a classic, has completed an 800-page biography of Henry Clay, to be published this fall. As for his next book, "I may want to write a history of UIC."

Legends

John Wayne

Chicago Sun-Times, 2/23/97

Director Howard Hawks once asked John Wayne to express fear during the filming of a scene for *Red River*. Wayne refused. Tom Dunson—the character he played—never would have displayed such an emotion. In shaping his own legend, writes Garry Wills, Wayne knew what he was doing.

The Northwestern University historian has written a fascinating and insightful study about the making of an American myth. Of more than a dozen books about Wayne, *John Wayne's America* is by far the best; it is a fresh and original interpretation of his film career and of his impact on American culture.

Wayne became a symbol of rugged individualism and American patriotism. Ronald Reagan tried to imitate Wayne both in his film and in his political careers, Wills writes. Richard M. Nixon defended his views on law and order by citing *Chisum*. Henry A. Kissinger described U.S. foreign policy in terms of Wayne's image. Newt Gingrich said *The Sands of Iwo Jima* was "the formative movie of my life."

John Wayne was born Marion Michael Morrison in Iowa and was known by that name through his early apprenticeship on Hollywood's back lots and sound stages. He recited Shakespeare as a high-school drama student and later played football for the University of Southern California.

Wills corrects the myth that John Ford discovered Wayne. It was actually Raoul Walsh who spotted Morrison moving props and decided to make him a star. In 1929 Walsh cast him in the lead of an epic Western, *The Big Trail*. A Fox press release described Wayne, somewhat ungrammatically, as "a handsome youth, weighing 200 pounds and all bone and muscle, a smile that is worth a million, a marvelous speaking voice, a fearless rider, a fine natural actor." The Fox publicist noted that Walsh had brought more unknowns to stardom than anyone in Hollywood and touted Wayne as "his biggest bet."

Though Wayne gave a good performance in *The Big Trail*, almost no one saw the film. Walsh had made his Western in 70 mm. for the wide screen. But only a handful of theaters were equipped to show it in this form. Unsurprisingly, the movie helped bankrupt the Fox studio— but, Wills writes, any blame attached to Wayne for the movie's commercial flop was unfair. Later, as Wayne became identified with Ford, his performance in *The Big Trail* often was overlooked.

In the 1930s there were few hints that Wayne was destined for stardom. He worked for seven studios in eight years. Most of his 65 movies of this time were produced for Saturday children's matinees. During this period, however, he formed close friendships with Yakima Canutt, a stuntman and former rodeo champion, who taught Wayne how to ride like a cowboy; and Harry Carey, a silent-film cowboy actor whose quiet style and graceful movement influenced Wayne's acting.

Wills credits Hawks, not Ford, with making Wayne a superstar. In the trail-driving film *Red River*, Hawks cast Wayne against type as the mean, tough Dunson. Wayne shows his humanity in a fight with his surrogate son, played by Montgomery Clift. "If you don't get a damn good actor [to act opposite] Wayne, he's going to blow him right off the screen, not just by the fact that he's good but by his power, his strength," Hawks declared.

Oddly enough, Ford was late in acknowledging Wayne's talent. Wills is particularly good in explaining the complicated relationship between Wayne and the director who defined him for the world. After Wayne made *The Big Trail* for Walsh, Ford didn't speak to the actor for three years. Wills discloses that Ford may have resented Wayne's success as the Ringo Kid in *Stagecoach* (1939). Ford still thought of Wayne as a character actor for secondary roles.

Wayne did not join the armed forces during World War II, which disappointed Ford, who served with the cloak-and-dagger Office of Strategic Services. Stars bigger than Wayne, including Clark Gable, Tyrone Power and James Stewart, also went to war.

Wayne, who feared that military service would affect his ability to win new roles, offered excuse after excuse. "He wrote to Ford that he was trying to fill out the proper forms to enter the military," Wills writes, "but he had no typewriter on location." Wayne also pleaded "that he had left [the] forms with [actor] Ward Bond, who couldn't fill them out; or that his wife, from whom he was separated, would not let him get essential documents that he had left at home. In short, the dog ate his homework."

After the war, Ford taunted Wayne for shirking his duty. "Duke, can't you manage a salute that at least looks like you've been in the service?" Ford barked during the filming of *They Were Expendable*.

Partly because Wayne had avoided military service, Wills writes, he became a virulent anti-communist after the war. Even in that he was late taking a stand; Wayne would later inflate his role in "standing up" to communist sympathizers and, in Wills' words, take credit "for wounds he never dealt." In the early 1960s, he did join the far-right John Birch Society. But his political activity consisted mostly of supporting conservative Republicans.

Wayne's worst films, *The Green Berets* and *Big Jim McClain*, were caricatures of his political philosophy. He was such a hawk on Vietnam that even Lyndon Johnson thought he was too hard-line.

As Wills also shows, Wayne's accomplishments were considerable. Though some critics have dismissively claimed that Wayne always played the same role, Wills convincingly demonstrates the actor's considerable range and emotional depth. In Wayne's 13 films with Ford, Wills notes, the actor was not typecast. He played widely differing characters in *Rio Grande*, *She Wore a Yellow Ribbon* and *Fort Apache*, Ford's great U.S. Cavalry trilogy.

Wayne perhaps gave his finest performance as Ethan Edwards in *The Searchers* (1956). Edwards, a former Confederate soldier, spends years tracking down his niece, taken captive by Indians who had massacred her family. "Wayne changes from a man with whom we are comfortable into a walking Judgment Day ready to destroy the world to save it from itself," the critic Greil Marcus wrote of Wayne's performance.

In Wayne's last film, *The Shootist*, he declined to shoot one of his assailants in the back in the final scene. "It's unthinkable for my image," the Duke explained. Wayne had learned from Marlene Dietrich, a former lover, the importance of exerting total control over the way the public viewed him.

There has never been a more enduring legend. Nearly 20 years after his death, polls still rate him the nation's favorite movie star. "He embodies the American myth," Wills concludes. "Our basic myth is that of the frontier. Our hero is the frontiersman."

Frank Sinatra

Chicago Sun-Times, 12/13/95

Each time he leaves, Chicago is tugging his sleeve.

For more than half a century, Frank Sinatra has had us under his spell. He owns this town.

It's not just the voice. Chicago also likes his style: the swagger and the tilted hat. More than any performer, Sinatra has enhanced Chicago's mystique as a world-class city. This town also has had something to do with shaping the Sinatra legend.

"I adore the place because it's a big city with the heart of a small town," Sinatra once said of his love affair with Chicago.

Sinatra, who celebrated his 80th birthday Tuesday, won't quit singing about this town. In his "Duets II" album, which was released last year, Sinatra and Frank Jr. collaborated on Jimmy Van Heusen and Sammy Cahn's "My Kind of Town."

In the movies, Sinatra has twice celebrated Chicago in song. Playing his friend, the late nightclub comedian Joe E. Lewis, in "The Joker Is Wild" in 1957, Sinatra made a new hit out of the old vaudeville tune "Chicago" with Nelson Riddle's Dixieland arrangement. Sinatra revived the city's image as a toddling town as he sang about State Street where they do things they don't do on Broadway. His humor came through when he wryly noted a man dancing with his wife. When he sang about Chicago as his hometown, Sinatra never sounded more genuine.

The best was yet to come. In the 1964 musical comedy "Robin and the Seven Hoods," which was filmed here, Sinatra played a '20s gangster who sought to minimize gangland violence. "My racket is hustling beer and running a gambling joint," Sinatra said in the film.

In the film's showstopper, Sinatra introduced "My Kind of Town." He sang about Chicago as a town that won't let you down, with "my kind of people," and "my kind of razzmatazz." It became an instant hit and this city's unofficial anthem. Sinatra liked the song so much that it became the final number at his concerts.

Not everyone was impressed. A critic for the *Chicago Daily News* wrote in 1964: "It's not a very good song, but like other unsingable anthems, 'My Kind of Town' will take root in Chicago."

The critic was wrong. Sinatra's song moved even New Yorkers to cheer for Chicago. Few cities have had a more wonderful tribute.

Sinatra's ties to this city are special. It was this town that gave him a brand-new start. He first sang here in 1939 at the Sherman Hotel with the Harry James band. Tommy Dorsey heard Sinatra at the Sherman and hired him as the vocalist for his band. Sinatra signed his contract with Dorsey at the Palmer House. He made his debut with Dorsey in Rockford. Sinatra recorded his first songs with Dorsey at RCA's Chicago studio in February of 1940. "What Can I Say After I'm Sorry?" and "The Sky Fell Down" were Sinatra's first two recordings. "Tommy taught me everything I know about singing," Sinatra said years later.

Like this town, Sinatra is a survivor.

In this town, nobody has had a better run.

Ella Fitzgerald
Chicago Sun-Times, 4/25/93]

She's no passing fancy.

Indeed, Ella Fitzgerald is the most enduring popular singer and greatest jazz vocalist of the 20th century, a shining star and inspiration. With clarity of tone and rhythmic style, she brings out the best in any melody. More than any other artist, Fitzgerald has defined the standard for America's music. Her musical personality is warmhearted and caring. When she laughs and cries during a performance, she means it.

Ella, who was born in Newport News, Va., on April 25, 1918, and is celebrating her 75th birthday Sunday, is in her seventh decade as a music legend. Her career was launched when the 16-year-old Ella won an amateur night competition at the Harlem Opera House. And she's still performing. Last year, though in frail health, she dazzled fans at Radio City Music Hall. The voice is still rich and her pitch is never less than perfect.

"Every night when I say my prayers I just thank God for the beautiful that happened too me and that I am here to see it," Fitzgerald once said of her career. "You know, so many things happen after people have passed, but here I'm seeing it. I just couldn't believe it."

From the Big Band era of the '30s and '40s and into the '90s, she has reigned as the first lady of song. "Ella Fitzgerald is a great philanthropist. She gives so generously of her talent, not only to the public, but to the composers whose work she performs," Duke Ellington said. "In terms of musicianship, Ella Fitzgerald is beyond category."

Bing Crosby, who could be a tough critic of other singers, described Fitzgerald as the greatest. As social commentator Murray Kempton observed, only Fitzgerald is "at once so simple and so complicated, so innocent and so sentient." A music critic once noted that Fitzgerald could sing a telephone directory with a broken jaw and make it sound good.

When she invites us to "Take the A-Train," her appeal is irresistible. Everybody is a passenger. Is there anyone who isn't moved when Fitzgerald sings about too much rain falling into her life? And who but Ella could make a smash hit about a little yellow basket?

After the teenaged Ella won the music contest, she was given a tryout with Chick Webb's band at a 1935 Yale University dance. "If the kids like her, she stays," Webb said. The applause has never stopped.

In honor of her 75th birthday, a new collection of Fitzgerald's more enduring hits has just been released on compact disc in a package that includes a booklet about her career and reminiscences of longtime associates.

Fitzgerald, who describes herself as a working musician, loves her work and also loves people. She said that the quality she most admired about Ellington was that he never rapped others. Fitzgerald, who is genuinely modest, still finds it difficult to accept praise. Once at a concert in Chicago, she noticed that a woman wasn't applauding at her bebopping and scat-singing numbers. Finally, Ella asked what was wrong and the woman said that she couldn't understand what Fitzgerald was singing. Ella responded with a ballad.

She's still got the world on a string.

Hank Williams
Chicago Sun-Times, 7/6/94

The life that Hank Williams Sr. led was sadder than any of the songs he wrote.

His recording career lasted only six years. He was only 29 when he died on Jan. 1, 1953, a victim of his own excesses. In the more than 40 years since his death, his legend has endured. He is remembered as a pivotal figure in the history of American popular music. He was country music's greatest performer and the most gifted songwriter of his generation.

Colin Escott, who recently produced and annotated a CD collection of Williams' songs, brings the singer into sharper focus than any previous biographer. It's a portrait of the artist with a talent for self-destruction.

For all his vitality and ability to put on a happy face for his audiences, Williams was also a very lonely man, who sang of robins weeping and losing the will to live, which told us a great deal about his own sadness.

Working in collaboration with Williams scholars George Merritt and William MacEwen, Escott has written a very compelling biography about this country music legend.

Escott chronicles the singer's childhood in Alabama and his musical roots. His father was a World War I gas victim. His mother was a church organist.

Among the disclosures in this biography is that Williams had a birth defect that was probably spina bifida occulta, a condition in which the arches of the spine don't unite. The crippling, degenerative illness took its toll on Hank's body and soul, according to the authors. But Williams had another illness. He began drinking hard liquor when he was 11 years old and was an alcoholic who couldn't overcome his thirst.

Growing up in rural Alabama, Williams couldn't play sports or become a logger because of his frail health. So he turned to music. His mother gave Williams a guitar when he was 8. His earliest musical influence was Rufus Payne, an African-American street musician.

"All the music training I ever had was from him," Williams said. When Hank Williams moaned the blues, it was Payne's legacy to American music.

His talent was recognized. After Williams cut his first record in 1946, Billboard magazine had this assessment: "With real spiritual qualities in his pipes, singing with the spirit of a camp meeting, Hank Williams makes his bow an auspicious one." He soon stormed the charts. As Escott writes, Williams "came closer to hitting a home run every time at bat than anyone in country music before or since."

Williams wrote with passion about a wide range of human emotions: "Cold, Cold Heart," "Hey, Good Lookin'," "Your Cheatin' Heart," "Why Don't You Love Me Like You Used to Do," "Howlin' at the Moon," "I Saw the Light" and "Mansion on a Hill."

Most of these songs were written in the front seat of Hank's sedan while he was touring. "There wasn't even room to break out a guitar in the sedan, so he'd beat out a rhythm on the dashboard and someone would get something like a cardboard stiffener from a pressed shirt and take the words down. Hank would come back off the road with a billfold full of scraps of paper on which he had verses, half-completed songs and abandoned ideas. The band would kid him because his billfold was so thick."

"People don't write music. It's given to you," Williams once confided. "You sit there and wait and it comes to you. If [a song] takes longer than 30 minutes or an hour, I usually throw it away."

Williams was ill prepared for fame and fortune. Escott provides the details of his stormy marriages, his declining health and his erratic behavior. At the peak of his popularity, Williams was bounced from the Grand Ole Opry. He showed up at his own concerts about half the time. He died in the back seat of his Cadillac while being driven to a concert in Ohio. Escott's book separates the man from the myth. It's a valuable contribution to the history of American popular music.

Patsy Cline
Philadelphia Inquirer, 10/9/94

In the summer of 1953, a 20-year-old woman singer dazzled and overpowered the audience at the National Country Music Championship at the Warrenton (Va.) Fairgrounds. Wearing a red-and-white cowgirl outfit, Patsy Cline held nothing back as she belted out "Bill Bailey, Won't You Please Come Home."

"She was an unknown—we had never seen her before and she just stood us on our ears," recalled Marvin Carroll, who played steel guitar for the Texas Wildcats in the same competition. But even then, the first pop-and-country singer wasn't easy to categorize. Despite Cline's winning performance, she lost the championship to a fiddler because she had sung a pop tune in bluegrass country.

The following summer Cline returned to the Warrenton Fairgrounds and easily won the national country music title with a soulful rendition of the Bob Wills classic "Faded Love."

With her full-throated singing voice and a remarkable range, Cline went on to become the first woman to achieve stardom on the pop and country charts. Her music is timeless and ageless.

More than 30 years after her tragic death in a plane crash at the age of 31, Cline is bigger than life. Her albums are more popular than ever. More than four million copies of her greatest-hits compact disc have been sold. The U.S. Postal Service issued a stamp in her image. She has twice been portrayed in the movies, first by Beverly D'Angelo and then by Jessica Lange.

But as Margaret Jones demonstrates in her superb biography, the movies only told part of the story. *Patsy* is a masterful study of an American master. It's the most meticulously researched and insightful of the three Cline biographies. Jones captures Cline in all of her vitality and passion, while showing how Cline rose from poverty to stardom.

There was much tragedy in Cline's life. The country singers Loretta Lynn, who wrote a foreword for the book, and June Carter Cash, who were among Cline's confidants told Jones that Patsy was a victim of incest. "By the time she was eleven years old she had already lived a woman's life," said Lynn. Jones writes that the director of *Sweet Dreams* cut scenes from the movie that alluded to Patsy's troubled relationship with her father.

Her formative years were a bad dream. Her family moved 19 times while Patsy was growing up. An indifferent student, she dropped out of school as a high school freshman and never went back. But, as Jones shows, Patsy had drive and ambition. While singing in a church choir as a youngster, Patsy's talent was recognized. Jones writes that among the singers who influenced Patsy's style were the country star Patsy Montana and torch singer Helen Morgan.

In her rise to prominence, Patsy showed extraordinary determination. But she also had fun with her music. "When Patsy went out on the stage she forgot about everything else," writes Jones. Among her breaks was an appearance on the "Arthur Godfrey Show" in which she won the talent competition by singing "Walkin' After Midnight."

Though the song became an immediate hit, Cline got ripped off by her record company, 4 Star Records. Jones discloses that the head of the record company, Bill McCall, deducted every conceivable expense and incredibly had Cline owing money for her hit. Her lifetime royalties for "Walkin' After Midnight" were less than $900, according to Jones.

Cline was among the few country superstars who wasn't a songwriter. But with her great singing talent, Cline was courted by writers who knew that she could make their compositions into instant hits. Cline, who endured much pain and heartache in her life as in her songs, lucked out in teaming up with the legendary producer Owen Bradley. Their sessions produced some of our more enduring music.

Unthreatened by younger country artists, Cline became a big sister to Lynn, Barbara Mandrell, Dottie West, and others. When country star George Jones attempted to make a play for the 13-year-old Mandrell, Cline intervened and became her "den mother."

Cline's own personal life was unhappy. She was battered by her husband Charlie Dick, whose relationship with Cline is chronicled in *Sweet Dreams*. Seriously injured in a car accident, Cline became addicted to pills including speed. When Patsy gave June Carter Cash a pill to calm her, Cash told Jones that she was wired for three days.

When Cline played Carnegie Hall in 1961, the New York gossip columnist Dorothy Kilgallen scornfully dismissed the show as "hicks from the sticks." But Patsy had the last laugh. Kilgallen is forgotten. Cline is an icon of American culture. Jones has brought the legend vividly to life.

Rock Garden

Chicago Sun-Times, 10/1/93

Rock on.

In recognition of the accomplishments of notable Chicago women, 100 boulders with names of women have been placed on Loop sidewalks. The Loop is being turned into a large rock garden "in the spirit of Jane Addams," according to Sculpture Chicago, the group behind the project. Not everyone is happy about it. Some people are tripping over the monuments.

There are boulders honoring such remarkable women as Addams, poets Gwendolyn Brooks and Harriet Monroe, social activist Ida B. Wells, the Lyric Opera's Ardis Krainik and Dr. Margaret Burroughs, founder of the DuSable Museum of African American History. Some rocks celebrate milestones: Comptroller Dawn Clark Netsch, the first woman in Illinois elected to statewide executive office; Susan Getzendanner, the first woman federal judge in Illinois; Carol Moseley-Braun, Illinois' first woman U.S. senator, and Aurelia M. Pucinski, the first woman clerk of the Circuit Court.

But in rocking around the block, some of the public-sculpture aficionados seem to have had an overdeveloped sense of their own importance. Socialites, heiresses and mediocrities are well-represented in the rock garden. So are political wives. That's not unusual. What is most intriguing about the 100 rocks is the women who weren't recognized. If there is a theme, it's who you know, not what you know or have accomplished, that's important.

In Chicago's 156-year history, only two women have been elected to citywide executive office: former Mayor Jane M. Byrne and City Treasurer Miriam Santos. Neither was given a rock by Sculpture Chicago's deep thinkers. Leaving them out is petty and silly. More books have been written about Byrne than any Chicago woman since Jane Addams, who would have been embarrassed by the shabby treatment of the former mayor. Without stones for Byrne and Santos, the Loop rock garden is a joke.

Community activist Nancy Jefferson, the West Side's Mother Teresa, couldn't even get a pebble from Sculpture Chicago. Jefferson's should have been among the first stones place in the Loop.

Mahalia Jackson, a rock of ages if there ever was one and America's most celebrated gospel singer, didn't get a stone. Neither did Dr. Hanna Gray, the first woman president of the University of Chicago; Ruth Page, the legendary dancer and choreographer; Mary Ann G. McMorrow, the first woman justice of the Illinois Supreme Court, nor Mother Frances Xavier Cabrini, the first American saint and the founder of Columbus Hospital.

The Loop's rock garden would have been richer if playwright Lorraine Hansberry and authors Edna Ferber and Sandra Cisneros had been given their due. There were no stones for blues legend Koko Taylor, the Chicago Opera's Mary Garden, Irish dancer Sheila Tully and Patsy Montana of the WLS Barn Dance. There should have been recognition for Olympic medal winners Barbara Ann Scott and Willye B. White and for TV's Oprah Winfrey, and actresses Mary Elizabeth Mastrantonio, Colleen Moore, Ann Margaret and Kim Novak.

It's useful to have friends at City Hall. Maggie Daley, the Mayor's wife, and her pal Lois Weisberg, the city's cultural affairs commissioner, are highlighted in stones at Daley Plaza. The Department of Cultural Affairs helped plan the rock garden. The planners took care of their friends and shunned Chicago's most accomplished women.

Steve Neal is the political columnist for the *Chicago Sun-Times*. He lives in the western suburbs with his wife, Susan, and their daughters, Erin and Shannon. Neal is a frequent panelist on the WTTW/Channel 11 program *Chicago Week in Review*. His previous books include *The Eisenhowers* and *Dark Horse: A Biography of Wendell L. Willkie*, which was named among the year's notable books by *American Heritage* magazine.